AF531797

FRANCE, GERMANY AND THE EUROPEAN UNION

Maastricht and After

FRANCE, GERMANY AND THE EUROPEAN UNION

Maastricht and After

Aparajita Endow

AAKAR BOOKS

FRANCE, GERMANY AND
THE EUROPEAN UNION
Maastricht and After

© Author, 2003

All rights reserved. No part of this book may be reproduced in any form without prior written permission from the author.

First Published, 2003

ISBN 81-87879-12-2

Published by
AAKAR BOOKS
28-E, Pocket-IV, Mayur Vihar Phase-I, Delhi-110 091
Phone : 22795505 Telefax : 22795641
E-mail : aakarb@del2.vsnl.net.in

Typeset at
Nidhi Laser Point, Shahdara Delhi-32
Ph. : 22825424

Printed in India on behalf of M/s Aakar Books by
Arpit Printographers, B-7, Saraswati Complex,
Subhash Chowk, Laxmi Nagar, Delhi-110 092

To my parents and Rajah,
For your support, encouragement
and lightening my burden.

Preface

European integration has been built around post-war Franco-German reconciliation. Ever since France and Germany began to play a crucial role in the European Union (EU), no major initiative has been possible, without their cooperation. The success of Franco-German relationship over the past decades is a record of determination to accommodate divergent interests through positive political action, to tolerate differences and to minimize the impact of their divergences. This has been largely possible due to the 'lowest-common-denominator bargains' between these two states. Despite the doubling of EU's Member States between the mid-1960s and thereafter to the mid-1990s, this pattern of Franco-German relationship seems no less marked even today. It is not the congruence of French and German objectives but positions of divergence on various issues that drove them to seek solutions and keep the European integration process on the track. When their conflictual positions could not be mediated, there were apparent deadlock in the EU (as was during the recent crisis over the Economic and Monetary Union during the 1996 Intergovernmental Conference). When they reached positions of convergence and cooperation, the rest of EU members had very little choice but to follow. On many of the oldest EU common policies (like the Common Agricultural Policy or on external trade policy) where the EU's competence are the strongest, it could be expected, on the basis of neo-functional rationale, that supranational governance would be dominant. On the contrary, there has been significant inter-governmentalism in EU politics, especially with France and

Germany playing a determining role (sometimes through a mutual bargaining process) in the EU.

The 1980s and 1990s witnessed some spectacular events in Europe with the democratic resurgence in the Iron Curtain countries in Central Eastern Europe, followed by the disintegration of the Soviet Union synchronising with the unification of Germany. The EU, on the other hand, was progressively becoming a dominant political and economic force, thereby reaffirming its stance as the most outstanding example of regional integration in human history. In view of the fact that the Franco-German core has been the main driving force of the evolution and growth of the EU, it is appropriate to critically examine the nature and dynamics of the cooperation and competition leading to inter-state bargains between these two countries in conditioning the scope and content of European integration in the 1990s. This book is an exercise in that direction.

The introductory chapter of the book presents a historical overview of Franco-German cooperation after the end of the Second World War—exploring the relationship in the context of external factors which prompted the *rapprochement* between these countries and it also takes into account the politics of cooperation and competition that has been the underlying basis of this alliance. After the end of the Second World War, it was French objective to regain its glory and prestige and German concerns to recover international recognition that made them embark on this partnership to harness German economic resources to meet French political objectives. The Federal Republic's limited foreign policy objectives in contrast to the broad foreign policy objectives and a weak economic base of France, made it a potential auxiliary to France. The chapter analyses the changing paradigms of the Franco-German relationship in the politically altered scenario of the late 1980s and early 1990s. The concluding remarks of the chapter identifies the impact of personality and political leadership of France and Germany as the continuing factors for shaping and reshaping the constraints under which the two governments operate.

The second chapter evaluates the Franco-German role in the formulation of the Maastricht Treaty. The late 1980s brought several new challenges into the EU which created incentives for greater cohesion and deeper integration. Faced with increasing global competition from the United States and Japan and hampered by rigidities in the industrial structure and labour market policies, EU's future economic and political policy demanded a renewed vigour and integrational thrust. With the end of the Cold War, the EU had new tasks in its agenda, primary of which was the consolidation of its economic and political integration. Under the aegis of Franco-German cooperation, the Treaty on European Union was signed in 1991. This chapter delves into the Franco-German motivations behind the Treaty and critically examines the response of the two Member States during the ratification of the Treaty. Finally, it concludes with a critique of the Treaty by highlighting those issues which the Treaty failed to resolve.

The third chapter deals with the challenge of enlargement that the EU is confronted with and Franco-German policies towards enlargement. The democratic resurgence in the erstwhile Iron Curtain countries coincided with the unification of Germany, while the EU was becoming a dominant political and economic force. It became a model for peace, prosperity and stability for the rest of the European countries whose aspirations to belong to such an order made the EU face a new challenge of enlargement. It came at a time when the EU was concentrating on its internal integration. The chapter at the outset, summarises the previous enlargements of the EU and their subsequent impact on the EU institutions. It further examines the implication of the changes in Central and Eastern European countries and the response of the EU in helping these countries attain political and economic maturity to qualify for membership. EU's well established credibility as an island of peace and stability is not only confined to Eastern Europe. The countries of Southern Europe (Malta, Cyprus and Turkey) and Russia also perceive themselves as potential members of the EU. In view of this, separate sections on prospects of EU enlargement to these countries, have been discussed. Major sections on Franco-German role towards enlargement have been devoted by bringing out their policies of competition over the future architecture of the EU. The chapter concludes with the institutional challenges that are likely to arise with future enlargement and the policies (like the Common Agricultural Policy, the Structural Fund and the EU budget) that might be affected when more countries become members of the EU. Finally, some perplexing themes that have emerged with EU's enlargement strategy have been examined.

The fourth chapter deals with the Common Foreign and Security Policy of the EU. The EU's economic weight makes it incumbent to play a commensurate political role in world affairs. The introductory section of this chapter makes a historical and analytical survey of the early developments of the European Political Cooperation (EPC) during the 1960s to the 1990s, culminating with the proclamation of a Common Foreign and Security Policy (CFSP) in the Maastricht Treaty. The performance and efficiency of CFSP has been examined with the help of a case study of the Yugoslav crisis. The prospects and role of the Western European Union (WEU) as a defence arm of the EU have been elaborately discussed. In keeping with the theme of this book, the Franco-German role in fostering CFSP have been dealt at length. The institutional loopholes, the budgetary problems, the lack of 'collectivity' amongst the Member States, the presence of a 'variable geometry' pattern and the existence of the 'capability-expectation gap' in the foreign policy of the EU have been examined in evaluating the prospects of a viable CFSP.

The fifth chapter reviews the IGC, 1996 which culminated with the Amsterdam Treaty. Even after the signing of the Maastricht Treaty, the Member States found themselves confronting the task of re-examining the institutions, reviewing the existing structure of the EU and seeking solutions to the unresolved challenges of the 1990s. Two most vital issues in the IGC, 1996 were institutional reforms to prepare the EU for the forthcoming enlargement and creation of a viable CFSP and justice and home affairs. The chapter explores the proposals put forward by the different Member States, who were the key actors in the IGC and whose positions and agenda underlined the diversity of views about the direction in which the EU is heading. The chapter concludes with a critical evaluation of the Treaty and reflects on the bargaining power of France and Germany in building a convergence from diametrically opposite positions.

The concluding chapter investigates into the present state of affairs of the EU and the challenges that it would confront in the years to come. The failure of institutional reforms in face of forthcoming enlargements, the power struggle between the Small and Big Member States, and the growing heterogeneity of the EU have been elaborately addressed.

In the course of my endeavour, my burden has been lightened by the contributions of those to whom I am greatly indebted. First and foremost, I express my profound gratitude to Prof. R.K. Jain, whose relentless assistance, constructive comments, illuminating criticism and recommendations greatly contributed in shaping the content and style of the book. I have come to depend on and respect his intellectual erudition and sharp but fair critiques.

I acknowledge the help I received from the staff of Jawaharlal Nehru University library, Hauptbibliothek, Humbolt University and University of Leipzig, Centre for European Integration (Bonn), and Stiftung Wissenschaft und Politik (Ebenhausen), British Council Library and Max Mueller Bhavan, New Delhi. I specially thank the staff of the Documentation Centre of the Delegation of European Commission, New Delhi. I am thankful to D.S. Rawat for his patience in typing, correcting and editing the work.

I acknowledge, with gratitude the help I received from several persons during the course of my study trip to Germany. I thank Prof. Dr. Hartmut Elsenhans, Institute fuer Politikwissen-schaft, University of Leipzig and Prof. Dr. Michael Kreile, Institute fuer Politikwissenschaft, Humbolt University, Berlin for all the help they rendered me. Their valuable suggestions and remarks on the topic of my research contributed immensely in the readability of this book. I also extend my thanks to Mr. Christian Sterzing, European Policy

Spokesman and Member of the Bundestag, The Green Party (Germany); Dr. Thomas Schiller, Spokesman of the Christian Democratic Union (CDU), Office of Karl Lamers, Berlin; Dr. Christoph Jessen, Head of Second Division in the Directorate of European Affairs, Auswaertiges Amt (German Foreign Office), Berlin; Dr. Ulrika Guerot, (CDU Parliamentary Group Member) Haus der Deutschen Wirtschaft, Berlin; Mr. Hubert Knirsch, Foreign Office Directorate, Chancellor's Office, Berlin; Dr. Carlos Jahnsen, European Afairs Advisor, Social Democratic Party, (Germany) and Dr. Michael Dauderstaedt, Friedrich Ebert Stiftung (Bonn), for giving me the opportunity to seek their views and opinions through a series of interviews. My conversations with them inspired me to rethink and reshape my arguments. I extend my hearty thanks to Ms. Viola Mittag and Mr. Fabian Becher and many others for their constant assistance, guidance and hospitality during my stay in Leipzig. A special thanks to Anja Gottschalk, Kristine Schierenberg, Mr. Amiya Paul, Mrs. Lipi Paul and friends for their care and concern in an alien land. I also express my gratitude to Dr. Volker Heins, Institute fuer Sozialforschung (Frankfurt). Most of all, I express my profound gratitude to the Friedrich Ebert Stiftung (FES), Germany, and in particular Mr. Horst Mund and Dr. Klaus Voll of FES, New Delhi and Ms. Karin Paffenholz, Department of Asia-Pacific Cooperation, FES, Bonn, for giving me this opportunity and material support to carry out my study in Germany. I thank those who were involved, in any way, with the European Union Studies Programme, Jawaharlal Nehru University. I also thank my publisher Mr. K.K. Saxena of Aakar Books.

I am deeply indebted to my parents and brother, Rajah, whose unflinching support and constant encouragement made this book possible.

New Delhi
2000

Aparajita Endow

Contents

Chapter I

Introduction

The heartland of Europe which has been engaged in the most successful experiment in regional integration in human history witnessed some spectacular events in the 1980s and the 1990s, which not only took the Europeans by surprise but also left the entire world in a state of amazement. Historically, European integration has been built around and identified with post-war Franco-German reconciliation. The success of the Franco-German relationship over the past decades is a record of determination to accommodate divergent interests through positive political action, to explain or tolerate differences and to minimize their impact.

HISTORICAL BACKGROUND

The end of the Second World War witnessed for the first time in modern European history, the shifting of gravitational centre of global power from the European heartland to the periphery or outside of Europe.[1] The Yalta and Potsdam Conference in 1945 divided the vanquished Germany into three parts, one each to be administered by the United Kingdom (UK), the United States (US) and the Soviet Union. On Churchill's insistence, France was given a portion out of the zone belonging to the US and the UK and was also admitted as member of the Allied Control Council for Germany. Despite being included in the Allied Military Command for Germany and accorded a permanent membership in the United Nations Security Council, France was relegated to the status of a medium power, contrary to the erstwhile French desire of being a world power, especially after Charles de Gaulle relinquished the French Presidency in 1946. Under the Fourth Republic (1946-58), France remained constantly under fear and uncertainty of Germany securing a prominent position in the North Atlantic Alliance. With the Communist rule in Czechoslovakia and Hungary and the outbreak of the Korean War, the US and the UK favoured the rearmament of Germany and its admission in the western defence apparatus against Soviet expansionism.[2] Since the late 1940s, France has been an uneasy ally of the western bloc,[3] due to the insufficient support extended by the Anglo-Saxon powers to the French colonial involvements in North Africa and Indo-China. However, the US and the UK sought to placate the French by encouraging them to pool up their industrial resources with those of the German within the framework of the European Defence Community (EDC) in the hope that these two powers would serve as a repository of the North Atlantic Treaty Organization (NATO). The EDC foundered as it could not survive the negative vote in the French National Assembly on 30 August 1954 due to French apprehension about their armed forces getting into the European command which they feared could be dominated by the Germans. In other words, there was the fear lurking in the French minds of a possible 'Germanisation' of European defence.[4] On further analysis, another reason why the French National Assembly failed to ratify the EDC Treaty was the emergence of the Gaullist Rassemblement du Peuple Francais (RPF), with anti-European stance.[5] Contrary to the German phobia of the RPF, French Foreign Minister Robert Schuman, who was the chief architect of the European Coal and Steel Community (ECSC), had announced an exchange of French coal against German steel in May 1950. The Schuman Plan which laid the foundations of the unification of Europe, culminated with the Treaty of Rome in 1957. In 1958, after the establishment of the European Economic Community (EEC) and the Euratom, concrete attempts with regard to European political unification were made by General Charles de Gaulle, who resumed French

Presidency in mid 1958. President de Gaulle's idea of a European political union were outlined first to Konrad Adenauer, the first Chancellor of the FRG, in their bilateral meeting of July 1960 where they encapsulated the French aim of building a 'European Europe' capable of dealing with the US on an equal footing. The mystical communion between President de Gaulle and Chancellor Adenauer of the FRG helped in the formation of the Fouchet-Cattani plans in 1961-62 with the object of setting up '1' Europe des parties', which however, failed due to the opposition formed by the Benelux countries who feared the emergence of the Franco-German axis.[6] The Fouchet Plan provided a model for European collaboration in foreign policy, in deliberated contrast to the Atlantic collaboration encapsulated in NATO. French perception of its foreign policy, of its association with nationhood, national pride and status made its relationship with the US peculiarly complex. As a dominant military and economic power in the inter-national system, the US provided the standard against which to measure French status, the foil for French efforts to demon-strate that status and the most immediately visible threat to the independence and autonomy which de Gaulle considered intrinsic to the preservation of French power and status.[7]

With the failure of the Fouchet Plans and President Kennedy's Independence Day Speech in July 1962 (calling for a Europe which included Britain as a loyal partner of the US), the perceived necessities of British dependence on the US made France reconfirm British preference for the Atlantic over the European connections. There followed, in quick succession, the French veto on British entry to the European Community (EC), the Franco-German Treaty of June 1963 and the Bundestag's addition to that treaty of a preamble which explicitly rejected the French model of transatlantic relations and reaffirmed the German commitment to the US.

COOPERATION AND COMPETITION

Unlike France, whose primary objective was to regain status

and prestige, the Federal Republic was concerned with the recovery of international acceptance and recognition. Therefore its approach to international and European issues were dominated by its twin concerns for security and for the maintenance of the principle of a united Germany. Unavoidably, therefore relations with the US was paramount.[8] The FRG needed US protection against Soviet threat and support for reunification relations with the US became a constant preoccupation for the two Member States of the EC. On the crucial relationship with the US, Germany occupied a position between the confident partnership to which the British declared there commitment and combative competitiveness of the French.[9] The French need to bridge the gap between their broad foreign policy objectives and relative weakness of economies and industrial base required them to find like-minded partners. The Treaty of Rome of 1957, amongst other things, successfully harnessed German economic resources to French political objectives in Africa, through the creation of the European Development Fund. The FRG appeared more easily available as a partner because of its limited international acceptance. Its confined foreign policy objectives made it a potential ally to France rather than a rival.

The Franco-German Treaty of 1963 was primarily concerned with foreign policy collaboration—with defence collaboration in accordance with the French strategic view. The French pursuit of reconciliation with Germany included a refusal to support German long-term aims of reunification with staunch and explicit support for the German position on Berlin, earning the reputation in Germany of a reliable though difficult ally as reconciliation and co-operation in other fields advanced in parallel. After the Elysee Treaty (Franco-German Treaty of Friendship) of 1963, it had been universally self-evident that the Franco-German link had become intrinsically closer. However, the relationship was not immune to the differences that arose from the international environment. The German Government opposed the French withdrawal from the integrated NATO structure in 1966, just as it had opposed the French Government during the quarrel on the structure and financing of the EEC in 1965. On this, as on a range of Community issues, the EEC Member States regularly split, with Germany or the Netherlands leading the opposition of French proposals. When Britain renewed its application to join the EC in 1967, the German Government offered its support against French resistance.[10] Throughout the 1960s and the early 1970s, marked disparities in their respective economic and political aims and structures one hindered effective co-operation, resulting rather in division and frequent conflicts of interest, counteracting the aspirations of the treaty between them.[11] Structurally, France and Germany are very different. A highly centralised and legislative administrative system in the France[12] contrasts with the devolution of many powers to the separate Laender in the FRG's constitution.[13] Centralization in France has generally been accompanied by a preference for *dirigisme* exemplified by the post-war *Commissariat du Plan* (Planning Commission), whereas the leaders of the FRG favoured an alternative path embodied in Chancellor Ludwig Erhard's free market economy. On the social level, difference in class structures and ideology remain far more apparent in France where deep cleavages amongst separate political parties and the rival Communist, Socialist and Catholic Trade Union groups striking for the homogeneity of its people and their aims, most vividly demonstrated in the consensus between workers and management.[14]

Differences between the two countries foreign policy aims and freedom of action were often no less marked during this period. Gaullist stress on national sovereignty and hostility to the 'apatrides' of Brussels stood fundamentally at odds with much more integrationist feeling in Bonn. Changes in the government in both France and Germany in 1969-70 led to significant changes in the orientation of their domestic and European policies. The pursuit of *Ostpolitik* turned the FRG in the perception of the French political elites, from a reliable junior partner to an 'unreliable and independent ally', competing for influence in Moscow. It reopened French fears of Germany with a resurgent economy facing an economically shaky France, and the old spectre of Germany 'turning towards the East'. Mistrust of German motives was strong in France and this was further strengthened by the poor personal relations between Brandt and Pompidou.[15] During this period, French shift towards Britain became a necessary counterbalance of the Franco-German relations as a certain convergence of British and French approaches to the transatlantic relationship and to the Middle East relations assisted the entente that was necessary for them.[16] Chancellor Brandt's *Ostpolitik* drew little enthusiasm and kindled the fear of an economically powerful and politically liberated Germany, perhaps marching to unification and these became significant factors in French acceptance of British membership of the EC.[17]

A factor which paved the way for renewed Franco-German rapport in Europe came from the more relaxed stance towards the EC under French President Valery Giscard d'Estaing and German Chancellor Helmut Schmidt, both of whom had shared experience as fellow Finance Minister in the early 1970s. Despite the constraints imposed by the nationalist leanings of the Gaullists and Communists alike, French European policy was placed on a more pragmatic surface, which falling short of more federalist feeling in Germany, had nonetheless come to put less stress on national independence and moved away from the legalistic formulase and strict demarcation between supranationality and inter governmentalism. Significantly, President Giscard accepted the creation of a directly elected European Council.[18] The Council may be seen as of evident Gaullian lineage, preserving the de facto power of each head of government to veto policies not deemed compatible with the national interest. But at the same time it may also be seen as constituting the European executive and providing the driving force behind any progress in the EC.[19]

Ever since France and Germany began to play a crucial role in the process of European integration, no major initiative within the European Community has been possible without their cooperation. This became particularly evident after Giscard d' Estaing's election to the Presidency in May 1974. Declaring his interest in closer cooperation with the FRG and improving relations with the US over the Atlantic Alliance, he also brought about new dimensions to economic policies by initiating stricter control over the EC budget. President Giscard's more favourable attitude to the US, which stemmed from an awareness of interdependence and less strict observance of the Gaullist doctrine of multipolarity, brought some convergence between France and Germany *vis-a-vis* the US. A greater European role in world affairs remained significant of Giscard's presidential platform, yet it no longer presented with a competitive edge towards the US as in the past. During his July 1980 state visit to Germany, President Giscard remarked that his desire for European independence did not imply independence 'from' anyone but rather an independent existence 'in itself' which was not incompatible with the Alliance.[20] On other international issues, French policy in Africa and the Middle East met with approval in the FRG.

French and German economic interests also came of overlap in the late 1970s, pushing the two countries closer. The replacement of Finance Minister Jacques Chirac, a Gaullist, by Raymond Barre, a former Vice President of the European Commission, in France to a certain extent helped foster French economic policy on *Modell Deutschland*. Although this did not prove entirely successful, it nevertheless indicated recognition of the need to modify thinking by removing price controls and reducing the government's role in the industry.[21] After the meeting in February 1977 in the framework of the Franco-German Treaty, a joint declaration by Giscard d'Estaing and Helmut Schmidt stated the hope that the EC might "renew in 1978, progress towards economic and Monetary Union, an obligatory passageway on the road towards the Union of Europe".[22] In December 1977, the European Council heard the Commission's proposal on the European Monetary System (EMS). It was after March 1978 elections in France, after fears of dividing further Presidential parties over European policy were dispelled (after the defeat of the Socialist Union), that intense consultation between Germany and France were initiated on monetary policy, and the EMS was announced in July 1978. In September 1978, the French government presented to the National Assembly its new macro-economic and industrial policies overtly modelled on the FRG.

As France sought to align domestic policies on the FRG, the latter distanced itself from the US. French foreign policy towards the US came to influence German attitudes towards the United States. At the core of German-American differences lay President Carter's 'dollar-and-defence-policy'. The one affected FRG's economic policies adversely,[23] the other threatened to introduce undesirable incalculability into German-Soviet relations.[24] Both contributed in bringing France and the FRG closer.

As global politics helped to shift West German foreign policy on a more regional focus, French European policies began to transform the political landscape in France. Both France and West Germany realised that the fall of the Mediterranean dictatorships implied an eventual enlargement of the EC to include Portugal, Spain and Greece. Both perceived parallel but different domestic costs and rewards; the West German trade unions feared the implications of the Mediterranean membership on free access to the domestic labour market of workers from the three candidates, while French farm organizations opposed Spain's request for membership for fear of competition from Spanish wine products. Conversely, Giscard d'Estaing's support for direct elections to the European Assembly stemmed from his long-term desire of meet long-standing West German requests for a more democratic community and also out of anticipation that the communist parties would be in a strong minority in a directly elected European Assembly.[25]

Notwithstanding the mutual relations of cooperation and adjustments, there still existed another aspect of French uncertainty *vis-a-vis* Germany. A less active role of the US in Europe or German disillusionment with the US enticements from the Soviet Union, hinting perhaps at improved relations with East Germany were treated in France as potential motives for a German drift to the East. These were all the more reasons for France to adopt a more community-minded stance to avoid estranging its partner and to co-operate with FRG in order to guarantee its links with Western Europe. Principally, there were still constraints on French European policy and on closer co-operation with the FRG, with regard to the integrationist-attitude of the FRG and the intergovernmentalist-minded France over European unification. On the wider question of Europe's position in the world, the French Presidents were obliged to conform to the board lines set out by Charles de Gaulle. Although improved relations between France and the FRG meant that France no longer needed to confront the FRG with the bare choice between France and the US, French calls for restoring greater Europe's power and influence required a delicate handling by the FRG as one of the Chancellor's aides quoted, "America is our most important ally. France is our closest ally".[26] Thus, while internal factors complicated French European policy, the FRG's exposed position and continuing dependence on the US for its security implied that German policy-makers were still obliged to shape their actions with broader considerations in mind.

Despite the divergences in their respective political aims, economic structure and philosophy, it was the cooperation between France and West Germany that paved the way for enlargement, EMS and the settlement of the dispute over the budgetary contribution. The agreement on the British budgetary issue represented a traditional Community package involving British concessions of France over lamb and farm prices and to the FRG on fishing, the latter in particular accepted a very large increase in its contribution to the EC budget. On enlargement, the role of France and Germany had not been collaborative so much as independent with the FRG being the most ardent supporter of new membership within the Nine, and France alternating between favouring and opposing the claims of the three candidates *i.e.* Greece, Spain and Portugal.

The modifications of the Common Agricultural Policy (CAP) and the restructuring of the Community budget also required the involvement of France and Germany. Despite Giscard's more liberal stance towards the EC, the agricultural policy was (and continues to be) a sensitive area for the French, while Chancellor Schmidt emphasised at the Venice Summit of 1980, his desire for action on the budget and an unwillingness to accept an increase in the one percent VAT contribution. This led to a co-ordinated demand by France and the FRG for maximum cuts in non-farm items in the Commission's 1981 draft budget–a stance not entirely favoured by some Member States.

In 1979-80 and in 1980-82, France was again preoccupied with the 'German problem' and with 'the threat of a new Rapallo'– of the FRG turning to the East and preferring the prospect of reunification to the maintenance of western solidarity and less well-established understandings between the new Mitterrand administration and its German counterparts led to a short-lived crisis in Franco-German relations after the imposition of martial law in Poland in December 1981. French attacks on the FRG for its failure to support the US firmly under conditions of East-West tension, repeated from 1981 to the change of German government in 1983. This reflected the perceived dependence of France on Germany for their security and cooperation. Such tensions indicated that not only their remained considerable differences of approach to foreign policy between the two countries and to the respective roles that they should play in transatlantic and East-West relations, but also that the sense of mutual dependence—of the necessity of maintaining the closest possible relations with Germany was the first priority of French foreign policy. French willingness to reopen a dialogue on defence policy between the two countries in 1982 and President Mitterrand's vigorous and politically valuable support for Chancellor Schmidt on the need to accept US intermediate nuclear missiles in Germany, were indicative of French adjustment to a more assertive and self confident Germany. A German government which was no longer subservient either to American or French pressures required a more vigorous and viable demonstration of French support for shared interests in order to maintain German support for the vital interests of France.[27]

THE EIGHTIES

By the early 1980s, Germany emerged a self-confident nation which stemmed from its economic strength and political respectability. There was an acceptance within the German elite that it was still convenient to follow France in European initiatives, although not in Eastern Europe or on transatlantic relations.

From the outset, West German leaders favoured integration, while at the same time eschewing a unilateral leadership role. They tend to accept their role as the paymasters of the EC. Bonn's European policy often appeared contradictory because the management of the EC business was highly fragmented at the level of the central government and within the Laender.[28]

The premise and practice of Germany's partnership in the EC revolved around its relationship to France. The EMS, the decisive proposals for political union and the expansion of the EC's international profile were all attributed to the Franco-German friendship which Chancellor Kohl declared in 1987, 'the dynamic force in the process of European integration'.[29] Beyond the Franco-German axis lay certain economic and political goals of Germany's European policy. Germany's economic goals with respect to the EC related to its pursuit of economic liberalism and growth, a social market economy and internal stability. By the beginning of the 1980s, Germany had established a pattern of balancing contradictory pragmatic needs, resulting from different domestic, political and economic pressures.[30]

As far as its political goals were concerned, Chancellor Schmidt had already rejected the common dual perception of Germany as an economic giant and political dwarf.[31] Germany moved beyond economic sphere to shape the framework of European Political Cooperation (EPC), that was the most viable demonstration that the EC was more than a Common Market and Custom's Union. The Genscher-Colombo Initiative of 1981, the Stuttgart Solemn Declaration of 1983 on the EC and the Kohl-Mitterrand proposals of 1985 all contributed to the conclusion of the Single European Act of 1986 which set the EC's agenda for the 1990s reiterating their commitment to political union. Germany's active pursuit of EPC and political union reflected the dual goals of national political and economic interests satisfied through an 'internally coherent and externally assertive EC, and an idealistic conviction based on German history, that the EC represented an antidote to excessive nationalism'.[32] The idea of the EC as an international actor presupposed a separate European identity different from other international actors.[33] The EC was viewed by German officials as a way to retain their own cultural identity as *Kulturnation* or *Staatnation,* and to develop loyalties that went beyond the nation.[34]

UNIFICATION OF GERMANY

With the unification of Germany, its relation with the EC showed signs of alternation. Until 1989, Germany's national unity was connected to its EC focus. Since 1990, with Chancellor Kohl's reaffirmation of Europe 'as every German's future' and the EC's acceptance of unification, the two have become intensely interlined. When Germany was divided some EC issues had special German dimension; with unification of Germany, almost every topic of EC's agenda became Germany specific.[35]

German unification required Germany to anew its commitment to universal values and democratic principles. For the other Member States of the EC, German unification accelerated the process of European integration. For Germany, however, it was an absolute priority. Germany's thrust during discussion over the Maastricht Treaty for a federal Europe, for increased supranationalism through a strong Parliament and Commission reflected Germany's will to blend self-interest with a larger vision. Through political union, Germany sought an enshrinement of its post-war ideals of muted national power and the opportunity to exert international influence.[36] During the negotiations of the Maastricht Treaty, German emphasis on federalism, 'subsidiarity' and a Committee of Regions enhanced the role of the German Laender. Consequently, Germany also expanded and institutionalised the participation of the Laender in the EC policy, ensuring the public concern that their interests and regional identities not be lost in the process of integration.[37]

The disintegration of the Soviet Union synchronised with the unification of Germany and brought with it old and new questions about the German factor in the Central European equation. With the political upheavals in the Central East European Countries (CEEC), Germany's *Ostpolitik* gained a new dimension and greater momentum. This was largely due to the fact that Germany being the closest Western neighbour of the volatile East was most vulnerable to any social, political and economic upheaval of that region. High unemployment, rising inflation and nationalist excesses led to a wave of migration from CEEC to Germany in the post Cold War era.[38] Germany's geopolitical and economic ties with the CEEC makes it indispensable for Germany to shoulder most of its financial aid and assistance to the CEEC. As the pivotal nation located in the heart of Europe, Germany is geared to use the next few years to prepare the EU for a decisive phase of enlargement.

Two other important objective for the German government seems to be revolving around narrowing the gap between the East and West, and to make Germany a more effective proponent of European integration.[39] To quote, Helmut Kohl: "It is neither in Germany's interest nor in Europe's interest that the Western border of Poland remains the Eastern border of the EC".[40]

Unification of Germany led other Member States to fear the rise of a *Mitteleuropa* which would drift to the East in search of markets. But German interest in an economically vibrant European economy has not been undermined by unification. The FRG's experience of federation with a diffusion of power throughout the political system, makes it less sensitive concerning sovereignty than its partners like France which has strong unitary political systems. Although there were inevitable fears of a resurgent German nationalism, there was considerable persuasive power in the assertion that Germany would co-operate with France to further integration.

FRENCH RESPONSE TO GERMAN UNIFICATION

The unification of Germany beneath the roof of EC brought new dimensions and controversies to European integration. In the post-Second World War era, it was felt by the West Europeans that Germany is safe when weak and divided. The special position that France enjoyed in a divided Europe built on a divided Germany in the post-Second World War period was severely challenged by the upheavals of 1989. Its political ascendancy over the truncated Germany, its status as a permanent member of the UN Security Council and its possession of a nuclear deterrent seemed to lose credibility with the changes in the European landscape. The dramatic shift in French foreign policy came with the unification of Germany. When the limited sovereignty of the FRG, hitherto a counterbalance to its economic strength, was replaced by a fully sovereign united Germany, France sought to bolster European integration as a necessary step to bind a unified Germany to European framework.[41] In the Bastille-Day Speech in 1990, President Mitterrand said :

> It is to turn the whole Europe into one space,... a single and vast market and at the same time constant and structural links established among all the European countries. This is why I have talked about a confederation....I would like the community of the twelve to strive for its own economic, monetary and political entity...[42]

This reflected a long-term view of the concentric circles of French policy for Europe—the Community within the confederation and the Franco-German axis at the centre. As in the decade prior to 1989, France was still a critical part of the equation for Germany in the years after 1989, as Foreign Minister Klaus Kinkel has noted,

> Our future lies in a European Union that is close to the people and open to the world... together with ours closest friend and partner, France, we will continue to be the driving force for European unification.[43]

TREATY ON EUROPEAN UNION

In April 1990, the Kohl-Mitterrand initiative to revive momentum towards the political union was followed by the Treaty on European Union which heralded a giant leap from the Community to the Union.[44]

The major objective of France was to create the Economic and Monetary Union (EMU) which was viewed as an attempt to curb the "predominance of the Bundesbank and the Deuschemark". Equally, the Common Foreign and Security Policy (CFSP) would also make it possible to channel the German dominance into the EC. Despite differences over the strength of the European Parliament, the independence of the Central Bank and the speed and scope of East European countries integration with the EC, France and Germany demonstrated the capacity for compromises necessary to propel the EC. The major examples were the 1990 initiatives on political union, the 1991 plans on CFSP, creation of the Franco-German corps, the joint attempt to support the ERM after 1991 and the combined effort after the French referendum on the Maastricht Treaty to make the integration process more democratic and transparent.[45]

Franco-German determination to seek solutions and improvise the somewhat intractable problems within the EC has made the relationship the motor of European integration.[46] Most alliances are made to advance or protect common interests. France and Germany has an alliance which not only seeks to find common interests but also reflect their political priorities and tries to ensure that the treaty outcomes are as close as possible to their interests. This is indicative of the on-going process of competition and cooperation between the two major forces of European integration. The agreement on monetary union and common defence policy during the Maastricht negotiations involved a concession and a bargain between France and Germany. The central advance at Maastricht for the French was the agreement on monetary union. By accepting a Single European Currency in 1999, Germany sacrificed the Deutschemark. Secondly, on agreeing with Germany to form an integrated military command tied to the West European Union, French obsession with maintaining a strict national defence was also sacrificed. The bargain amounted to German sacrifice of monetary sovereignty for French sacrifice of military sovereignty.

After more than 40 years, the Franco-German tandem which has been the basic ingredient in European integration is undergoing perceptible changes. The generational change between the Member States came with French reluctance to embrace the Germanic design which proposed a federal framework for the European Commission during the German Presidency in 1994. This design proposed that the EC should quickly embrace the CEEC, give real powers to the European Parliament and turn the European Commission into a federal government. The internal reform needed to prepare the EU for further enlargement has proved divisive. While former German Defence Minister, Volker Ruehe declared that the 'nation state is dead', former French prime Minister Edouard Balladur announced,

> France is the oldest nation in Europe.... and has given the rest of the world the concept of the nation and of liberty whose combination underlines our notion of democracy.[47]

The northern enlargement of the European Union (EU) in 1995 and prospects of future eastward enlargement is already proving decisive in shifting the weight and strength of the EU to Germany. Germany has already exhibited its overwhelming interest in expanding the EU eastward. To avoid being marginalised by EU's eastward expansion or in other words to counter Germany's domineering influence,

France has redressed the balance by securing trade concessions for its erstwhile colonies in the southern fringes.[48]

Unlike some of the other Member States, Germany considers 'deepening' and 'widening' as compatible with one another. Regardless of how problematic an intensification of the EU might be in view of the growing heterogeneity which would automatically accompany accession by new members, the simultaneous performance of both goals are important for Germany. Traditionally closed to the idea of an enlarged EU, France is apprehensive of the fact that subsequent expansion of the EU will run the risk of reducing the internal cohesion of the Union and convert it into nothing more than a free-market area. French advocacy of the EMU and supporting the political union in the IGC, 1996 stemmed from a commitment to strengthen the EU institutions before any further enlargements.

Prior to the commencement of the Inter-Governmental Conference (IGC) of 1996, Germany and France devised measures and offered proposals for reactivating European integration. In 1994, Germany's ruling Christian Democratic Coalition released a policy paper outlining a strategy aiming to create a 'hard-core' of European states around a Franco-German axis that would move towards deeper integration.[49] The CDU also came with proposals for a new structure which would not allow any country to block integration by those who choose to go ahead,[50] outlining a vision of a 'multi-speed' Europe thereby setting off fears in Britain and Italy of a Franco-German domination of the EU. Strains in Franco-German relations arose with respect to Germany's concerns over the EU budget and French sensitiveness over the CAP. Unified Germany's economic environment has noticeably affected its EU policies over the budget. Previous German concerns about being the main pay-master of the EU was demonstrated in Germany's opposition to the Delors II package to finance the Maastricht goals. The discrepancy between contributions and payments still exists. Germany contributed 25 per cent of the total budget in 1990 and received 12.9 per cent. The reality that the federal budget would increase by less than 3 per cent has rendered the EU's proposed budget of 10 per cent annual increase practically untenable and the suggestion of a ECU 6 billion increase in Germany's contribution between 1992 and 1997 politically impossible.[51]

While the Single Market has opened France to foreign investments, the EU has made it difficult to continue with its policies of state-subsidies and anti-competitive regulation. For all the modifications it has undergone, CAP still requires more reforms in EU's farm policy and farm prices in view of future enlargement to Eastern Europe. Ever since the EU accepted the idea that farming should be subject to world trade arrangements, there are continuous pressures for implementing further price cuts. Any efforts for the reform of the CAP is likely to meet with disagreements in an agriculture-sensitive France which has always had reservations concerning farm support and CAP budget. Germany, on the other hand, proposed reform of the CAP which has been taking away more than half of EU budget and seeks to ensure a strict budgetary discipline and fairer fiscal burden-sharing.

The road to EMU has generated some divisive tensions for France and Germany. Faced with soaring unemployment and budget deficits, France has begun to realise the shortcomings of being inside a currency-zone designed and likely to run along the lines of the Bundesbank. France is liable to suffer from more unemployment dislocation and restricted market-access than Germany.

CONCLUSION

Any study of the Franco-German co-operation should be identified with the impact of personality and political leadership as continuing factors for shaping and reshaping the constraints under which governments operate as they interact. Chancellor Adenauer and President de Gaulle, Giscard d'Estaing and Helmut Schmidt, Francois Mitterrand and Helmut Kohl stand out as examples of personalities between heads of governments which altered the configuration of relations. Other less successful personal links like Pompidou and Brandt with their suspicion and misunderstandings altered prevailing patterns of *rapprochement.*

Franco-German co-operation was based on the premise of French recognition of the necessity of harnessing German economic strength to French objectives. This was matched by German tolerance of French activism and awareness that French initiatives could also be harnessed to German ends.[52] In view of the fact that the attitude of the other Member States could present a restraining influence on Franco-German collaborations, both the countries are aware of the friction that could be caused by too blatant an impression of hegemony. Italy's preoccupation with domestic matters and Britain's undecided and unclear role in Europe leave with no alternative but to continuing the unhindered pre-eminence of France and Germany in the EU. Nevertheless, the Franco-German axis as the motor of EU would have been short-lived without the agreement of the other EU Member States, indicating the acceptance of the situation as it is and asserting rights of those left out.[53]

NOTES

1. Chopra, H.S., "European Policy Options: An Indian Perspective" in K. Subramanyam and Jasjit Singh (ed.), *Global Security: Some Issues and Trends-An Indo-German Dialogue* (New Delhi: Lancer International, 1987) p.82.
2. Jordan, Robert S., (ed.), *Europe and the Super Powers: Perception of European International Politics* (Boston : All You & Bacon, 1971) pp. 30-31.
3. Theodore C.Sorensen, *Kennedy* (New York : Harper & Row, 1965) pp. 644-45.
4. For details see, H.S. Chopra, *De Gaulle and European Unity* (New Delhi : Abhinav, 1965).
5. Jules Moch, *Historie du Rearmament Allemand Depuis, 1950* (Paris : Robert Laffort, 1965), p. 333 as cited in H.S. Chopra, "The Franco-German Reconciliation : its relevance to the Indo-Pak perspective on South Asian Peace Order", Paper

presented in the seminar SAARC 2000 and Beyond, IIC New Delhi, 24 March 1995, p.15.

6. See Robert Aldrich and John Connel (ed.), *France in World Politics* (London : Routledge, 1989) p.47.
7. Wallace, W., "Foreign Policy the Management of Distinctive Interests", in Roger Morgan & Carolyn Gray (ed.) *Partners and Rivals in Western Europe* (Aldershot: Gower, 1986) p. 206.
8. See for background details, R. Morgan, *The United States and West Germany, 1945-1973: A Study in Alliance Politics* (London: Gower, 1974) and James L. Richardson, *Germany and the Atlantic Alliance,* (Massachusetts: Cambridge, 1966).
9. Wallace, n. 7, p. 206-207.
10. Wallace, W., "Introduction : The Shaping of Close Relationships", in Morgan and Gray, (ed.), n. 7, p. 1
11. For a closer analysis of these factors in the past, see Robert Piche (ed.), *Deutschland-Frankreich-Europa : Bilanz einer schwierigen Partnerschaft* (Munich : Piper, 1978) pp. 19-239.
12. See, Roy Pierce, *French Politics and Political Institutions* (New York: Harper and Row, 1973).
13. Alfred Grosser, *The Federal Republic of Germany: A Concise History* (New York : Praeger, 1964).
14. Simonian, Haig, "France, Germany and Europe", *Journal of Common Market Studies,* Vol. 19, no. 3, Mach 1981, p. 205.
15. For Pompidou's attitude and the friction that developed in Franco-German relations in mid-1973, see M. Ullmann, "Security aspects in French foreign policy", *Survival,* vol. 15, no. 6, Nov.-Dec. 1973, pp. 262-267.
16. A considerable evidence to indicate the effect of German economic strength on French attitude towards British membership in the EC dates back to the Bonn IMF Conference of November 1968 and the Soames Affair of 1969. The latter which involved de Gaulle and the British Ambassador in Paris, Sir Christopher Soames focussed on the future of Atlantic Alliance and the need to forge a closer tie between a weakened France and Britain to help maintain a balance in Europe with Germany. In this context see, *Le Monde,* 11 March 1969 and Sulzberger's interview with de Gaulle in *International Herald Tribune,* 11 November 1970.
17. For a more detailed examination of the motives surrounding the French desire for enlargement see, Vincent Berger, *Pompidou and the Construction of Europe* (translated), (Paris : University of Droit, 1973).

18. For the development of the European Council, see, Annette Morgan, *From Summit to Council: Evolution in the EEC* (London: Chatham House, 1976).
19. *Le Monde,* 7 December 1978.
20. *The Times,* 12 July 1980.
21. The theme 'German Model' came to dominate political debate in France. Both the Gaullists and the Communists dealt with growing vehemence on the President's alleged subordination to German interests as the Gaullist's developing the argument that Giscard was preparing the 'subservience' of France to Germany. Cf Jonathan Story, "The Franco-German Alliance", *The World Today,* vol. 36, no. 6, June 1980, p. 214.
22. *Le Monde,* 6-7 February 1977, cited in Story, n. 21, p. 212.
23. See, T. de. Vries, "Saving the Dollar", *The World Today,* January 1979.
24. On differences over detente between the US and the FRG, see David Watt, "The Atlantic Alliance needs leaders who face the facts", *The Economist,* 11 October 1988, pp. 19-28.
25. See Julian Crandall Hollick, "Direct Elections to the European Parliament : the French Debate", *The World Today,* December 1977.
26. Cf. Simonian, n. 14, p. 216.
27. Wallace, n. 10, p. 6.
28. Though the reform of the CAP was a major German goal in the 1980s, yet Ignaz Kiechle, the German Agriculture Minister, used the veto to block the agreement on cereal prices on the eve of the Milan European Council Meeting in 1985. The needs of the Bavarian cereal producers took precedence over the Community's concerns. See, G. Hendricks, "Germany and CAP: National Interest and the EC", *International Affairs,* vol. 65, 1988/89, pp. 75-87.
29. Germany, "Policy Statement by Helmut Kohl to the Bundestag, 18 March 1987, *European Political Cooperation* (Bonn : Press and Information Office, 1988), pp. 378.
30. Simon Bulmer and W. Patterson, *The Federal Republic of Germany and the* European Community (London : Allen and Unwin, 1987).
31. For text see, Wolfram Hanreider (ed.), *Helmut Schmidt : Perspectives on Politics* (Boulder : Westview Press, 1982), p. 209.
32. Roger Morgan, "Federal Republic of Germany", in C.Twitchett and K. Twithet (ed.), *Building Europe: Britain*

Partners in the EEC (London : Europa, 1981) pp. 61-66.

33. Feldman, Lily G., "Germany and the EC : Realism and Responsibility", *The Annals of American Academy,* vol. 531, January 1994, p. 31.
34. Eberhard Schulz, "Unfinished Business : The German National Question and the Future of Europe, *International Affairs,* Vol. 60, no. 3, 1984. During the Solemn Declaration of 1983, Helmut Kohl and Foreign Minister Genscher amplified their goals on EC to develop a sense of common cultural heritage among Member States. See *EPC*, n. 29, pp. 349, and 378."
35. Feldman, n. 33, p.33.
36. See for details, D. Rotfield and W. Stuezle, *Germany and Europe in Transition* (New York : Oxford, 1991).
37. Jeffrey, Charles, "Towards a Third level in Europe? The German Laender in the EU", *Political Studies,* Vol. 44, no. 2, June 1996, pp. 253-66.
38. See, Gerd Langguth, "Germany, EC and the Architecture of Europe", *Aussen Politik,* vol. 42, no.2, 1991, pp. 137-146.
39. *Financial Times,* 14 October 1994.
40. *International Herald Tribune,* 24 November 1994.
41. Buchan, David, "Mitterrand Urges Early Talks on EC Monetary Integration", *Financial Times,* 26 October 1989.
42. R.Tiersky, "France in new Europe", *Foreign Affairs,* Vol. 71, no. 2, Spring 1992, p. 139.
43. Klaus Kinkel, Verantwortung, Realismus Zunkunftsschwierung : Deutsche Aussen Politik in einer sich neue ordnenden Welt", *Frankfurter Allgemeine Zeitung,* 19 March 1993.
44. See, L. Kellanway, "Kohl backs Mitterrand in support for Union", *Financial Times,* 23 November 1989; *The Economist,* 4 November 1989, p. 58.
45. Deubner, C., "The Role of the French-German couple in European Integration in the 1990s : Disruption or Continuity?" Washington: International Conference on European Community Studies Association, May 1993.
46. For historical background see, Haig Simonian, *The Privileged Partnership : Franco-German Relations in the European Community* (New York : Oxford, 1985).
47. *The Economist,* 3 December 1994, p. 60.
48. Chancellor Kohl's decision to invite CEEC at the Essen Summit in December 1994 raised hopes for a German led

strategy to build a wider Europe. To counter this, France aimed at balancing the priorities by allocating ECU 5.5 billion to the Mediterranean states and embrace North Africa and Middle East in a free trade zone. See, *Financial Times,* 12 December 1994.

49. For text see, "Agence Europe", *Europe Documents,* no. 1895/96, 7 September 1994.
50. *The Times* (London), 2 September 1994.
51. See Anita Wolf, "Bundesrepublik Deutschland" in *Jahrbuch der Europaeische Integration, 1991/92* (Bonn : Europa, 1992) p. 315.
52. Wallace, n. 10, p. 217.
53. *The Times,* 13 August 1980.

Chapter II

France, Germany and the Maastricht Treaty

In the European Community (EC), the outcome of integration had always been related to a particular pattern of institutional and constitutional development.[1] The form of integration launched by Robert Schuman in 1950 was characterized by a transfer of powers from the Member States to the Community. Since its inception, the Community has seen an expansion of its policy, scope and membership while other West European organizations, like, the Council of Europe, European Free Trade Area (EFTA) and the Norden have found themselves adapting to the development of the EC. The late 1980's brought in several new challenges which created incentives for greater cohesion and deeper integration. Faced with increasing global competition from the United States and Japan and hampered by rigidities in industrial structure and labour market policies, Europe's future economic policy demanded a renewed vigour and integrational thrust. The 'European malady' which the Albert and Ball Report spoke of, engulfed the EC.[2] Although the Treaty of Rome set out to establish a Common Market, a host of non-tariff barriers to trade remained and free movement of goods and capital was not fully achieved. It was the Single European Act of 1986 that installed an area without frontiers in which the free movement of goods, persons, services and capital was ensured in accordance with the provisions of the Treaty.

THE EUROPEAN COMMUNITY AND THE END OF THE COLD WAR

A year of revolutionary change has given both East and West Europeans a new vision of common destiny distinct from the needs and ambitions of the Soviet Union and the United States. The year 1989 heralded a glorious upheaval against a dying order in Eastern Europe and in the prosperous Western Europe, it brought an adjustment replete with apprehensions, hopes and new challenges. While visible and radical changes were occurring behind a collapsing Iron Curtain, more subtle and fundamental shifts in power balances were under way in the western part of the continent. West German influence on European events became dominant, filling much of the vacuum created by the collapse of the Soviet Union. Gorbachev's "Common European Home" and Bush's "Europe Whole and Free" produced by an economic and ideological collapse of the Soviet power, appeared to be gaining new dynamism and economic clout.

The EC's decision to embark on the completion of the internal market by 1992 gave renewed impetus to economic integration. It led to a reassessment of policies on economic and social cohesion, on the environment and social issues. However, there was one aspect of the Community which, despite all the strenuous efforts and setbacks and sporadic bursts of optimism, could never be touched. The preamble of the Rome Treaty about the "ever closer union of the peoples of Europe " was something no one could really say how and whither it was really moving.[3] Economic integration was all that was promoted. The political structures which formed a system of traditions was an extremely sensitive zone. Convinced Europeans consoled themselves over and over again with the idea that economic integration would sooner or later be followed by political union. But as all the wars of this century revealed, how quickly the network of economic cooperation is hampered by political antagonism, the idea of political union gradually gained predominance in order to retain the economic integration in a tighter framework.

The idea of European Union (EU) suddenly received a special, new and unexpected thrust when the Soviet Union began to disintegrate in the autumn of 1989. The European idea which had hitherto rested on the premise of a divided world found itself faced with pressures, no longer from outside but from within, from the United Germany which was already beginning to haunt some Member States in the shape of a "Fourth Reich".[4] The most pertinent of all was France which suddenly found itself abruptly forced into the periphery.[5]

The profound political changes in Europe along with the Gulf War provided the motivation for renewed interest in the international role of the EC. The Gulf War highlighted how diversity rather than coherence characterized the Member States' responses to the war. It also demonstrated the striking gap between EC's economic weight and political capacity.

The decline of the Soviet threat and acceleration of disarmament also changed Europe's security environment in a profound manner. The former Soviet Union's formidable nuclear arsenal, the fear of a unified Germany and a destabilized Eastern Europe bringing in the question of minorities, frontiers and self-determination gave rise to new pleas for restructuring European security.[6] While the EC was characterized by integration, high levels of material welfare and political stability, the Eastern bloc was characterized by political turbulence, destruction of civil society, economic stagnation and revival of ethnic tensions. The EC became a central pillar in the reconstruction of Eastern Europe and an anchor of stability in a rapidly changing continent. The EC established itself as a point of reference for the future stabilization of eastern Europe through its democratic credentials and its resources for economic opportunities for trade.[7]

The key question in the early 1990's was whether or not the EC could amass sufficient political and economic capacity to tackle the multiple challenges facing it — the challenge of internal integration, and the demands of the East Europeans and the European Free Trade Area (EFTA) group who sought to refashion their relation with the EC for better access in the Community's Single Market. On the face of it, there was a tussle between the impulse towards deeper integration through Political Union and Economic and Monetary Union and the aspiration of the non-members for membership in the EC. With the end of the Cold War, the EC had new tasks in its agenda:

- consolidation of its economic and political integration;
- to assist the East European countries in transition to a free market economy and pluralist civil society;
- to find means of socio-economic and political rehabilitation of Soviet Union, the failure of which might have led to a resurgence of nationalist forces;
- to restructure its capabilities as a world economic power in the emerging new world order;
- to confront a cluster of issues that emerged with the blurring of the political boundary of the East and the West. Enlarging its domain geographically became a potent factor.

It was no longer the internal market, with the famous four freedoms which was to be effected on schedule: monetary union with a common central bank became the target. At the same time the first steps were to be taken towards political union through a Common Foreign and Security Policy (CFSP), including common justice and home affairs.

FRANCO-GERMAN CO-OPERATION AND EUROPEAN INTEGRATION

European integration has always received a special impetus from the Franco-German axis.[8] From the very outset, Germany has been the driving force of European integration and whenever it has teamed up with France, the rest of the EC has had very little choice but to follow. The decision to establish the European Coal and Steel Community (ECSC) in 1951 was based on a realization by the French that integration produced the best anchor for the new and truncated West Germany. The Elysee Treaty of 1963 on Franco-German cooperation provided an institutional basis for the development of an intensive bilateral relationship between these two countries at political levels. The Franco-German relationship has not only been critical in fashioning major political initiatives in the EC but also enabled the two governments to ensure that bilateral disputes on various policy issues did not prevent agreement on a wider forum. During the 1970s, the Paris-Bonn axis was cemented by a very close relationship between Chancellor Helmut Schmidt of the Federal Republic of Germany (FRG) and President Giscard d'Estaing of France. In the 1980s, Chancellor Helmut Kohl and President Francois Mitterrand undertook major policy initiatives in European integration which bore the stamp of Franco-German accord.

Faced with multiple challenges in the 1990s, it became a major issue for France and unified Germany to amass the EC with sufficient political and economic strength to help face the challenges.[9] United Germany's keenness to enhance European integration and French eagerness to bind a united Germany within the European framework came in the form of a Kohl-Mitterrand resolution of April 1990 which called for a Intergovernmental Conference (IGC) on political union which was to run parallel to the Economic and Monetary Union.[10] The IGC was essentially a strong political statement that the Franco-German axis had partly overcome the uneasiness created by German unification. Following the two IGC on Economic and Monetary Union (EMU) and European Political Union (EPU), the Maastricht Summit culminated in December 1991.[11] It was a giant leap for the Community to gradually transform into a Union.

FRENCH MOTIVATIONS BEHIND THE MAASTRICHT TREATY

Since the end of the Second World War, France supposedly had a geopolitical interest in avoiding German unification. In a divided Europe with divided Germany, French overall interest was maximized. It pursued three policy options in order to check an over-powerful neighbour:

— form an alliance with the eastern neighbours of Germany to contain Germany from both sides;
— draw Britain and the US into a tight commitment to maintaining the European balance against German power;
— draw Germany itself into an intimate partnership with France, forging bonds of economic and political interdependence.[12]

The French argument against a centralized Germany was two fold: that Germany in the past was peaceful when decentralized and that a unified Germany could pose a threat in Europe.

The unification of Germany beneath the roof of the EC brought new dimensions and controversies to European integration and to Franco-German cooperation. When unification became a *fait accompli*, many West European states, particularly France sought to bolster up European unity and include a unified Germany in the European framework as a necessary step to persuade Europe that Germany can and will be accommodated as part of a wider structure. Germany's remarkable involvement with Eastern Europe, its strategic location at the centre of Europe and its demographic and economic weight made France fear that a united Germany could be tempted to strive for a hegemonic role in Europe. The consequences of German unity was in Pierre Lellouche's pungent words:

> an economically super-powerful Germany, politically dominant in Central Europe and France reduced to a secondary role, an end to Gaullist dreams of a Europe directed politically by a nuclear France.[13]

This brought out a long term view of the concentric circles of French policy for Europe: the community within the Confederation and the Franco-German axis at the centre. The 'grand design' which Mitterrand sought to give the EC could be realized by assuming the leadership role which France coveted so much. The Maastricht Treaty, a by-product of Franco-German cooperation came at a time when the need to further European integration became the foremost goal for French European policy.[14]

GERMAN MOTIVATION BEHIND THE MAASTRICHT TREATY

From the outset, the Federal Republic of Germany (FRG) has been closely involved with European integration. The essential feature of FRG's policy towards European integration was that Germany must never find itself again in the situation which led to the outbreak of both world wars, not float aimlessly and become a danger to peace. This implied a rejection to neutrality and entering into the EC and membership of the western defence alliance. In the 1950s the FRG saw the political momentum towards economic and political integration in Western Europe as a means for re-establishing its credentials as an independent state in the international community.

The collapse of the Soviet Union which synchronized with the unification of Germany increased the significance of Germany and heralded a new phase in the country's history. In terms of its population, its economic power and geographical location in Europe, Germany became a power factor which in the views of its partners, required a counterbalance.[15] The history of the two world wars which still looms large in the minds of Germany's neighbours, made them view unified Germany with mistrust and scepticism. The rejoining of the two German states gave the neighbours the impression that Germany could, yet again pursue a policy geared to purely national goals, create new spheres of influence, and foster the intention of shifting the already changed balance of power in Europe in a stronger manner. The 'bridge-head function' propagated by some Germans between Western and Eastern Europe was viewed as an attempt to move along special ways and to ensure a new hegemonic status in Europe.[16] Fiscal and monetary strength had aroused suspicion that unified Germany could in future, again concentrate to a greater extent on interests viewed in a purely national light and ruthlessly play its power against its partners.[17]

In order to nip in the bud the fears of a new German hegemony or a new German megalomania, Germany's primary intention after unification was to counter this suspicion harboured by its neighbours. Therefore, its policy towards Europe was to strike a balance between "clarity on issues, restraint, in style and sensitivity towards its neighbours".[18] There were considerable persuasive power in the assertion by Germans that a united Germany would be frightening for many Europeans and therefore Germany can actually exercise that power more effectively, without endangering fear within and outside as a member of the EC.[19] The concerns evoked by unification of Germany brought about an acceleration in the movement towards European integration. This was explicit from Hans Dietrich Genscher's statement at a meeting of the WEU, in March 1990, when unification became a *fait accompli,* he stated:

> We seek the process of German unification in the context of EC integration, the CSCE process, East-West partnership for stability, the construction of the common European house and the creation of a pan-European peaceful order. We Germans do not want to go it alone or to follow a separate path. We want to take the European path.[20]

German motives to deepen integration struck a familiar chord with French concern to bind united Germany in a European network and this joint endeavour culminated in the draft Treaty on European Union at Maastricht. West Germany's experience with federalism, and a distribution of power throughout the political system made it less sensitive concerning sovereignty than its partners. This was probably one reason why Germany was the only Member State which proposed political integration in the EC, without which monetary integration did not hold much meaning. Moreover for the EC aspiring for supranationalism in a federalist structure, political union would be a necessary prerequisite to achieve its goal of an "ever closer union of the peoples of Europe".

THE MAASTRICHT TREATY

The aim of the draft Treaty on European Union (TEU) was

to unify the basic elements that would entail in supranationalism in the EC.

These are as follows:

- to bring about the EMU over three stages; between 1992-94,
- to strengthen the fixed exchange rate parity of currencies through the Exchange Rate Mechanism (ERM);
- to promote the convergence of monetary and fiscal policy;
- to establish a common currency and a central bank by 1999;
- to initiate a design for the EPU which aimed to harmonize foreign policy interests of the Member States and establish a Common Foreign and Security Policy (CFSP) and create common policies in justice and home affairs;
- to include the eventual framing of a common defence policy and in time lead to a common defence;
- to adopt a Social Charter to standardize health and labour laws.[21]

The principal intent at Maastricht was to constitute a federal Union and to transform portions of national sovereignty to the EC's centralized agency. The Maastricht European Council meeting of December 1991 marked the end of year-long negotiations on EPU and EMU. A substantial agreement on the timetable for the EMU was created. A single currency was decided to be introduced in 1997, if seven states conform to the convergence criteria concerning economic performance laid down in the Treaty. In case this did not materialize then a single currency would be established in 1999 by those states who were capable of it. Following British reservations about a single currency, a protocol included to the treaty, allowed Britain to opt out of the move to a single currency. The inclusion of a date in the Treaty regarding the introduction of the single currency was the most important decision taken by the Member States since the foundation of the EC.[22] It also signified a political commitment to hand over responsibility for exchange rates to a European system of central bank.[23]

The TEU differed from the Treaty of Rome and the Single European Act in the following aspects. It introduced a Regional Cohesion Fund for the poorer members of the EC, due to the demands made by the Southern members of the

EC. However, this provision was not a part of the Treaty but annexed as protocol which promised a thorough evaluation of Structural Funds.[24]

The inclusion of the opt-out clause in a protocol following British reluctance to accept the social charter, was an entirely new concept. It led the other Member States to agree to proceed on matters of social policy on the basis of eleven Member States.[25]

The TEU sought to establish for the first time a direct relationship between the EC and the peoples of Europe. The goal for 'an even closer union of peoples' found more credence with the introduction of a common citizenship of the Union which intended to protect the rights and interests of the nationals of the Member States not only as workers but also as individuals.[26]

The TEU created two new pillars for the EC which extended its policy scope of the Union on the basis of an even stronger role for the Council of Ministers. These new pillars which provided for the creation of CFSP and Justice and Home Affairs was an attempt of bringing uniformity of policies and practices into the Community fold. While these new pillars sought to increase the policy scope of the new European Union in comparison to the old Community, they also illustrated the weakness of the 'single institutional structure' which the Union aimed to achieve.[27] The diversified structure of the Union could lead to the weakness in its ability to act ineffectively.

ECONOMIC AND MONETARY UNION

Under the Maastricht Treaty, the Member States of the EC were committed to an Economic and Monetary Union (EMU) by the end of the century. The EMU implies three stages as envisaged in the Delors Report of 1989.[28] Stage I was meant to comprise the consolidation of the Exchange Rate Mechanism (ERM), removal of the remaining exchange controls and passage of the other EC legislation, to complete the Single European Market in goods, services, labour and capital. It was almost flown off the track by the currency turmoil of 1992-93 due to some delays in the ratification of the Treaty. During the period, the lira and the sterling were forced out of the ERM, several other currencies were devalued, and the mechanism only survived by resorting to massive widening of the fluctuation bands. Stage II of the EMU process came into effect in January 1994 which implied the transition between Stage II and full EMU. The essential objective of transition was to achieve close convergence of economic performance among the states which were candidates for EMU. The Treaty set out four main criteria by which convergence was to be attained. They were as follows:

- The respective national rate of inflation should not exceed the average rate of inflation of the three best performing Member States in terms of price stability by more than 1.5 percentage points,
- the long-terms nominal interest rate level should exceed the corresponding average of the three best performing Member States in terms of price stability by at the most two percentage points,
- the level of public debt should not be excessively high (annual new borrowings should not exceed 3 per cent and the total government debt 60 per cent of national gross domestic product), and
- the national currency should stay within the fluctuation margins provided for the EMS without devaluation during the past two years.

Otherwise, the Treaty's regulations required entry into the final stage of the European Monetary Union by 1 January 1999 at the latest. As specified in Article 109J(4) of the TEU, only those EU Member States could participate in this case which have fulfilled the aforementioned convergence criteria.[29]

Apart from the convergence criteria and the 'excessive deficit' procedure aimed at limiting fiscal deficits, the main innovation in Stage II was the establishment of the European Monetary Institute (EMI), a new body empowered with the tasks of strengthening the monetary policy coordination during the transition and making the technical preparations for Stage III.

The essential feature of Stage III would be the pooling of responsibility for monetary policy in the hands of a new European Central Bank (ECB). Its chief function would be to formulate and administer the single monetary policy, managing short-term conditions in all the Member States participating in the EU. Stage III implied the irrevocable locking of exchange rates between participating currencies. The ECB has the absolute commitment to convert currencies at those rates without limit and without margins.[30]

The EMU aspects of the Treaty implied the creation of a 'multi-speed Europe'. From the outset, it was obvious that some states would be unable to meet the convergence criteria. At the time of the Maastricht Treaty, only the Benelux countries were eligible to meet the convergence criteria while Greece, for instance, had little chance of meeting this criteria. If EMU resulted in close economic integration and speedy growth in the participating countries but slow growth in the countries which remained outside the Union, it would become more difficult for those outside to catch up with the pace of the Union. It could also lead to a "Europe a la carte" or of "variable geometry". Given the development of EMU in some parts of the EC and the exclusion of some would violate the notions of equal standing and change the spirit of a uniform Community.[31]

COMMON FOREIGN AND SECURITY POLICY

The second major decision taken at Maastricht was the inclusion of a chapter on CFSP. Art J.1 of the TEU states that the main treaty revisions were designed to define and implement a CFSP covering all areas of foreign and security policy. Setting the Objectives of the CFSP, it called upon the Member States :

— to safeguard the common values, the fundamental interests and the independence of the Union;

— to strengthen the security of the Union and its Member States;
— to preserve peace and strengthen international security;
— to promote international co-operation, to develop and consolidate democracy and rule of law, respect for human rights and fundamental freedom (Act J1.2)

The provisions of CFSP as embodied in the TEU called for stages to consult within the Council in order to ensure that their combined influence is exerted as effectively as possible by means of concerted and convergent action (J.2.1); it required national foreign policies to conform to the EC's common positions (J.2.2.) and instructed the Member States to coordinate their actions and promote common positions in international organisations (J.2.3).

An important aspect of the Treaty was the demarcation between the economic and political aspects of security and the defence aspects. The dividing line between the two became very thin. The Treaty referred to the Western European Union (WEU), which despite having a shadowy existence so far, emerged as the implementing arm of the Community concerning defence and security matters.[32] In view of the ongoing split among the EC members between an 'Atlantist' or a 'European' defence strategy, the TEU sought to establish a framework for the elaboration of a European defence strategy.

It was more or less agreed at Maastricht that foreign and security policy would subsequently pass to the jurisdiction of the EU. However, there was more of ambiguity centering the CFSP and the absence of a cohesive foreign policy was evident in the discord between the EC Member States that followed the Yugoslav crisis.[33] The EC proved ineffective in face of German recognition of Croatia and Slovenia, while Britain and France disagreed upon the role of North Atlantic Treaty Organisation (NATO) and the United Nations (UN) peacekeeping forces. As far as security was concerned, the hopes of a common European defence remained an empty phrase. The Franco-German plan to form a joint Eurocorps collapsed with the intensification of the Yugoslav crisis. It became clear that neither the WEU nor the Eurocorps could be a possible supplement to NATO as a bedrock of European security. While Britain and Germany and the 'neutral' EFTA states agreed on the continuation of US presence in Europe, France maintained its historical thrust of opposition to the security umbrella providing US nuclear hegemony.[34]

Another syndrome which emerged to block a smooth movement towards European unity in 1992 was the demand made by the Southern members of the EC for more regulation and structural aid from the richer north and applicant countries of EFTA. The budget which had always been the cause of conflict for many years within the EC did not provide any better ground for peace. The more affluent states in the north were unwilling to hike community-wide taxes and spending, while the poorer states continued to make their demands.

Apart from the Articles which formed the basis of the Treaty, 17 Protocols and Declarations were attached to the Treaty covering matters ranging from the EMU and Social Charter to special provisions giving the Danes privileged access to second homes in parts of rural Denmark. These Protocols, however, represented serious challenge to the *acquis communautaire*.[35] The Protocol on EMU allowed the United Kingdom to decide not to participate in the monetary union. The Protocol on social policy by which the eleven members would attempt to implement it gave the impression that parts of the Community law may not have application throughout the EC territory. The Protocol on the acquisition of property in Denmark which allows the Danes to buy certain property in Denmark is a derogation of the general principle of free movement in economic activity. These Protocols attached to the TEU also showed that the Member States could undermine the general application of Community law.[36]

INSTITUTIONAL REFORM

As far as institutional changes were concerned, the TEU

allowed for more majority voting, one Commissioner per Member State and a limited form of co-decision for the European Parliament. Though this reflected a continuation of the process started with the Single European Act in matters concerning institutional changes, but through the provisions of the Maastricht Treaty, the institutional capacity of the EC was meant to be strengthened.[37]

The introduction of majority voting implied an exacerbation of the powers of the Council of Ministers. This move could be interpreted as a strong step towards the federal direction. At the same time, it weakened the already feeble control of national parliaments over the Council of Ministers. The increase of the powers of the Council of Ministers and the simultaneous decrease of the mechanism of accountability represented an aggravation of the democratic deficit. The Commission was not expected to be able to operate effectively as a counter weight to the Council of Ministers for the former lacks the democratic characteristics of an institution. The Commission would have to be drastically overhauled to match up the standards of transparency and democracy in order to safeguard the credentials of a more federal state of the EC. The Maastricht Treaty did not entail a significant increase of the Parliament's powers apart from introducing the co-decision procedure. This allowed the Parliament to reject legislations over which an agreement could not be made between the Council and the Parliament. Nevertheless, the Treaty did not seek any solutions to the problems of democratic accountability.[38]

FRANCE AND THE RATIFICATION OF THE MAASTRICHT TREATY

On 20 September 1992, the French electorate voted 51 per cent to 49 per cent to ratify the Maastricht Treaty in a referendum. It was the eighth referendum held in France since the creation of the Fifth Republic in 1958, which produced one of the narrowest of approvals.[39] The referendum campaign over the Maastricht Treaty had given rise to a public debate for both the proponents and the opponents of the Treaty. At the core of the debate was the question of French national identity in a post-1992 Europe. The fears of French national identity focussed on the EC which:

> often decides against French interest which moves towards a concept of European citizenship that goes against the Jacobian strain... and whose institutional system is far closer to the German federal model than to the French unitary one.[40]

The Treaty required a ruling from the Constitutional Council of France to set out the yardsticks by which its compatibility with the French Constitution could be measured. The Council found three sections of the Treaty to be controversial in French constitutional terms. These included common citizenship of the European Union, the EMU and Immigration. 8b(1) which dealt with common citizenship stated, "every citizen of the Union residing in a Member State of which he is not a national shall have the right to vote and stand as a candidate in elections in Member States in which he resides under same conditions as the nationals of the state".[41]

This aroused the most intransigent among those favouring a centralized notion of state and citizenship. Opposition to this provision came especially from the Communist Party (PCF), a minority in the Socialist Party (PS), most of the Gaullists (RRP) and the National Front.[42] The immigration clause which read in Act 100c(1) of the TEU stated:

> The Council acting unanimously on a proposal from the Commission after consulting the European Parliament shall determine the third countries whose nationals must be in possession of a visa, when crossing the Member States.[43]

This issue raised by Le Pen of the National Front brought in the question of French national identity. Gaullists argued that this would weaken the state and lead to separatism on the part of ethnic minorities and contribute to their ghettoization and permanent impoverishment.[44]

The pro-Maastricht campaigners consisted of the political

establishment who then comprised the French Government, the Socialists, RPR and UDF, the business community and the Church. The 'NO' campaigners consisted of the 'excluded' and the 'peripheral'. The main spokesmen of the rebel left-wing were Jean-Pierre Chevenment, Phillipe de Villiers, a right wing nationalist (UDF) deputy and Phillipe Sequin and Charles Pasqua. The 'NO' campaigners made a considerable impact on the public mind. Phillipe de Villiers who sought a "Europe of sovereign states", rejected Maastricht Treaty as deflationary, encouraging immigration diminishing sovereignty and increasing technocracy.[45]

A similar chord was struck by Le Pen who identified Maastricht Treaty as a world wide conspiracy organized by "Maastricheurs" leading France to national suicide. The Communists concentrated on Maastricht as the Europe of bankers and of job losses of public sector employees by EC competitive rules. Chevenement, a left wing member denounced Maastricht as a masochist propaganda which would lead a number of Member States into real austerity thereby threatening French export markets.[46]

The basic reservation towards the Maastricht Treaty was that it would have a negative impact on the essential attributes of sovereignty.[47] The question of sovereignty which was raised by many revolved around the European Parliament which as multi-national body lacked legitimacy. They believed that "democracy is inseparable from national sovereignty".[48] The debate in France was between the Gaullist support for "l Europe des patries", or "Europe of nation-states" versus some form of supranationalism."[49]

Pro-Maastricht elements in France readily admitted the limits of national sovereignty in a complex and interdependent world. In support of the Maastricht Treaty, former Prime Minister Biregovoy argued:

> The most enterprising go as far as recommending a confederal Europe to which they contrast a federal Europe....But we are going further than a Europe of nations, because we accept in sharing the competencies in those areas where one can do better with twelve than going alone and failing..... What is

> necessary for us to refuse, in all cases, is a return backwards.[50]

The political debate over EMU also brought in questions of financial sovereignty. Industry Minister Dominique Strauss-Kahn justified the EMU as follows:

> .....whether one deplores it or applauds it, our states hardly constitute any longer, and will allow Europe to create itself in the same manner as the franc, lira, mark allowed the development of France, Italy and Germany.[51]

The 'YES' campaigners did not fail to hammer on German domination which they hoped would be enabled by the implementation of the Maastrich Treaty. Prime Minister Rocard said that Maastricht had to be approved in order "to preserve Germany from its demons, for after two generations of democracy, Germany might be tempted by romantic irrational forces and pursue interests backed by the all powerful D-Mark".[52] In a similar vein, it was stressed that a 'NO' vote would bring a divorce between Paris and Bonn and that Germany would look more to the east, "probably encouraging an anti-democratic ferment."[53]

The referendum results showed that the 'YES' vote was more urbanized, professional and well-educated, while, the 'NO' vote was mostly rural which reflected farming hostility to current EC policies and the working classes who were disenchanted by high unemployment.[54]

The motivation of French voters in the French referendum on the Maastricht Treaty was largely determined by the prospects of peace, prosperity and competitiveness. The protesting character of the 'No' vote was in the form of hostility to Mitterrand and the political class in general. Beyond the pro-Maastricht debate, a constitutional argument supporting a transfer of sovereignty had also been developed. It was felt that implementation of the Treaty would entail a 'transfer of competencies' and a 'limitation of sovereignty' and hence a constitutional revision in France was incumbent which would allow for sovereignty to be ceded in relation to provisions of the Treaty that were earlier found incompatible with the Treaty.[55] The new Title XIV, Art

88(1) of the French Constitution which mentions the EC in the Constitution for the first time removed the old distinctions between limitations of sovereignty and transfers of sovereignty.[56]

GERMANY AND THE RATIFICATION OF THE MAASTRICHT TREATY

When the Maastricht Treaty came up for ratification in Germany, there seemed to be two rather thorny issues which led to intense debates. The Opposition had mounted a vigorous campaign in Germany against the proposal for a single currency and the central bank. 70 per cent of Germans refused to trade off their national crown jewel, the strong D-Mark for a dubious and untested unit--the European Currency Unit (ECU).[57] Many spoke of a compelling national interest: to curb the alarming surge of money supply and an inflation rate rising towards 4 per cent. Germany was making public transfers of $100 billion a year to build the Eastern *Laender* (States) and running a deficit equal to 4 per cent of the Gross Domestic Product.[58]

The second debate centred around political union, which was a poorly defined concept in the Maastricht Treaty. It entailed a greater democratic input into decision-making by recognizing that the power of European Parliament remained weak in relation to other European institutions. Maastricht seemed to lose its psychological credibility when the Christian Social Union (CSU) Bavarian Minister, Edmund Stoiber attacked the idea of a European federal state which he said, ran the risk of a democratic deficit so far as decision-making is concerned.[59] For Stoiber, democracy for the nation comes first and he wanted Germany's internal state position to be based on democracy and majority decision before Germany supports a position in the European confederation. It was primarily the fear of Bavaria, a state with 12 million people and historical tradition of 100 years old, being stripped off her statehood as the European super-state emerges. The CSU leader justified his position on the ground that since the

European Parliament was not a directly represented body, it lacked "democracy and transparency".

The German Laender which maintained liaison offices in Brussels complained of the rigid centralized institutional structure and stressed subsidiarity as an inviolable principle. They argued that by conforming to the directive decisions of the EC, they would be denied the right to decision-making in this centralized system. This debate took the Treaty to the constitutional court.

After a prolonged judicial procedure on the debate over the democratic deficit, the Federal Constitutional Court at Karlsruhe unanimously declared the Maastricht Treaty to be in conformity with the Basic Law. After months of speculation over the awaited discussion from Karlsruhe, the Court found that the objections raised were unfounded. The Federal Court stated in its verdict that the Union founded in Maastricht Treaty, remains an "association of states and is not a state that can be based on a European population in as much the EC Member States remain masters of the Treaty".[60] On the issue of democratic deficit, the Court declared that the European institutions obtained their legitimacy from the democratically elected national parliaments for that reason responsibilities and powers that are of substantial importance must be left upto them. The judges found that there was sufficient democratic control over the development of the Union but warned that an "over preponderance of tasks and responsibilities at the European level would weaken democracy at the state level".[61] On German pressure, the principle of subsidiarity[62] was strengthened to control any excessive centralization of power. Fears that Germany was subjecting itself to an automatic process towards a monetary union which no longer could be steered were dismissed. The Bundestag stipulated that it would be consulted on whether or not to proceed to the third stage of Monetary Union involving the introduction of a single currency.

The Karlsruhe Court's decision of 12 October 1993 finally removed the hurdles on the way to the European Union. However, Helmut Kohl's speech in the Bundestag on 11

November 1993 lent a new dimension to German initiatives towards European Integration. Kohl asserted:

> We want a Europe—a unified Europe. We want a political union that concentrated its powers but at the same time preserves the diversity and identity of its Member States. In this Europe, we of course remain French, Italian, Dutch and German and at the same time Europeans. Unity in diversity is the only reasonable alternative to an empty centralism.[63]

Though the ratification seemed to lose its psychological credibility when the CSU Bavarian Minister Stoiber raised these debatable issues thereby making the process cross bumpy stretches, yet it strengthened the influence of the Laender within Germany. The Laender gained extensive co-determination rights with regard to European political decision-making at the federal level.[64] The German model of federalism cannot simply be transferred to the European Union but it did represent a source of varied experience in the practice of federalism which could be used to help shape Europe.[65]

The Karlsruhe judgement on the Maastricht Treaty did not place any insurmountable problems, on the contrary, it conferred legal legitimacy on the Treaty. This shifted the debate out of the courtroom to where it really belonged—the political arena. The fact that only 17 per cent of German populace saw advantage to the EC membership and over half were concerned about German independence demonstrated the extent of the need for consciousness and commitment towards European integration.[66] There were of course reasons for a growing coolness of the Germans towards the EC—the tragedy in the Balkans, mass unemployment and infiltration of refugees which made the Germans more inward looking.[67]

However, in Germany, there was no major disagreement between the political parties over the Treaty and all the political parties agreed to the Maastricht Treaty without much controversy. They were probably aware that they could not afford to let the Treaty founder lest it aroused the suspicion that a united Germany wanted to withdraw from

Europe and tread the old *Sonderweg* (special way). Germany also was aware of the nightmare of history, not so much because it had learnt more from the past than others but because the horrors of history start on its immediate borders.[68]

A CRITIQUE OF THE MAASTRICHT TREATY

The Maastricht Treaty was supposed to capitalize upon the triumph of the Single European Market by opening the way to a political union that would complement the economic union that was virtually complete by December 1991.[69] In a clear illustration of the logic of 'spillover'[70], the true completion of the Single European Market required a single currency which in turn required a single central bank and thereby a single monetary policy. A per-requisite of a single monetary policy is a coherent policy-making in political matters. So the Treaty on European Union was in some way a natural follow-up of the Single European Market project. The TEU was not only supported by the EC Member States but also by a vast majority of political forces throughout the EC. However, in some countries, there was a formal requirement to hold a referendum before the document could be ratified. The initial accomplishments of the draft treaty received its first setback when a wave of popular opposition emerged, the volume of which raised questions about the underpinnings of EC.

In June 1992, the Danes rejected the Treaty in a referendum, held as a constitutional necessity for ratification and in September 1992, the French came within a hair's breadth of doing the same. It was obvious that voters resented discretionary power passing to the Commission in Brussels. The public opinion in Europe turned against the 'federal dream' of Chancellor Kohl and President Mitterrand. The Maastricht Treaty pushed the hitherto existing 'permissive consensus' regarding Europe beyond is limits.[71]

European integration which was originally established as an elitist project,[72] confronted with the basic question of political legitimacy during the ratification of the Maastricht Treaty. The political actors who shaped European integration had relied on persuading the masses that integration was directed towards the general welfare. As long as people did not perceive themselves as being directly affected by European decisions, they went along without opposing the elite decisions. This scenario which posited a 'permissive consensus' for accepting, although not necessarily embracing the EC policies,[73] enabled the elites to carry on the integration without any restraint from the people. With the entry into force of the Treaty, European integration amassed an ever-widening range of policy competence.[74]

This proved that the 'permissive consensus' was incapable of providing sufficient support to sustain the Maastricht Treaty agreements. The referendum in Denmark and France made it clear that the elite-driven process no longer was enough for further integration. These also indicated that the question of the policy legitimacy needed to be tackled more directly in view of the gulf between the perceptions of decision-making elites and the public. The ratification process also widened the credibility gap and aggravated the problem of legitimacy.[75]

Lindberg and Scheingold had earlier pointed out that the 'permissive consensus' might not withstand a major increase in the scope or capacity of the EC.[76] The debate on the Treaty made the people realize that the European project was developing in ways which they did not favour.[77] When 'permissive consensus' gave way to squabbling divisiveness over each component of the Treaty, it was rightly pointed out as to how:

> decisions that will profoundly change the way Europe works, are being taken in tortuous negotiations behind closed doors. That is why some puzzled Europeans have been slow to appreciate the scale of what is happening. How, they wonder, has Europe come to this?[78]

The institutional ambiguity and combination of confusion, fuss and empty phrases which was created by the Maastricht Treaty raised questions amongst Europeans as to whether the TEU was the beginning or the end of a development. At the heart of Western European integration policy lies the intention of creating a supranational federal structure which can be realized by Member States' initiatives to relinquish their sovereignty. In principle, a state restricts its sovereignty in some form through every international commitment into which it enters. The significance of Maastricht Treaty can also be assessed from the extent to which the EC moved towards supranationality. The CFSP proved impossible to include any unanimity in foreign policy matters and to form any concrete security policy, let alone a relinquishment of sovereignty, beyond the creation of a new acronym.

Even after 43 years of integration, Member States of the EC resolved to carry on the process of an "ever closer union of the peoples of Europe", in which the decisions were taken as close to grassroot level as possible in line with the 'subsidiarity' principle. The inclusion of this principle was not only a response to public fears of over centralization, but it also was a retrogressive move with regard to integration. As opposed to the centripetal policy of integration which aimed to transform nation-states into supranational federal state, the application of the centrifugal principle of 'subsidiarity' sought to transfer competence back to the nation-states.[79] Subsidiarity also proved to be a 'double-edged weapon' which, although originally initiated by the federalists, was used by the intergovernmentalists to restrict integration. The reference of the 'subsidiarity' principle in the Treaty reflects the Member States' political message that they are not prepared to accept an unlimited extension of EC powers.[80]

Maastricht Treaty failed to resolve the debate between the federalists and intergovernmentalists.[81] The opt-outs which Britain, Portugal and Denmark pushed through during the Treaty negotiations, can be viewed as "breaches of contract". The predictable inability of some of the stages to meet the convergence criteria of monetary union demonstrated that there would be a possibility of a Europe of different speeds.[82]

Maastricht was not a departure to new shores but, as a

French observer said:

> only a calculated move against the predominance of the Bundesbank and against the existence of an independent German currency.[83]

A French newspaper spelt out more blatantly what France expected from monetary union : "Maastricht is the Treaty of Versailles without war." Incessant reference to the "return of Germans" revealed how the abysses of the past opened up all over Europe, with the loudest fears coming from France, Britain and Italy. Maastricht reflected the political priorities of the Member States where each of them tried to ensure that the Treaty outcomes were as close as possible to their national interests. The Treaty also increased the existing divisions between the potential beneficiaries and the potential loosers, *i.e.* the unskilled labourers, the farmers and immigrants.[84]

Unlike the Treaty of Rome of 1957 and Single European Act of 1986, which laid down a precondition for peace creating Euro-phoria and a revival of enthusiasm amongst the Europeans, the Maastricht Treaty came at a rather inauspicious time. Europe was facing not only an economic crisis characterized by high rate of unemployment and inflation, but also a problem of political legitimacy amongst the discredited Western political class. Much of the resentment which came from the non-receptive audience was due to their disenchantment with the state of affairs in the heart of Europe.

The Maastricht Treaty was expected to lay down provisions to enable the EC to tackle the challenges that arose in Eastern Europe with the collapse of Communism and also draw an agenda on possible eastward enlargement of the EC. However, the Treaty could not even provoke a common European consciousness which was the much needed design for a wider Union. In view of the changed European scenario, all that was left was "yesterday's answers to yesterday's problems". No constitutional debate arose over the eastern enlargement nor did a decision materialize on the ongoing theme "widening versus deepening". The Treaty did not provide a clear enough strategy for dealing with the surge of membership requirements from the aspirant countries of Europe. Europe remained a mere "nameplate behind which the old nation-states continued to live as silent ghosts".[85]

The Treaty remained silent while contradictions continued between national and supranational policies and between a federal state and a confederation of states. Above all, the Treaty on European Union, apart from coining a loosely defined term "union" also proved how a 'European identity' cannot be introduced by decree.[86] The loopholes of the Treaty which became prominent even before the ink was dry, made the Europeans wake up to the risks that a defective structure carries with it. Once the triumph of short-sighted affirmations was over, a new period of reflection began with the awareness that the second stage of creating an "ever closer union of the peoples of Europe" had to be opened with the IGC of 1996 in order to review the TEU, tackle those issues that EU continued to confront and find solutions to the unanswered questions of institutional reforms, enlargement and integrational challenges which the Maastricht Treaty failed to resolve.

NOTES

1. Helen Wallace, "The Europe that came in from the cold", *International Affairs,* vol. 67, no. 9, no. 4, 1991, p. 647.
2. For details see, M. Albert and J.R. Ball, *Towards European Economic Recovery in the 1980s* (Luxembourg : European Parliament, 1983) p. 11.
3. Joachim Fest, "Europe in a Cul-de-sac" in Arnulf Baring (ed.), *Germany's New Position in Europe* (Oxford: Berg Publishers, 1994) p. 54.
4. See, Elizabeth Pond, "Germany in the New Europe", *Foreign Affairs,* vol. 71(2), Spring 1992, pp. 114-130. Also see, Jochen Thies, "German Unification: Opportunity or Set-back for Europe", *The World Today,* vol. 47, no. 1, January 1991, pp. 8-10.
5. See, D. Moisi, "French Answer to German Question", *European Affairs,* vol. 4, no. 1, Skewing 1990, pp. 33-35.

6. See, G. Wetting, "Security in Europe : A Challenging Task", *Aussen Politik,* vol. 1, January, 1992, pp. 3-11.
7. EC, Commission, *The European Community and its Eastern Neighbours* (Luxembourg: Office for Official Publications of the EC, 1990), European Documentation Services, 8/1990, p. 10.
8. For background see, Haig Simonian, *The Privileged Partnership: Franco-German Relations in the European Community, 1969-84* (New York : Oxford, 1985) and Brigid Laffan, *Integration and Cooperation in Europe* (London : Routledge, 1992), pp. 181-183.
9. Rudolf Scharping, "New Challenges for Franco-German Cooperation", *Aussen Politik,* vol. 45, no. 1, 1994, p. 3.
10. See the Kohl-Mitterrand letter published in *Agence Europe,* no.5238, 20 April 1990.
11. See for background EC, "Political Union: Structure of the Draft Treaty, Contribution by the European Commission to the IGC, 21 May 1991", Agence Europe", *Europe Documents,* no. 1715, 31 May 1991.
12. Roger Morgan, "French Perspectives of the New Germany", *Government and Opposition,* vol. 26, no. 1, Winter 1991, p. 18. See in this connection, Reinhard Meier, "Germany, France and Britain on the Threshold to a new Europe", *Aussen Politik,* vol. 43, no. 4, 1992, pp. 334-42. For a historical background on Franco-German relations, see, Omer Bartow, "Nations in arm: Germany and France 1789-1939", *History Today,* vol. 44, no. 9, September 1994, pp. 27-33.
13. "Cette grande Allemagne qui inquiete", *Le Point,* 5 March 1990,p. 44, as cited in David Yost, "France in a new Europe", *Foreign Affairs,* vol. 69, no. 5, Winter 1990-91, pp. 107-28.
14. For an assessment on Mitterrand's policy see, Elizabeth Haywood, "The European Policy of Francois Mitterrand", *Journal of Common Market Studies,* vol. 31, no. 2, June 1993, pp. 269-282.
15. Gerd Langguth, "Deutschland, die EG, und die Architektor Europas", *Aussen Politik,* vol. 2, 1991, pp. 140 and 145.
16. Christian Hacke, "Deutschland und die neue Weltordnung", *Das Parliament,* 6 November 1992, p. 15.
17. Helmut Schmidt, "Deutschlands role im neuen Europa", *Europa Archiv,* no. 21, 1991, p. 622.
18. Rudolph Scharping, "New Challenges for Franco-German Cooperation", *Aussen Politik,* vol. 1, 1994, p. 6.

19. R. Keohane and S. Hoffman, "Institutional Change in Europe in the 1980s" in Keohane and Hoffman (ed.), *Decision making and Institutional Change in the EC* (Colorado: Westview Press, 1991) p.26.
20. *Irish Times,* 24 April 1990, p. 5.
21. Walter Goldstein, "Europe After Maastricht", *Foreign Affairs,* vol. 71, no. 5, Winter 1992-93, p. 119.
22. Brigid Laffan, *Integration and Cooperation in Europe* (London : Routledge, 1992), p. 224.
23. Ibid., p. 224.
24. Laffan, n. 22, p. 225. See Protocol on Economic and Social Cohesion attached to the Treaty on European Union. The Member States recognised their need to promote economic and social progress and strengthening social and economic cohesion agreed that a Cohesion Fund was to be set up before 31 December 1993 which would provide Community financial contribution to environmental and trans-European network projects in those Member States with a per capita GNP of less than 90 per cent of Community average.
25. See *Protocol on Social Policy* of the Treaty. It reads, "The United Kingdom of Great Britain and Northern Ireland shall not take part in the deliberations and the adoption by the Council or Commission proposals made on the basis of this Protocol and the above mentioned agreement *i.e.* Social Charter".
26. Art. 8(1) of Part II of the Treaty states, "Citizenship of the Union is hereby established. Every person holding the nationality of a Member State shall be a citizen of the Union."
27. Art. C of Title I dealing with Common Provisions states, "The Union shall be served by a single institutional framework which shall ensure the consistency and the continuity and building upon the *acquis communautaire*".
28. EC, Committee for the study of Economic and Monetary Union (Delors Committee), *Report on Economic and Monetary Union in the European Community* (Luxembourg: Office for Official Publications of the European Communities, 1989).
29. Cf. Andreas Knorr, "The European Economic and Monetary Union", *Aussen Politik,* vol. 4, 1995, p. 340.
30. See, Christopher Taylor, "EMU the state of play", *The World Today,* vol. 51, no. 4, April 1995, p. 75.
31. Laffan, n. 22, p. 211. Also see, N. Berthold, "Europe after Maastricht : Have the Monetary Questions been Settled? ", *Intereconomics,* vol 27, no. 2, March-April 1992, pp. 51-56. For

a critical analysis on EMU, see, N. Thygesen, "Towards Monetary Union in Europe", *Journal of Common Market Studies,* vol. 31, no. 4, December 1993, pp. 447-72 and Jacof Frenkel and M. Goldstein, "Monetary Policy in an Emerging European Economic & Monetary Union, Key Issues", *International Monetary Fund Staff Papers,* vol. 38, no.2, June 1991, pp. 356-73.

32. See Title V, "Provisions on a Common Foreign Security Policy" of the TEU. Treaty provisions on CFSP are covered from Art. J-J9. Also see "Declaration on Western European Union" of the TEU, which separately states WEU's relations with the EU and the Atlantic Alliance.
33. Goldstein, n. 21, p.126. For an assessment of EU's response in the Balkan crisis, see, D. Owen, *Balkan Odyssey* (New York: Harvest, 1995).
34. Goldstein, n. 21, p. 127. See, T. Taylor, "West European security and Defence Cooperation, Maastricht and Beyond", *International Affairs,* vol. 70, no. 1, January 1994, pp 1-16.
35. Daniel Wincott, "Is the Treaty of Maastricht an adequate Constitution?" *Public Administration,* vol. 72, Winter 1994, p. 580.
36. Ibid, p. 582.
37. Art. 137-238 of Part V of the Treaty consists all provisions dealing with the Institutions of the Community.
38. Wincott, n. 35 Also see, K. Neunreither, "Democratic Deficit of the EU: Towards Closer Cooperation between the European Parliament & National Parliaments", *Government & Opposition,* vol. 29, no. 3, Summer 1994, pp. 299-314.
39. B. Criddle, "French referendum on Maastricht Treaty", *Parliamentary Affairs,* vol. 46, no. 2, 1992, p. 228.
40. Stanely Hoffman, *French Dilemmas and Strategies in New Europe,* Harvard University, Working Paper, no. 38, 1992,p. 33.
41. Peter Oliver, "French Constitution and the Treaty of Maastricht", *International and Comparative Law Quarterly,* vol. 43, no. 1, January 1994, 25 pp.
42. Robert Ladrech, "Europeanization of Domestic Politics and Institutions. The Case of France ", *Journal of Common Market Studies,* vol. 32, no. 1, March 1994, p. 73. For detailed analysis see, W. Safran, "State, National Identity and Citizenship: France as a Test Case", *International Political Science Review,* vol. 12, 1991, pp. 219-39.

43. Ladrech, n. 42, p. 74.
44. Safran, n. 42, p. 226.
45. Criddle,n. 39, p. 232.
46. Ibid., p. 233.
47. *Le Monde,* 3 March 1992.
48. Criddle, n. 39, p. 234. Refer, S.Hoffman, "The Institutions of the Fifth Republic" in J Hollifield and G. Ross (ed.), *Searching for the New France* (New York: Routledge, 1991) pp. 50-70.
49. Ladrech, n. 42, p. 75.
50. *Le Monde,* 7 March 1992.
51. *Le Monde,* 15 May 1992.
52. Criddle, n. 39, p. 234.
53. Ibid., p. 234.
54. Ibid., p. 236.
55. Ladrech,n. 42, p. 76. For a background appraisal of sovereignty of the Member States *vis-a-vis* the EU, see, S. Williams, "Sovereignty and Accountability in the European Community" in R. Keohane and S. Hoffman (ed.), *The European Community Decision-making and Institutional Change* (Boulder: Westview, 1991), pp. 150-165.
56. A report from the National Assembly Commission in charge of the Constitutional revision relative to the Maastricht Treaty confirmed the jurisdictional evolution of the concept of sovereignty. Commenting on the Constitutional Council decision of 9 April 1992, Commission spokesman Gerard Gouzes stated "It is not illegitimate to give the notion of sovereignty a new meaning (in which France) by a sovereign consented act, the signing of a treaty, accepts the limitation of its sovereignty in view of realising an objective of higher interest". *Le Monde,* 6 May 1992.
57. Goldstein, n. 21, p. 121.
58. Ibid., pp. 121. Also see, Karl Cordell, "Birth Pangs of the new Germany", *International Relations,* vol. 11, no. 4, April 1993, pp. 381-92.
59. Stoiber threatened non-ratification three times in one session of the Joint Commission on 12 March 1992. For an essay on democratic deficit see, Georg Ross, "The Constitution and the Maastricht Treaty: Between Cooperation and Conflict", *German Politics,* vol. 3, 1995, pp. 56-68.
60. Commentary by Gwenther Neunmacher, "Foundation Stones on the way to Europe", *Frankfurter Allgemeine Zeitung,* 13 October 1993, in *Foreign Broadcasting Information Service,*

WEU, 93-209, 1 November 1993, p. 29.

61. Ibid., p. 29.
62. 'Subsidiarity' has been described as a larger unit which assumes functions in so far as the smaller units of which it is composed are unable or less qualified to fulfill their role. See in this contest K. Neunreither, "Euphoria about Subsidiarity : A Constitutional Debate in the European Community", *Political Science and European Unification*, no. 2, 1991, p.1. Subsidiarity was incorporated in Art, 3b of the Maastricht Treaty.
63. Speech by Helmut Kohl in the Bundestag, 11 November 1993, *FBIS, Western Europe*, 15 November 1993.
64. Charles Jefrey, "Towards a third level in Europe? The German Lander in the European Union", *Political Studies*, vol. 44, no. 2, June 1996, pp. 253-266.
65. See, A.B. Gunlicks, "German Federalism after Unification. : The Legal/Constitutional Response," *Publius*, vol. 24, no. 2., Spring 1994, pp. 81-96.
66. Commentary by Dieter Buehl, "Who's afraid of the Super-State? The Constitutional Court has cleared the way to Europe.....", *Die Zeit*, 15 October 1993, p.1, *FBIS-WEU-93-209*, 1 November 1993.
67. Ibid. For a critical assessment on the problems and uncertainties connected with Germany's response to the Maastricht Treaty see, Reinhard Stuth, "Europe-Tired of Change", *Aussen Politik*, vol. 45, January 1994, pp. 30-39.
68. Joachim Fest, "Europe in a Cul de Sac", in Arnulf Baring (ed.), *Germany's New Position in Europe* (Oxford : Berg Publications, 1994), p. 63.
69. Mark Franklin, "Uncorking the Bottle: Popular Opposition to European Unification in the Wake of Maastricht", *Journal of Common Market Studies*, vol. 32, no. 4, December 1994, p. 455.
70. For a theoretical approach on European integration see, E. Haas, *The Uniting of Europe : Political, Economic and Social forces 1950-1957* (Stanford : Stanford University Press, 1958). Also see for neo functionalist approaches to integration, Keohane and Hoffman, n. 19.
71. L. Lindberg and S. Scheingold, *Europe's would be Polity* (New Jersey: Prentice Hall, 1970) pp. 40-45.
72. Haas, n. 70, According to Ernst Haas, the political actors in the Community's decision-making process are essentially

the leaders of political groups and in definition are elites.

73. Lindberg and Scheingold, n. 71, . 41-42.
74. Daniel Obradovic, "Policy Legitimacy and the European Union", *Journal of Common Market Studies*, vol. 34, no. 2, June 1996, p. 192.
75. Ibid., p. 193.
76. Lindberg and Scheingold, n. 71, p. 277.
77. However, another view holds that the apparent unpopularity of the Maastricht project reflected the unpopularity of the governments in France and Denmark. The referendum in Ireland, where the government was more popular, received a good majority just as it did in the referendum conducted a year later in France and Denmark after a more popular government assumed office. This view is sought from Mark Franklin, M. Marsh and L. Mclaren, "Popular Opposition to European Unification," *Journal of Common Market Studies*, vol. 32, no. 4, December 1994, pp. 462-68.
78. *The Economist* (London), 30 November 1991.
79. Ibid., pp. 272-273. Keohane and Hoffman, n. 55, argue that in many respects the TEU is more intergovernmentalist than the Single European Act.
80. This view has been expressed in several articles in Renaud Dehousse (ed.), *Europe after Maastricht: An Ever Closer Union?* (Munich: 9 Wilhemstrasse, 1994).
81. European integration has always been influenced by the federalists (integrationists) and the funtionalists (intergovernmentalists). See in this connection, Paul Taylor, *The Limits of European Integration* (Kent: Croom-Helm, 1983) and Martin Holland, *European Community Integration* (London: Pinter, 1993).
82. Fest, n. 3, p. 59.
83. Quoted in Joachim Fest, "Europe in a Cul-de-Sac" in Arnulf Baring (ed.), *Germany's New Position in Europe* (Oxford : Berg Publishers, 1994) p. 58.
84. For instance, the 'NO' vote in France was basically rural-reflecting the farmer's hostility to EC policies and the worker's against problems of unemployment.
85. Fest, n. 3, p. 59.
86. A reference can be made to Chancellor Kohl's speech on Bundestag, November 1993, Footnote n. 63.

Chapter III

France, Germany and the Enlargement of the European Union

The cascading events in Europe following the collapse of the socialist system, the completion of the Single Market and the signing of the Maastricht Treaty rendered the EU with sufficient dynamism to sustain its integrationist momentum and draw attention from its northern and eastern neighbours. Before the end of the East-West conflict, the option of integration was not available to all Europeans. The members of the European Free Trade Area (EFTA) deliberately chose to be left alone, some South European states were kept at a distance while the East Europeans were segregated from the West during the Cold War.[1] The thaw in the East and the emergence of the EU as a dominant trade bloc which brought the Eftans close to the latter implied a more inclusive interpretation of the EU. The EU found itself facing a new challenge of enlargement and this eventually gained prominence in the EU agenda.

The European Community of Six, after the First Enlargement in January 1973, became the EC of Nine (with the United Kingdom, Denmark and Ireland). The Second and Third Enlargement, from the EC of Nine to the EC of Twelve took place in January 1981 with the addition of Greece and in January 1986 with the inclusion of Spain and Portugal. The Fourth Enlargement, from the EC of Twelve to the EU of Fifteen (with Austria, Sweden and Finland), took place from 1 January 1995. A fifth and subsequent enlargements of the EU are likely to take place at the turn of the century.

Prior to the 1990s, discussions of enlargement primarily focussed on the applicant states either from the Union's southern periphery or northern states of the EFTA. With the spread of democratization throughout the Central East Europe, the form, speed, scope and need for enlargement has become EU's pressing problem.

The EU was envisaged as a wider family of European states with flexible institutional relations. The Treaty of Rome (1957) adequately accommodated the original six members all of whom shared relatively similar economies and levels of development. Both the Single European Act (1986) and the Maastricht Treaty (1991) introduced policy and reforms to assist the EU with its increased membership of Twelve and to prepare it for further enlargement. Maastricht of course fell far short of radical measures needed to prepare the EU for the subsequent expected enlargements over the next decade. The Maastricht Treaty, taking into consideration only the EFTA applicants, incorporated Article O, stating: "Any European state may apply to become a member of the Union."[2] The term 'European' combines geographical, historical, cultural elements which all contribute to the European identity. Other essential conditions for membership as referred to in the Maastricht Treaty are the principles of democracy and free market economy, the respect for human rights and the acceptance of the Union *acquis, i.e.,* the legal, economic and political framework of the EU, including the ability to implement the CFSP.

IMPACT OF PAST ENLARGEMENTS

In order to understand the issue of future enlargements, it is necessary to discuss it within the context of EU's past experience of enlargement from Six to Twelve and Twelve to Fifteen. The EU has significant experience of increasing its domain geographically. Enlargement has successfully taken place on four successive occasions (1973, 1981, 1986 and 1995). Despite the unique features of each, the themes common to all three enlargements can be identified: thc level of commitment to the European ideal, economic and political compatibility and the impact on existing policy frameworks.

FROM SIX TO TWELVE

The political content of EU membership, particularly in 1973, had been under-emphasised in comparison with economic aspects. Britain's isolation from the EC would have relegated it to a 'second class European', on the other hand, economically, the Common Agricultural Policy (CAP) was ill-adapted to the British needs, and Britain was sensitive about relinquishing is national sovereignty. Given this attitude towards the EU, it is hardly surprising that a significant percentage of the British population still remain ambivalent to membership. Denmark also displayed a similar level of attitude towards the political vocation of the EU but sought EU membership in a bid to extend EU's influence northward in the Nordic region.

The decade that followed the first enlargement lent support to those who argued that "widening" would be incompatible with "deepening". The EU underwent a period of stagnation although steps such as the first direct election to the European Parliament and the creation of the European Monetary System (EMS) were taken. Britain and Denmark resisted proposals, that they felt, would erode their national sovereignty. Both Denmark and the UK, two enthusiasts for a widened EU preferred to see it as a loose inter-governmental structure with an expanded free trade area.[3]

The enlargements in 1981 and 1986 also had to face the question of commitment to the EU ideal. The theme common to the second and third enlargements was that of economic and political compatibility. For different reasons, the three applicants—Greece, Spain and Portugal—were delayed on the grounds of compatibility with the EU. The three states were free from dictatorial strongholds and the EU was a symbol of democracy which would help consolidate their newly formed democratic system. For the EU, the political factors, like, maturing of these fledging democracies was essential.[4]

The Southern enlargement brought with it a new kind of economic divergence which generated new policy in new areas. The economies of the three new members were at a premature stage of development. These members and Ireland pressurized the EU for regional development and social cohesion to complement and balance the economic consequences of the Single Market. After the Maastricht conference, the Council agreed on a "Cohesion Fund" for the poorer states.

The three successive enlargements of the EU have had significant impact on EU politics. The CAP, which is EU's most controversial and yet most developed policy area, went through major structural changes. The first enlargement saw the Irish and Danish dairy sectors integrated into EU's agricultural support system, together with Britain's farming enterprises, but the latter did not benefit from its financial contribution to the CAP. The economic disparity between the Nine and the new members had detrimental consequences for the CAP.

EU's successive enlargements have tended to strengthen intergovernmentalists, like the U.K., Denmark and Greece, in areas like decision-making, the limited roles ascribed to the Parliament and Commission and the political authority of the Council. Though these enlargements of the EU may have dissipated much of its dynamism upto the mid 1980s, but conversely, without these enlargement-caused-crisis, the EU may never have been able to address the structural loopholes in its institutions.

FROM TWELVE TO FIFTEEN

With the completion of the Single Market, there have been major implications for EU's trading partners of which the EFTA countries were the most important ones. The Single European Act (SEA) of 1986 which created new challenges for the EFTA's previous relations of bilateral free trade with the EU proved to be too inadequate. Lacking a strong foothold and facing a discriminatory potential in view of

EU's internal market programme, the EFTA countries sought to re-fashion their relationship with the EU. Their disappointment with the European Economic Area (EEA) which was set up to ensure a "more structured partnership" made the EFTA states seek a more palpable alternative in the form of full membership into the EU.[5] For the EU, there was a noticeable change in its perception towards the EFTA countries. The proximity of their socio-political and economic set up with that of the EU, made the later move closer to their more affluent neighbours, whose inclusion would not only expand the revenue base of the EU but also help share the burden of reconstruction of Eastern Europe.

With the application of membership coming from Austria, Sweden, Finland and Norway, the EU started negotiation with each of them on its own merit. The other EFTA countries, namely, Iceland, Switzerland and Liechtenstein decided to remain outside the EU due to their respective national restrictions against joining a supranational organization. The referendum held in the four applicant states became the deciding factor for EU membership. Austria, Finland and Sweden voted in favour but Norway rejected EU membership. On 1 January 1995, the three countries joined the EU and the EC of Twelve expanded to the EU of Fifteen.

The Nordic members of the EU who are by nature confederalists with a clear sense of identity, entailed a change in several structures of the EU institutions. A new set of problems centering around the rotating Presidency of the EU Council, the functioning of the Commission and the European Parliament with the increase in the number of members, came to the fore. The European Parliament has already been plagued by a quantity problem. The enlargement of the EU had a danger of the Parliament suffering from a "paralysing hypertrophy" and possibly a lack of unanimity in policy formulation.[6]

A decisive issue that came up with the accession of the three states, mainly Austria, was with regard to the implementation of the CFSP. A Member State which has legal status for maintaining permanent neutral status could create hurdles in reaching a consensus on the issue.

Apprehensive of some of the institutional challenges that a geographical expansion would entail, the EU agreed to examine them in the 1996 Inter-Governmental Conference (IGC).

PRINCIPLES OF EU ENLARGEMENT

The challenge of enlargement which the EU faces today with the changes in the European landscape, raises questions about the way in which the EU has traditionally managed the enlargement process and whether this is an appropriate framework for the future. The classical method of enlargement has been based on five key principles,[7] which though often reluctantly accepted, have been the underpinning principles of the integration process.

The first principle implies the full acceptance of the *acquis communautaire,* by the applicant states. This principle found expression in de Gaulle's rejection of the UK's application to EC membership in 1963 on grounds that the UK was incapable of adapting to the *acquis.*[8] In more recent enlargement, this *acquis* has been expanded in order to strengthen EU institutions.

The second principle is based on the premise that formal accession negotiations focus solely on the practicalities of the applicants taking on the *acquis*. The EU manages this process by setting up transitional periods, target dates for reducing tariffs and quotas. This principle was tested when it was believed that Greece, Spain and Portugal would have more difficulties in adjusting to the *acquis.* In the case of Greece, it was overridden by the political priority given to locking Greece's new democracy into the Union. The budgetary burdens of Spain and Portugal also made the negotiations protracted.[9]

Each enlargement has brought into fore the possibility that hard won agreements between Member States might have required a reform in order to integrate new members, if their economic structure does not fit into the existing patterns of the EU-expenditures etc. This issue was raised during the Spanish & British cases of enlargement. UK's high level of food imports from cheaper producers and Spain's competitiveness of agricultural exports threatened to undermine the CAP. Strict application of the *acquis* either imposed domestic adjustment costs on existing Member States as was the case with French farmers during the Spanish enlargement or imposed high budgetary burden on new members, as was with the UK. In these cases, the Union's preference has been to stretch the adjustments and transitional periods of the *acquis* and unburden the problem of adjustment on to the applicant states and refashion the *acquis* once the new members joined. The establishment of the Regional Development Fund in 1975 and Structural Funds in the late 1980's addressed the issues created by UK's membership and the Iberian enlargement respectively.[10]

EU's previous enlargements have pointed out that the Union prefers to negotiate with groups of states which already have close relations with each other.[11] Despite this, preference, policy and issue linkage between applicants can hamper the enlargement process. The negotiation process of EU's first enlargement was determined by issues raised by the UK's application. The Danish and Irish applications were linked to a series of issues over which they might not have had any control.[12] During the Mediterranean enlargement, the difficulties created during the Spanish negotiations tended to undermine the negotiations with Portugal.[13] The EFTA enlargement presented the EU with a close grouping whose experience in the European Economic Area (EEA), facilitated convergence in EFTA's negotiations with the EU.

CHALLENGE OF FUTURE ENLARGEMENT

Future enlargements presented the EU with more choices, although some sub-groups were identified like the four Visegrad States or the Baltic States. EU's policy objective was geared to strengthen these linkages within a coherent framework before accession negotiations began.[14] The EU on completing the first stage of its post Cold War reconstruction by embracing three states of EFTA had to shift its gaze to its East in response to the emerging challenges that came with the transition in the erstwhile communist countries of Central and Eastern Europe.

1989 was the *annus mirabilis* of the postwar era of Europe. The democratic resurgence in East Europe blurred the political boundary between the East and the West. The chief event in this period was the transformation of Hungary, Poland, Czech and Slovak Republic, Bulgaria and Romania into nascent democracies and the disintegration of Soviet Union. In the wake of the collapse of the socialist system in Central East European Countries (CEEC), the EU was confronted with a new set of challenges in the form of political and economic instability, resurgence of nationalism, resulting in an exodus of refugees from the East to the West. These issues, if neglected had the potential of spilling over to the West and jeopardizing its peace and stability.

IMPLICATIONS OF THE CHANGES IN THE CEEC

Central East European Countries in the aftermath of the 1989 revolutions represent on the one hand, an assertion of a historical and cultural identity distinct from that imposed for 45 years by the Soviet Union. On the other hand, it is also a part of the continuing political search for an alternative to the partition of Europe.[15] Their economy is characterized by a high rate of inflation, growing unemployment, decline in real income, steeply rising public debt, and unfruitful transition to hard currency. All these offer a fertile ground for the resurgence of traditionalist and nationalist forces which are often seen to be reversing to old historic designs.[16] The Yugoslav crisis bears testimony as to how a failure to cope with these threats could spillover to the EU and jeopardize the peace and security of its neighbouring areas. The transformation of CEEC, which has been considerably impaired by ethnic and nationalistic elements, accentuated the problems of mass migration from East to West.

MOTIVATIONS OF THE CEEC FOR EU MEMBERSHIP

The countries of CEEC, which emerged from the shackles of communism, considered membership of the EU an anchor for political and economic stability and greater regional security.[17] The EU is a model which the CEEC aspired for, in terms of high living standards, economic growth and a long record of democratic credentials. Moreover, the Single Market project, by putting East Europe before the prospect of having to face a powerful and compact economic bloc, probably made these ex-communist regimes aware of their near bankrupt state of economies. In the East European states it was assumed that the removal of internal frontiers within the EU would lead to trade divisionary effects and that market access for EU would be impaired. From the point of view of the East European states, the worst possible outcome would be to find themselves isolated between West European states and a problematic Russia.[18]

EU'S RESPONSE TO THE CEEC

The explosive potential of this situation was initially contained by a European political order and also dominated by one of its former Cold War features, viz., the institutionalized political and economic interdependence of West European states. The question was whether this order could be successful without its extension to Eastern Europe. When ex-Foreign Minister of Belgium, Mark Eyskens remarked, "what has to be prevented at all costs in tomorrow's Europe, is the rekindling of nationalism as the result of a renaissance of the nation state",[19] it rang a bell of alarm amongst West Europeans, who, as a result of this could be infected by the emerging risks of Central and East Europe.

The EU faced a sensitive question whether to proceed with the internal integration or to open itself for new candidates and thus enable the process of economic and political consolidation of the former socialist countries. On the one hand, a stable and firmly integrated EU could certainly be a reliable support to market and democratic changes of East Europe but that would postpone possible admission of these countries for many years resulting in a long period of economic and political instability of a large part of the continent. On the other hand, early admission of these countries to the EU would permit their problems to enter the EU, which would postpone the strategic goals of its integration for a longer period of time.

The acceleration of the process of internal integration in the EU was also coupled with the realization that as the true centre of gravity of future developments, the EU not only had to meet the challenge of internal integration but its commitment in CEEC. In view of a lack of mutual support amongst the East Europeans to create a firm basis for amalgamation, it became imperative for the EU to respond to the challenge in the political, economic and security fields. A failure to create a civil society and pluralist structure with market economy could lead to a consolidation of a new European poverty-line. Shaping the relation between Europe's developed centre and semi-developed periphery in a socially compatible way was one of the biggest challenges confronting the EU.[20]

The EU, thanks to a shared tradition of common heritage and culture, was uniquely placed to help the European neighbours on their way back to democracy and free market economy. The revolution in CEEC and the completion of the Single Market changed the political and economic architecture of Europe. The Single Market became an opportunity for CEEC once the economic reforms were pushed resolutely. The CEEC provided a huge growth potential at the EU's doorstep—especially in the Visegrad states namely Poland, Hungary and the Czech Republic due to their developed heavy industries and rapid progress of economic reform.

Another concept for the future relation between the CEEC was the notion of "Mitteleuropa", *i.e.*, a political group of those states with historical and cultural bonds in the centre of Europe. Given the wide scale of involvement of Germany in the economic development of East Europe, an expanded network of connections led to link these states of EU in a special way.

The initial reaction of the EU to the historic changes in the former Iron Curtain countries was more of a conglomeration of discrete activities instead of a well developed strategy. The Member States seemed unable to overcome their political differences over the appropriate strategies. The task was left to the EU Commission which resorted mainly to well established means and procedures in the foreign relations of the Union. There were two dimensions for western interests in CEEC, viz., protection against dangers resulting from neglecting the CEEC and of capitalization of profits resulting from the integration of CEEC into Western structures. The Strasbourg Declaration on CEEC, by the European Council on 8 and 9 December 1989, recognizing the EU's responsibility towards the CEEC stated:

> The community and its member states are fully conscious of the common responsibility which devolves on them in this decisive phase in the history of Europe. They are prepared to develop with the USA and the other countries of Central and Eastern Europe, and with Yugoslavia, in so far as they are committed to this path, closer and more substantial relations based upon an intensification of political dialogue and increased cooperation in all areas.[21]

Based on the conclusions of the Strasbourg European Council Meeting of 8-9 December 1989, the Council of Ministers agreed on 20 January 1990 to prepare a draft on concluding Association Agreement with these countries.[22]

Depending on the geographical proximity and progress in economic transition, the EU negotiated with three types of agreements with the CEEC. *The European Agreements* were created for potential East European applicants. They were meant to foster their integration by lowering trade barriers and establishing a framework of political dialogue. Poland, Hungary and former Czechoslovakia (CSFR) signed bilateral Europe Agreements in December 1991. Romania and Bulgaria signed it in February and March 1993 respectively.[23]

Trade and Cooperation Agreements which were signed with the Baltic Republics and Albania in March 1993 and with

Slovenia in July 1993 were seen as a step towards Europe Agreements. These agreements grant Most Favoured Nation (MFN) status rather than free trade with the EU, excluding the sensitive sectors like textiles, steel and agriculture.[24]

Partnership and Cooperation Agreements were a new form of agreement announced by the EU in October 1992. They were concluded with Russia in 1994, Ukraine and countries of the Commonwealth of Independent States (CIS). The central issue in these agreements was market access.

TRADE AND AID

Following the collapse of the Council of Mutual Economic Assistance (CMEA), the countries of Eastern and Western Europe became the most important trading partners. With the nordic enlargement of EU, its external trade accounts for roughly 87 per cent in case of Slovenia, 70 per cent in the case of Poland, 60 per cent for Hungary and almost 55 per cent for Czech Republic. This means that the four countries of Central and East Europe, with the most pronounced EU orientations reveal an extent of external trade ramification already resembling that of most EU Member States. The greater the degree of economic interpenetration, the greater the advantage of membership. The CEEC extended trade with the EU despite the fact that the latter erected trade barriers which do not exist within the EU. The Europe Agreements merely envisaged a step-by-step reduction of tariff and quantitative restriction until a free trade area was created. The four Visegrad countries—Poland, Czech Republic, Hungary and Slovakia—were given unimpeded access to the EU market for industrial goods from 1 January 1995,[25] the corresponding access date for iron and steel products was in 1996 and for textiles until 1998. Imports of agriculture are however subject to the restriction of the CAP for an unlimited period. The same regulations applied to Romania and Bulgaria.[26]

The countries of Central and East Europe were often seen as exporters of raw materials and agricultural products. These countries however had a much more advanced production structure than the Southern members of the EU. Machinery and transport material from the three Visegrad states had tremendous access to the German markets. Intra-industrial trade was more significant between the EU and the Visegrad states than in the case of the Member States—Portugal, Greece and Finland. Hungary's intra-industrial trade with the EU reached the levels recorded by Denmark and Ireland.

The CEEC became important for the strategic locational planing of companies. The shift in their external trade to industrial goods was motivated by the fact that wage-intensive production and foreign investment were moving to an increasing extent to these countries. The wage costs in Poland and the Czech Republic were roughly 7 per cent of the West German level, while roughly 50 per cent of the West German productivity level was achieved.

Following Europe Agreements, EU imports from the CEEC increased from 15.4 per cent in value terms in 1989 to 23.6 per cent in 1993. Poland recorded the highest share of imports to the EU followed by Hungary and the Czech Republic. EU exports to CEEC increased from 13.1 per cent from 1989 to 29.4 per cent in 1993 with the three Visegrad states recording the largest share of EU exports.[27]

In a bid to bail out the CEEC from economic impoverishment, the EU assumed a key role in coordinating the overall Western aid efforts for CEEC. These efforts were centred around Poland-Hungary Assistance for Reconstruction of the Economy (PHARE), European Investment Bank (EIB), the European Bank for Reconstruction and Development (EBRD) bilateral and schemes from donor countries, *i.e.*, Group of 24 (G-24).[28]

Originally set up for Poland and Hungary, the PHARE Programme was extended to Bulgaria, CSFR and Romania. The PHARE programme surpassed EU's trade agreements with Poland and Hungary by abolishing all specific quantitative restrictions imposed by EU Member States on Polish and Hungarian products excluding the sensitive goods.[29] The treatment gane Poland and Hungary equal to that accorded to most of EU's other General Agreement on Trade and Tariff (GATT) trading partners.

The G-24 assistance to the CEECs in 1990-93 was ECU 33080.81 million out of which ECU 23663.01 million were alloted to the Visegrad states while ECU 9417.75 million were given to the other states of the region.[30] As far as loan from the EIB is concerned, from 1990 to 1993, the Visegrad states received the maximum loan from the EIB. In 1993 Poland received ECU 2300 million, Hungary received ECU 72 million and ECU 100 million was allotted to Czech Republic while Romania and Bulgaria received ECU 65 million and ECU 51 million respectively.[31] Poland and Hungary had been the two most beneficiaries of the EBRD loan. In August 1994, the EBRD decided to give a credit of $38 million to Poland over a period of 10 years for developing energy[32] while loans worth ECU 75,000,000 was granted to Hungary in 1993 for restructuring transport.[33]

Recognizing the possibility of eastward expansion of the EU, the Member States and their officials went on record to reassure some potential states of the CEEC of their entry into the EU. In his meeting with the Polish Deputy Prime Minister in September 1994, EU Commissioner Jacques Santer confirmed the opinion that Poland may become a full-fledged member of the EU by 2003-2004 AD.[34]

Britain's preference for a loosely structured but geographically wider EU could be gauged from Leon Britan's keenness towards embracing the East. He stated, "we have taken a quantum leap towards bringing the Central and East European countries into the EU.....".[35]

The EU's dealings with CEEC, through its trade relations, aid, investment and loans, revealed a clear differentiated approach which the former adopted *vis-a-vis* the three Visegrad states, *i.e.* Poland, Hungary and the Czech Republic and also Slovenia. The three states, owing to their relatively developed economy than Romania & Bulgaria, were in a better position to be considered for EU membership.

TURKEY

The Southern enlargement of the EU which brought in Greece, Spain and Portugal into its domain, necessitated additional consequences from other neighbouring countries which found themselves being engaged in a competition for development. Other Mediterranean countries like Turkey were particularly hit hard by the repercussions of EU's Southern enlargement because of their geographical proximity and a fairly similar economic structure. Turkey was a special case with which the EC maintains ties following the Ankara Agreement of 1968. Article 28 of the Ankara Agreement envisages Turkish accession to the EU, once the country is in a position to fulfil the *acquis communautaire.*[36]

Turkey's external relations after the Second World War were determined by both national security and economic cooperation. Feeling directly threatened by the Soviet expansionism, it joined the North Atlantic Treaty Organisation (NATO) in 1952. Henceforth, Turkish governments maintained fostering ties with Western Europe-by seeking membership of the Council of Europe and Conference on Security and Cooperation of Europe (CSCE). The disintegration of the Soviet Union left a political vacuum in the Trans-Caucasian belt and Central Asia, which Turkey sought to replace. Its myriad domestic problems coupled with unfriendly relations with Greece over Cyprus, and terrorism on Kurds triggered problems for Turkey.[37]

Turkish interest in seeking EU membership, nevertheless, remained one of its foremost priorities. Advocates of joining the EU view membership of the EU as a culmination of their process of Westernization in which Turkey was engaged for so long and it was a matter of Turkey being acknowledged as a member of the west and as a European country. Another major political move governing Turkish interest towards the European Union is the "Greek factor". Turkey's bid to apply for Association Agreement with the EU in 1959 only eight weeks after Greece, reflects its efforts to ensure that the other side of the Aegean does not gain an edge in world affairs. Since Greece became a member of the EU, Turkish representatives have constantly voiced fears if Greece was using its membership to keep Turkey out of Western Europe.[38] Aspirations for EU membership are also motivated by economic factors, which include better access to western markets, export of labour (migrant workers) easing Turkey's burden on the domestic labour market and boosting economic development by financial aid from the EU. These interests formed the background for EU-Turkey relations. Since September 1971, the EU has abolished all import tariffs and other levies in non-agricultural goods from Turkey other than textiles and petroleum products.[39] EU also established a customs union in 1995 with Turkey introducing the EU's common external tariff and abolishing quotas on imports from EU.

The present ruling coalition of Germany have assented to bring Turkey within the European perspective. Backed by the Social Democratic Party (SPD) government of Germany, the EU agreed, in the Helsinki Summit of December 1999 to grant the status of a candidate country to Turkey as the isolation of Turkey could be risky on geopolitical grounds.[40] The Christian Democratic Union/Christian Social Union (CDU/CSU) remains critical to this approach as they feel that if Turkey is granted membership, it would be the biggest country in terms of size and poorest in terms of economy, which in turn would take a large share of the EU budget as a net recipient.[41]

Despite the recent proclamations of increasing ties, prospects of Turkey's membership into the EU does not seem optimistic for several reasons. Turkey's main shortcomings, as perceived by the EU, has been its failure to draw consequences for national economic development policies from its treaty commitment to aim at an eventual membership. The most important factor which does not allow the EU to cherish thoughts of Turkish membership is the religious and cultural difference between the former and the latter. During the Fourth enlargement, EU's worries about the influx of Protestants from Sweden and Finland in a predominantly

Roman Catholic society was a clear indication of its desire to maintain a uniformity in the religious and cultural landscape of the Union. It is seriously felt in the EU that the inclusion of a Muslim country would not only introduce asymmetrical sets of values but also cause cultural invasion in a "Christian Europe". Many observers, both from the European left and right parties have suggested that "Europe" was a homogenous continent with single religion and civilisation, and that the integration of an alien religion would represent serious challenges to the societies, thus forbidding to some extent the admission of a country with a dominant Muslim population.[42] In Turkey, too, there is a constant contradiction between the Kemalist inspired philosophy of etatism alongside a pronounced nationalism and the achievements of Western orientation by means of association with the EU. Turkey therefore faces the task of reconciling two basic features of its political culture that in principle defy reconciliation.[43]

MALTA AND CYPRUS

Besides Turkey, Malta and Cyprus were also aspiring and waiting for EU membership for long. The European Council in its meeting at Lisbon on June 1992 agreed to consider their applications for EU membership on its merits. As regards Malta, the EU had agreed on starting accession negotiations six months after the 1996 IGC on the basis of the Commission's proposals. Meanwhile, the Commission continues to monitor Malta's implementation of reforms to prepare its economy for accession.[44] The per capita GNP of Malta estimated at ECU 5630 is lower than the EU average, less than that of Spain and Ireland but more than that of Greece. Membership of Malta to the EU would mean an additional expenditure between ECU 60 to 70 million from EU's Structural Fund while a net revenue of ECU 25 to 30 million will flow from the EU budget, making Malta a net beneficiary.[45]

Although Malta applied for EU membership back in 1990

after its Association Agreement in 1970, the EU was not too enthusiastic about its membership. This could be due to Malta's exceptionally small size of 316 km and its leanings towards Libya, a terrorist state. Italy in particular had been often threatened by Malta's links with Libya with whom the former shares a common cause of the Mediterranean security.[46] Domestic politics which often sees confrontations between the anti-EU Socialist Party and the Nationalist Party have also hindered the democratic credibility of the state.

Cyprus and the EC have been linked with each other ever since the Association Agreement of 1972. Cyprus which has a predominantly agricultural economy sought to enhance its economic development by getting access in EU markets and also be included in EU's Mediterranean Policy. The *de facto* division of Cyprus between Greece and Turkey following the Turkish invasion in 1974 caused a set-back in EU-Cyprus relation.[47] EU however concluded a Customs Union in two phases with Cyprus in 1978 after the former's Southern enlargement. The first phase marked the adoption of the Common Customs Tariff by Cyprus while the second phase which extended from 1997-2002 included the free movement of industrial and agricultural product.[48] The situation in Cyprus worsened after the unilateral declaration of independence of Turkish occupied Cyprus in 1983. In view of its application for membership to EU in July 1990, the EU agreed to start accession negotiations by mid 1998, six months after the 1996 IGC. Without a settlement between Turkey and Greece over the *de facto* division of Cyprus, it would be practically impossible for EU to consider Cyprus as a potential candidate. All evidence suggested that Turkey would not easily cede the northern territory of Cyprus as it considers Cyprus "an island which pierces the middle of Turkey like a dagger" and the "existence of Turkey in northern Cyprus is a guarantee against any enemy."[49]

EU's cast-iron promise to open accession talks with Cyprus which also happens to be the world's most densely militarised confrontation zone, has been considered by many Member States as rash. To quote former German Foreign

Minister Klaus Kinkel:

> Anyone who wants to join the EU must know that the EU cannot deal with the accession of new members that bring in additional external problems.[50]

EU faces a crucial issue as the Greek Cypriots were pressurizing the former to open talks on making Cyprus member of the EU, while the Turkish Cypriots have not reached any kind of reconciliation with the Greek Cypriots.

RUSSIA

EU's well-established credibility as an "island of peace and stability" has not only been confined to the countries of Central and Eastern Europe. Russia too perceives itself as a potential member of the EU, although from EU's stand-point this is a far-fetched expectation. EU is Russia's largest trade partner accounting for 45 per cent in 1995. Germany is Russia's biggest trading partner accounting for 40 per cent of EU trade. Russia attracted $ 700 million as foreign investment from EU in the first half of 1995.[51] EU had earlier signed a Partnership and Cooperation Agreement with Russia in 1994. On 17 July 1995, it enhanced its partnership with Russia by signing an Interim Cooperation Agreement on trade. This agreement which enables the elimination of quantitative restrictions and tariff provisions, came into force on 1 February 1996.

Given the massive size of Russia and its economy grappling with reforms, membership is more than a distant prospect. There is a virtual unanimity amongst the EU Member States of Russia being "a bull in a china shop". The regional conflicts in Bosnia, Chechnya had led to a revival of nationalistic flavours in Russia. This syndrome coupled with the parliamentary debut of a Right-Wing extremist Vladimir Zhirinvosky also put into question the democratic credibility of Russia. It has been stated that trade itself is not a sufficient ground for complacency. Russia figures well below the potential required for mutually profitable business and attracts fewer funds than other East-European economies.[52] Since a complete political and economic isolation of such a vast country would be detrimental for the whole continent, EU has adopted a strategy through Cooperation Agreement to retain ties with Russia to foster stability and security in the country.

GERMANY AND ENLARGEMENT OF THE EU

With the political upheavals in CEEC, Germany's *Ostpolitik* or eastern policy gained a new dimension and greater momentum. This was largely due to the fact that Germany being the closest Western neighbour of the volatile East is easily jeopardised by any kind of political, social and economic and adversities of that region. High levels of inflation rates, nationalist excesses leading to outbreak of violence brought in a wave of migration from CEEC to Germany. Between 1989 to 1992 a significant 1.35 million refugees who sought asylum in Germany came from CEEC. The same year witnessed 22,000 crimes against foreigners and electoral successes of right wing parties. In 1993, a trend towards political polarization continued as an increasing number of citizens voted for parties of extreme Right and the Greens.[53]

The disintegration of the "Yalta system" brought with it old and new questions about the German factor in Central European equation. For historical and cultural reasons it is impossible to reclaim a Central and East European identity without its essential German component.[54] Germany has had an inextricable link with the East ever since the end of the Second World War. In the beginning of the 1980's, Konrad Adenauer, the first Chancellor of FRG, initiated a "policy of strength" by assuming that the EC's magnetic attraction would fade communism. This policy gave way to Willy Brandt's "chance through *rapprochement*" which was based on the premise that the EC was a catalyst for creating an all-European peace and stability zone. Chancellor Helmut Schmidt continued the notion of "West Europe's windows, doors and passageways to the East Europeans". This theme still ran strong and was enhanced by Helmut Kohl.[55] Before 1989, Germany's eastern policies aimed at bringing about a change in the Soviet bloc, legitimately. With the upheaval in the East, the questions of stability and security in the East became incremental for Germany. To Germany, European integration and progress in Eastern Europe were locked in a symbiosis of stability. Political union was deemed to provide an "anchor of stability to deal with the immediate risks and uncertainties" of East European countries and to stimulate the long-term political and economic stabilization that would permit their entry into the EU. This change in priority towards the East was largely due to the fact that Germany is the closest Western neighbour of the volatile East and is easily jeopardised by any kind of political, social and economic adversities of that region.

Germany's geopolitical and economic ties with CEEC made it indispensable for Germany to shoulder most of its financial burden in the provisional aid and assistance of CEEC.[56] From 1989 to 1993 Germany paid ECU 7.3 billion as aid to CEEC. Germany was also the main donor and investor in CEEC. Foreign Direct Investment (FDI) flows from Germany to CEEC increased from DM 103 million in 1989 to DM 4.2 billion in 1995. In Hungary, where FDI has been the highest in CEEC, out of $ 7.5 billion recorded till the 3rd quarter of 1994, 20 per cent of the total came from Germany. In the Czech Republic 39.9 per cent of total investments between 1991-1992 came from Germany.[57] Germany was the largest member of foreign capital partnership in Poland, which figured over 3000 in 1994.[58] German exports to CEEC increased from ECU 13.1 percent in 1989 and reached ECU 28.9 per cent in 1994.[59] German over all trade with Eastern Europe reached DM 100 billion in 1994. Germany accounts for nearly half of the EU's total trade with CEEC. The total trade in 1995 was DM 120 billion with German exports totalling to DM 58.5 billion. Germany's trade with CEEC exceeded its trade with the United States or Great Britain and Germany's trade with CEEC doubled by the year 2000.[60]

The outcome of German elections in 1994 had an impact

well beyond Germany's borders. Germany took up the task of using the next 3-4 years to prepare the EU for a decisive phase of enlargement. Germany's special interest in Eastern Europe has been emphasised by former German Foreign Minister, Klaus Kinkel:

> ... in achieving political unification we derived a maximum gain from the end of the East-West conflict. On the basis of our central location, our size and our traditional relations with Central and East Europe, we are predestined to derive the primary advantage from the fact that these countries have intervened from Europe.[61]

Two most important objectives of the German government seemed to be narrowing the gap between East and the West to make Germany a more effective proponent of European integration.[62] In a speech Chancellor Kohl, after emphasising on his pledge to intensify his commitment to European integration, said he would bring the young democracies of CEEC closer to the EU, in view of the risks and uncertainties which the East may pose for Germany. To quote Helmut Kohl, "it is neither in Germany's interest nor in Europe's interest that the Western border of Poland remains the Eastern border of the EU.[63]

Germany's tilt towards Eastern Europe gained momentum in the Essen Summit of 9-10- December 1994. An invitation to the six CEEC to attend the Summit on the one hand, raised hopes for a German-led strategy to build a wider Europe and on the other, signified the relevance and importance of keeping eastward expansion of the EU on track. Helmut Kohl, on sending the message to the CEEC, stated that the EU was not running a closed shop. He said:

> We want to show these countries (CEEC) that they will be welcome if they want to join the Union when their domestic and economic situation permits it. [64]

The Central and East European countries also look up to Germany to act as a "bridge-head" between the CEEC and the EU. drawing the historical and cultural ties of Germany with the East, Czech president, Vaclav Havel, after a meeting with German President, Roman Herzog said that Germany wants to reflect truthfully about history and wants Germany to be a "real trustworthy European country who does not have any problem with it neighbours."[65]

On one of his visits to Germany, Hungarian Prime Minister Gyualla Horn stated:

> The German government is our partner in this and indeed it is one of the main initiators and supporters of Hungary's membership in the EU. We also fully agreed that there was no need to wait until all countries, even the Visegrad simultaneously meet EU membership conditions, but what must be considered is the extent to which the individual countries can fulfil these conditions.[66]

This statement reveals the underlying desire harboured by the Central European countries who do not want to be treated as one bloc or one single region as and when the EU negotiates on the enlargement strategy with them. They would rather choose to be considered as individual countries. The EU has earlier demonstrated its preference to negotiate on enlargement with group of states which have geographical proximity with on another. A similar policy towards the CEEC might hamper the process due to the complex issue linkages and the varying degree of development in these states which could undermine the negotiations with the more progressive states of Central Europe.

In view of its traditional links with CEEC, Germany emerged as a bridge between the East and West of Europe and a vehicle of integration for the "other Europe".[67] Enlargement would expand the internal European market for German goods. German manufacturers are already taking advantage of the much cheaper skilled labour to be found just over the border by relocating production there. Last, but by no means least, Germany would be at the centre of this wider Europe.[68] Regardless of how problematic an intensification of the EU might be in view of the growing heterogeneity which would automatically accompany accession by new members, the pursuance of the two goals of widening and deepening is in-keeping with the German interests.

FRANCE AND ENLARGEMENT OF THE EU

For France, the idea of a European Community has always been one of an able political actor, a distinct defence identity and a cultural mission. In view of this, the "French-Europe" has necessarily been Western Europe; for only Western Europe has had the potential to attain these qualities.[69] Thus, France has always been reluctant to have a European Community or European Union with a blurred border or unclear membership. With the changes in the political map of Europe, Eastern Europe has entered the French domain of debates and discussions.

In the early 1990s when there were debates concerning the eastward expansion of the EU, France preferred to take a restrictive approach towards this issue. Rather, it favoured an intensification of the EU structures and institutions. The fears of escalated German sphere of influence in the heart of Europe, once the CEEC were brought within the EU fold, loomed large in France. With the advent of the neo-Gaullists Rassemblement pour la Republique (RPR) Party in 1994 under Prime Minister Edouard Balladur and President Jacques Chirac, there were perceptible changes in French attitude towards the eastern enlargement. Distancing himself from the provocative remarks made by President Mitterrand in June 1991 that it would be "decades and decades" before the erstwhile communist countries would be ready for accession to the EC, Prime Minister Edouard Balladur reiterated his view on 8 April 1993, that the countries of Eastern Europe should be welcomed into the EU, first politically and later economically.[70] On May 1994 Prime Minister Balladur stirred the Conference for a Pact on Stability in Europe, which focused on the CEES's vocation to belong to the EU.[71] The Copenhagen meeting of the European Council on 21-22 June 1993, lent a thrust to Balladur's design on Stability Pact. An underlying idea of Balladur's initiative was the idea of admitting those countries with Europe Agreements as "associate members" into the WEU, so as to bolster security in East and Central Europe.[72]

The Paris-Bonn axis pushed forward EU's eastern agenda, when Kohl and Balladur jointly declared that:

> it is Union's historic obligation and common goal to help the states of Central and Eastern Europe, which have embarked upon the road of reform to rejoin the European family and to include them in the unification process underway.[73]

Nevertheless, both the leaders warned that the "road to membership will be long and hard". There was a joint proposal by Kohl and Balladur to include the heads of government of applicant countries once a year at European Council Meetings to strengthen cooperation. Jacques Chirac, on assuming office, too championed the cause of CEEC. His call for closer ties with CEEC has been reflected in his book, "Une nouvelle France : Reflexious". In one of the sections entitled, "The East is our new frontier.., Europe should forge is identity", he stated:

> Europe cannot be content to be a club for the privileged, condemning a part of the European family to wait patiently for an audience.... The EU must open its doors to all the countries of the European continent, provided of course they have adopted democracy and the market economy and they show their readiness to participate in the shared adventure.[74]

France also appeared as a third force between German and Polish relation. This "Euro-Trio" comprising German-French-Polish cooperation was an outcome of a tripartite meeting in Paris on 3 March 1994.[75] From a Polish perspective, a third partner like France could help normalise the relation between Poland and Germany, which could run the risk of being impaired by the burdensome historical legacy. Declaring Poland as its first partner in CEEC, France confirmed its commitment towards the economic development of Poland through cooperation. Polish expectations of EU got a boost with Balladur's comment that Poland is qualified to be a full member of the EU as it is a democratic state with market economy and sustains "friendly relations with its neighbours".[76]

France which is more extensively represented in

Hungary, Czech Republic and Slovakia in cultural and also economic spheres, has acknowledged the achievements in those countries in their endeavour to come closer to the EU.[77]

In view of Germany's endeavours in the East, France found itself as providing a supportive role in Germany's pursuit in the Eastern enlargement of the EU. However there is a sharp contrast between the French and the German approaches to enlargement of the EU. Germany's unquestionable position in the centre of Europe and a shared historical, cultural and geographical proximity with the East coupled with its enormous economic and trade ties with CEEC, made it the indisputable spokesman of eastern enlargement in the EU.

German Presidency's preoccupation with the CEEC, which became even more prominent at the Essen Summit of 1994, when the heads of six CEEC were invited by Chancellor Kohl, was apparently followed by a "strategic bargain" between France and Germany. France aimed at balancing the priorities of Eastern Europe and the Southern Mediterranean countries with regard of trade concessions and aid from the EU. During the French Presidency of the EU, France redressed the balance by turning southwards due to its colonial links with that region. At a EU meeting in Brussels, the EU Foreign Ministers agreed to allocate ECU 5.5 billion and ECU 7 billion to the Mediterranean States and the CEEC respectively between 1995 to 1999.[78] In lieu of this compromise, Germany won an agreement for weakening anti-dumping provisions against the CEEC. The European Commission also agreed to submit proposals for phased modification of rules-of-origin in order to stimulate trade and investment in the CEEC.

France also won $1 billion standing loan from the International Monetary Fund and persuaded the Paris Club of creditor countries to reschedule $5 billion worth of Algerian debts.[79] Moreover, France succeeded in securing for the three Maghreb countries namely Algeria, Morocco and Tunisia, a fund from the EU to promote economic reform which would bring peace and stability in the region. Just as

Germany has the maximum stake from any instability in the CEEC, so also peace and stability in the Maghreb countries of southern Mediterranean was essential for France. France was already facing problems with a heavy inflow of migrants from the Maghreb countries and North Africa. There were nagging concerns amongst the French, particularly by the cultural purists, of an intrusion by an immigrant alien culture in the French territory,[80] which could increase the economic hazards with in the country and serve as a "fifth column of Islamic fundamentalism".[81]

French interest in the Mediterranean region is gaining importance in the EU agenda just as Germany's involvement in CEEC has become significant in EU's enlargement strategy. In view of the fact that if priority is given to the extension of the EU to the East, problems in the balance of the European architecture might emerge. In order to avoid such problems and to maintain a balanced European architecture, a periphery for the "Latin Arch" should be envisaged. France became the most vocal proponent of this agenda and political reasons were proposed for the extension of the EU to the South. The French scholars urged the necessity to promote to the greatest extent the association of the Southern European countries with the EU, without threatening the extension of the EU to the East. The German preference for opening to the East is not primarily the consequence of geographical proximity, but a result of a lack of openness for non-European cultures. This seems to be consistent with respect to the two regions' various positions in economic development, geopolitical location and historical heritage. The French preference of favouring the Mediterranean option reflects a difference in the orientation of the European identity to be forged. The German preference reveals a short-term logic; the French preference reflects a 'return of Europe' into the world arena, a sort of European superpower, which is possible only if European integration has reached a degree of cohesion which would allow a European identity to emerge which does not yet exist.[82]

INSTITUTIONAL CHALLENGES

Enlargement is also a major challenge for the institutions of the EU. The accession of more countries is widely perceived as an external shock which carries the risk of institutional paralysis. Without changes in the composition and working methods of the Commission, the Council, the Parliament, the increase in membership threatens to undermine the decision-making capacity of the main EU bodies.

However, previous enlargements of the EU have not demonstrated any kind of detrimental feature for the EU. Past experience suggests that the future widening of the EU would not be incompatible with its deepening. However, any subsequent enlargement would demand a reconceptualisation and readjustments of its policies, interests and institutions.

With greater diversities amongst the Member States, unanimity in the Council will be harder to attain. This will apply in particular to the CFSP and cooperation in the field of justice and home affairs, where unanimity is to be the general rule and in those cases, where unanimity applies in the Union's affairs.

Enlargement can make the system of rotating Presidency even more difficult. The problem is how to reconcile considerations of efficiency with the recognition of equality among Member States. Excluding the small Member States from the Presidency would be incompatible with the second criteria. Extending the present system to the new members would lead to a poor management of the Council. It also raises new questions about the inability of the system of supervision of the Commission and the European Court. In spite of an expansion of functions and a functional shift from policy initiation to policy implementation, the organisation of the Commission have been left largely unchanged, although the bureaucracy has grown in size. The problem of enlargement for the European Court of Justice is not one of adequate powers of procedures. On the other hand, the application of the EU law depends heavily on the Court's and legal systems of the Member States.[83] Some of the judiciaries of the applicant states may not have the competence to play the role satisfactorily. The implication is that the applicant states must attain reliable judicial standards before they can accede to the EU.

Large countries are currently under-represented (relative to their population), in the Council and the European Parliament. Since most of the potential members except Poland are small countries, their entry would exacerbate the large Member States' under-representation. Any politics of institutional reform would be marked by the defence of interests by those Member States who would fear a loss of power and status, especially in matters which affect the distribution of power between big and small Member States. In relation to the demographic size, the smaller states are over represented in the Council when it comes to Qualified Majority Voting. A re-weighting of votes would be resisted by the smaller states. On the other hand, a voting system that includes a dual majority is likely to be opposed by the big Member States.

Language questions may prove harder to solve with further enlargement. With the present number of official languages in the EU, any meeting of the ministers or officials required 27 interpretations. The entry of new states would create probably 16, 18, 20 language-EU, needing more than 42 interpreters and involving exorbitant costs.

The most pertinent problems caused by enlargement in the EU institutions is with regard to EU decision-making capacity, which has been far from optimal in the EU of 12 to 15 and its efficiency is likely to decrease if more countries join. Some new decision-making structures will become imperative for the Council, since it safe-guards the interests of the Member States. In view of the impact that enlargement would have on EU institutions, EU Commission President, Jacques Santer said on the German Radio:

> We will do everything to be able to lead these countries (CEEC) upto the EU around the end of this century. We must get our house in order from an institutional perspective.[84]

PROPOSALS FOR INSTITUTIONAL REFORM

The implications of enlargement make further institutional policy reform of the existing structure imperative during the IGC, 1996. In the opinion of former EU Commission President, Jacques Delors, substantial enlargement would demand considerable institutional change otherwise the EU:

> would return to a simple free trade area and ...we (EU) would lose all the acquisitions gained from thirty years of political economic integration.[85]

The first salvo of proposals for constitutional reforms of the EU in the 1996 IGC which came from the French government, called for more flexible integration in a non-federal Union and for reforms of the institutions to make them more democratic so as to cope with an enlarged EU. The French Prime Minister Edouard Balladur asserted that an enlarged Europe "could not be federal". A federal state, he added, "would mean an expansion of majority voting", therefore, the five big states representing four-fifths of EU's population could be put in a minority. He also stressed that enlargement would require the Union to be more modest in its funding and called on the pooling of resources of Member States.[86]

The French European Affairs Minister, Allain Lamassoure emphasized that "subsidiarity" should be made more precise, more homogeneous and more restrictive in the 1996 IGC, as bringing in more states into the Union would reduce the subjects of common interest between them. In order to solve the problems of decision-making and to extend democracy in the EU, the French government suggested reducing the Council of Ministers' management role from its legislative function. Balladur stressed the need for more coherent security and defence policy in the 1996 IGC, just as the Maastricht Treaty emphasized on the Economic and Monetary Union.

With regard to the powers of the Parliament, a decision which may appear unfavourable to the nationalist French has been more or less agreed by those in Brussels. There was a plan of introducing the right of "co-decision" with the Council. With a view to consolidate the power of the Parliament, President of the EU Commission, Jacques Santer suggested that the future Commission President should be elected by the Parliament from candidates proposed by governments.[87] This could perhaps give way to the Parliament's demand for a "new code of conduct" that would require the Commission to treat it equally with national governments and to abandon any legislation rejected by an absolute majority of the Parliament and this would extend the Parliament's limited right of veto to all legislation.

In Germany, the Government of Chancellor Gerhard Schroeder stressed that institutional reform must be tackled as soon as the negotiations on Agenda 2000 (covering the reform of CAP, Structural Funds and the budget) was completed.[88] The German government advocated the extension of decision-making by Qualified Majority Voting and restriction of unanimity.

CAP AND EASTWARD ENLARGEMENT OF THE EU

Extending the EU eastward is no longer an impractical proposition but the question is how to prepare these countries and accommodate them into the EU. The political promises have been made and several strategies worked out but for one—farming. For all the modifications it has undergone, the Common Agricultural Policy (CAP) remains an inexpensive way of support for a fairly small number of farmers. East Europe is much poorer as compared to the EU and has a large number of farmers. Simply integrating them into the CAP with its high food prices is prohibitively expensive. Neither East European consumers nor the EU's farm budget would be in a position to build CAP-like policies in the belief that it will prepare them in a better way for membership. But neither their budgets nor their consumers can afford it. The CAP's 1992 reforms have already lowered farm prices. Now that the EU has accepted the idea that farming should be subject to world trade arrangements, there will be continuing pressures implementing further price cuts.

With reference to the convergence between the CEEC and the EU in matters of agricultural policy, EU Commissioner Rene Steichen proposed that partners should adopt substantial components of the EU measures.[89] The result however would be unacceptably excessive subsidies and a surplus production stimulated by the high prices. The convergence of the CAP would be difficult and reduction of subsidies would meet with stiff opposition in the EU. As Baldwin pointed out:

> ....even the Visegrad Four are two and half times more agricultural and less than one-third as rich as the EU. They could not enter the EU without threatening two powerful interest groups–the incumbent farmers and poor regions, during the decades they will need to catch up.[90]

Extending to the east or not, the EU farm policy will become more market sensitive. EU's accession agreements with Austria, Sweden and Finland have introduced even higher levels of farm supports and prices than the EU. To bridge the gap, the new Member States have been given considerable freedom to top up farm incomes. Some support will come from Brussels but much of the cost will fall on national budgets. This principle could be extended to CEEC farmers as well. Lowering CAP prices would prevent farm output in CEEC from soaring. But this proposal is susceptible to risks, as opening more national support could lead to subsidised competition in CEEC. Any attempts for the reform of the CAP will inevitably be subject to a debate of agreements and disagreements between France and Great Britain as both countries have certain reservations concerning farm support and CAP budgetary.

TIMING AND DATE OF MEMBERSHIP

The highly demanding and structured process which the CEEC has to undergo in order to join the EU requires the adoption of the *acquis communautaire* which has been laid down in the European Council of Copenhagen in 1993. The

Copenhagen criteria specifies the following conditions for membership :

- stability of institutions guaranting democracy, rule of law, human rights and respect and protection of minorities,
- the existence of functioning market economy as well as the capacity to cope with the competitive pressures of the market forces in the EU,
- the ability to take on the obligation of membership, including adherence to the aims of political, economic and monetary union.[91]

On the basis of the Commission's recommendations, the European Council held at Luxembourg in December 1997 decided to open negotiations for accession with the six applicant countries (Poland, Hungary, Czech Republic, Estonia, Slovenia and Cyprus).

When assessing the ability of the candidate countries to take on the obligations of membership, the Commission based its judgement on the performance of a country in implementing the 'Europe Agreements' and its record in adopting the *acquis communautaire*. The core of the *acquis* is embodied in the internal market legislation the phased adoption of which is the essential element of the pre-accession strategy launched by the Essen European Council in December 1994.[92]

The adoption of the internal market *acquis* not only requires that the associated countries adapt their relevant legislation but also adequate institutional measures which ensure the effective implementation of community laws and regulations. Applying the *acquis* therefore, requires efforts in institutional building and administration and judicial reform which often put under strain the human and financial resources of the candidate countries. However, about 30 per cent of the *acquis communautaire* has been incorporated in the Europe Agreements.[93] These agreements have aided the transition to the market economy in the associated countries by promoting legal and institutional convergence with the EU. The pre-accession strategy adopted by the Luxembourg of European Council in December 1997 provides for bilateral agreements with the applicant countries which include a National Programme for the Adoption of the *Acquis* and financial assistance made contingent on the progress in implementing the Europe Agreements. Such an approach reflects the gap in economic and institutional development between the EU and the candidate for accession as well as the asymmetry in the bargaining capacity between the parties to the enlargement process.[94] Ambition to join the EU has clearly determined the path of political and economic transformation of several CEEC.[95] Having entered a 'patron-client' relation with the EU, they had to commit to invest heavily in an economic constitution and regulatory regimes of great legal and institutional complexity. The EU, has been extremely reluctant to accept any binding commitments as far as the timing of enlargement and its own preparation for the same are concerned. This complicates the task of adjustment for the applicant countries, as the EU presents itself as a moving target.[96]

ENLARGEMENT AND CONFLICTUAL INTERESTS AMONGST MEMBER STATES

As and when the EU includes the new members, differences of interest amongst the Member States will become more evident. Enlargement has potentially huge implications on various levels which are bound to provoke conflicts among Member States as well as between the Member States and applicant countries. Full membership implies complete freedom of movement. Given the huge wage differentials, this could lead to substantial migration flow from the new eastern members of the EU, primarily into Germany. Among the applicant states, only Poland poses a problem in this context. Population is declining in most CEE countries and unemployment rates are at more or less the same level as in Western Europe. In this regard the picture is completely different from that in the Mediterranean with its massive population and high unemployment. Turkey's migration potential is probably the main reason for her not becoming a full member of the EU. The EU budget could increase substantially, if certain policies, like the CAP are not reformed before enlargement. Governments under severe pressure to raise their fiscal policies and reduce expenditure find new contributions to the EU a daunting task. The CEEC would be net recipients of the budget and Germany as the biggest net contributor will have to bear the burden.

The old Member States mostly benefiting from EU Structural Funds will lose transfers as thresholds will increase with the entry of poorer regions into the EU. With the average EU income decreasing, some regions now eligible for assistance will no longer benefit from the funds.[97] For the countries like Ireland, Greece, Spain and Portugal, the EU has functioned as a "development assistance community" and this will also apply to the new members of CEEC. The struggle for budgetary resources will thereby intensify, pitting the new periphery against the old.

IMPACT OF TRANSFORMATION AND INTEGRATION IN THE CEEC

Ten years after the revolutions in the CEEC, these countries made wide progress in the transition to free market democracies. Even these relatively stable democracies contain features that analysts[98] find pessimistic when looking at developments in CEEC. These include a conjunction of challenges to democracy both traditional (centralism, voter turn-out, minority questions) and modern (over extended social welfare systems, lacking international competitiveness) in the context of a legacy of old structures and entirely different historical experiences and expectations.

Even in the case of sustained economic growth, the transformation process in CEEC has increased economic and social differentiation and created a significant group of worse-off and disgruntled individuals.

Because of specific structural problems (missing democratic traditions, value patterns, party system, and in general, a weakly developed civil society), the emerging democracies in East-Central Europe are particularly vulnerable to those groups who have suffered under the reforms and become critical of the new system.

Transformation and social differentiation are thus eroding popular support for democracy in East-Central Europe. Moreover, these democracies do not have a cushioning social welfare system nor fresh democratic political alternatives.

Joining the EU would have ambivalent consequences for the democratic stability of East Central Europe. While it would provide an anchor of stability, it would at the same time accelerate not only the transformation process, but social differentiation and political polarization.[99]

CONCLUSION

It has been suggested that with its northward enlargement in 1995, the "EU's eyes have grown a little bluer, and its skin a little fairer, its religion a little more Protestant and its political centre of gravity has moved to the Nordic states".[100] The enlarged EU would, to some extent tilt the majority of Europeans to the north and eventually to the east and Germany. This is proving enough to make the Southern fringes of the EU feel queasy.[101] The Southern Member States have already started thinking of means of tackling the problems emerging from their southern frontiers. The EU leaders have allowed their commitment to the southern neighbours by approaching a plan to embrace North Africa and Middle East in a free trade zone and pledging to "maintain an appropriate balance in the geographical commitments".[102] EU's ultimate aim is to create a Euro-Mediterranean Economic Area and contribute more than double aid to those regions.[103]

The northward enlargement of the EU and the inclusion of Austria in the east and prospects of future eastward enlargement could prove decisive in shifting the weight and strength of EU to Germany making it the hub of European politics. To avoid being marginalised by EU's eastward expansion or to counter Germany's domineering influence,

France hinted at its desire to cooperate with Britain, strengthen ties with Spain and Italy in order to boost is Euro-Mediterranean policy. The head of the Invest in French Bureau and Ambassador Jean-Daniel Tordjman commented:

> The French have no wish to find themselves in a permanent tete-e-tete with the Germans and we would very much like Britain to join us wholeheartedly in the movement towards European Union. The German alliance is important, but a counterweight to German economic strength would also be valuable.[104]

The debate amongst EU Member States over enlargement clearly reflect that applicant states not only have to fulfil the formal conditions of accession but also the less formal conditions arising from the national interests of the existing Member States. The national priorities of the Member States have always dominated the integration process of the EU. With regard to future integration, the division within the EU have become so acrimonious that the idea of a "two-speed" or "multi-speed" Europe for those favouring deeper integration on the one hand, and for those tied to intergovernmentalism, could become a possibility and some have argued this as the most likely and preferable alternative. The idea of a "multi-speed" Europe which was signalled by the Maastrich Treaty has the potential danger of leaving behind those who are slower in integration. Moreover, a "multi-speed Europe" would not fulfil the traditional homogeneity which the EU has always aspired to attain.

As the EU is formally negotiating not with a group but with individual applicants who will be treated according to their performance in meeting the criteria for membership, such selective demotion would be unexceptionable, but the transaction costs of the ratification process are likely to promote a group-approach rather than a series of ratification procedures for individual countries.[105]

EU's preferential treatment *vis-a-vis* the potential candidates presents a likely scenario of the EU breaking up into three distinct political and economic zones: the new entrants of EFTA forming the middle circle around the original Twelve Members to be followed by the Visegrad states in the periphery and the remaining applicant states in the extreme outer fringe. The idea of a "EU of concentric circles" was raised when Chancellor Kohl and his associates called for a core-group of countries led by Germany, France and the Benelux countries.[106] Britain, in particular, has been critical of such a project where all the Member States would benefit economically, but those in the periphery would undoubtedly remain politically isolated.

EU's enlargement strategy largely depends on the 1996, IGC. Clearly, the EU is attracted by proposals for institutional reform before it absorbs new members. This deepening process will appear to reinforce the worry of a "Fortress Europe" and also that the EU is becoming a "rich-man's protectionist club". The idea of a European economic core, periphery and outer-rim being comprised of the original EU twelve, the Nordic Members and the CEEC respectively, is likely to be replaced by a much more basic division of Europe: perhaps a rich "West" and a relatively poor "East".

Enlargement in the past had multifarious affects on the EU and even in future, enlargement will entail changes and remodeling of existing EU structures and institutions. The success of the EU, which lies in enhancing economic prosperity and stability of the region will be determined largely by the manner in which EU tackles this pertinent issue in the 1996 IGC and beyond.

NOTES

1. See, Helen Wallace, The Europe that came in from the cold", *International Affairs,* vol. 67, no. 4, October 1991, pp. 647-663.
2. EC, Commission, "Europe and the Challenge of Enlargement", *Bulletin of the European Communities* (Luxembourg: Official Publications of EC, 1992) Supplement 3, p 11.
3. Martin Holland, *European Community Integration* (London : Pinter Publishers, 1993) p. 167.
4. For details, see, P. Laurent, "European Community: Twelve becoming One", *Current History,* vol. 87 (532) November 1988, pp. 357-60 and C. Brewin, "European Community: A Union

of States Without Unity of Government", *Journal of Common Market Studies*, September 1987, p. 1-23.

5. See, T. Osmundsen, "A United Europe: Where does EFTA fit in?" *European Affairs*, vol. 4, no. 2, Summer 1990, pp. 73-77 and S.Gstohl, "EFTA and the EEA or the Politics of Frustration", *Cooperation and Conflict*, vol. 29, no. 4, 1994, pp. 331-361.
6. See, Trevor Meridian, "How will the EFTA four affect the EU Twelve? " *European Trends*, (EIU), 2nd quarter 1994, pp. 53-62.
7. Christopher Preston, "Obstacles to European Union Enlargement", *Journal of Common Market Studies*, vol. 33, no. 3, September 1995, p. 352.
8. UK's commitment to the European Community was also questioned by France due to the former's "special-relation" with the US and ties with the Commonwealth countries.
9. Preston, n. 7, p. 454.
10. Preston. n. 7, p. 454.
11. As was the case during the Iberian enlargements when the EC negotiated with both Spain and Portugal together, or the recent EFTA accession.
12. Preston, n. 7, p. 456.
13. For details on impact of Spanish enlargement, see Robert Hine, "Customs Union, Enlargement and Adjustment: Spain's Acession to the EC", *Journal of Common Market Studies*, vol. 28, no. 1, September 1989, pp. 1-28.
14. Ibid., p. 456.
15. Jacques Rupnik, "Central Europe or Mitteleuropa" in Stephen Granbard (ed.), *Eastern Europe, Central Europe....Europe* (Boulder: Westview, 1991) p. 234.
16. For background see, G. Schopflin, "The End of Communism", *International Affairs*, vol. 66, no.1, Fall 1990, pp. 3-16 and W. Wesolawski, "From Authoritarianism to Democracy", *Social Research*, vol. 57, no. 2, Summer 1990, pp. 435-62.
17. EC Commission, *The European Community and its Eastern Neighbours* (Luxembourg: Office for the Official Publications of the EC, 1990) Supplement 9, p.10.
18. A. Karkhoza, "Transition of the East: A New Beginning for Europe", *Adelphi Paper*, vol. 247, Winter 1989-90, p. 90.
19. Flora Lewis, "Bringing in the East", *International Affairs*, vol. 66, no. 4, Fall 1990, p. 19, Also see, G Wettig, "Political Implication of Changes in East Europe", *Aussen Politik*, vol. 41,

no. 23, 2nd Quarter 1990, pp. 107-117.

20. Heinz Kramer, "The EC's Response to the New Eastern Europe", *Journal of Common Market Studies,* vol.31 No. 2 June 1993, p. 6.
21. EC, Commission, The European Community and its Eastern Neighbours (Luxembourg: Office for Official Publications of the EC, 1990) Supplement 8,1990, p. 6.
22. Ibid.
23. EC, Commission, Association Agreements with Poland Czechoslovakia and Hungary, Brussels, 9 March, 1992, p.1.
24. EC, Commission, *Annotated Summary of Agreements Linking the EU with Non Member Countries, 31 December 1992,* 351/930, Brussels, January 1993, p. 98.
25. EC Commission, Directorate General for Economic and Financial Affairs, "Trade Liberalization with Central and Eastern Europe: An Assessment of the Interim Europe Agreements", *European Economy,* Supplement 4, no 7, July 1994, 88 pp.
26. Ibid.
27. Source : EUROSTAT, No. 07, 1994, Commission of the European Union.
28. EC, Commission, General Report on Activities of the European Union, 1994 (Luxembourg: Office for Official Publications of the EC, 1995) 560 pp.
29. *Council Regulation* 3381/81, 32 O.J. European Commission (No. L 326) 6(1998).
30. EC, Commission, Directorate General X, "EU Assistance to Central and Eastern European Countries, 1990-1993",12 July 1994, *Background Brief* 22, 18 pp.
31. *European Investment Bank Information,* November 1992.
32. Pap News Agency, (Warsaw), 8 August 1994 in BBC, *Summary of World Broadcasts* (SWB), EE/.0345, 11 August 1994, p. A/2.
33. MTI News Agency (Budapest), 25 April 1993, in BBC, SWB EE/W.0280,6 May 1993,p. A/2.
34. Pap News Agency (Warsaw), 8 September 1994, in BBC, *SWB,* EE/2097,10 September 1994, p. A/1.
35. *Financial Times* (London), 1 November 1994.
36. For a text on EC-Turkey Association Agreement, See *Official Journal of the European Economic Community,* no. 217, 29 December 1964.
37. Bahri Yilmaaz, 'Turkey's New Role in International Poli-

tics", ,*Aussen Politik,* vol. 45, no. 1, 1st Quarter 1994, pp. 90-98.

38. Mehmet A. Birand, "Turkey and the European Community", *The World Today,* vol. 34, no. 2, February 1978, pp. 52-61.
39. Heinz Kramer, "Turkey and EC's Southern Enlargement", *Aussen Politik,* vol. 35, no. 1, January 1984,p. 107.
40. Interview with Prof. M. Kreile, Institut fuer Politik Wissenschaft, Humboldt Universitaet, Berlin, 18 November 1999, and Christian Sterzing, Member of Bundestag and European Policy Spokesman, The Green Party, Berlin, 29 November 1999.
41. Interview with Dr. Ulrika Guerot,, Former Member of CDU Parliamentary Group, Haus der Deutschen Wirtschaft, Berlin, 1 December 1999.
42. Hamit Bozarslan, "Integrating the Muslim Mediterranean : The Non Obstacles and Obstacles", in Harmut Elsenhans (ed.), *A Balanced European Architecture: Enlargement of the European Union to the Central East European Countries and the Mediterranean* (Paris : Publisud, 1999).
43. Kramer, n. 39, p. 109.
44. EC, "Commission's Report to the Council on the implementation of Economic Reform in Malta", *Press Release,* IP/95/198, Brussels, 1 March 1995, 2pp.
45. EC, *Commission's Opinion on Malta's Application for Membership,* Com (93), 312 final, Brussels, 30 June 1993, 23 pp.
46. Edit, "Malta's Testing Time", *The World Today,* vol. 3, no. 1 January 1987, pp. 15-17.
47. For background on Greek-Turkish conflicts over Cyprus, see, Andrew Margo, "Greek-Turkey Unfriendly Allies", *The World Today,* vol. 43, no 8-9, 1987, pp. 144-147 and Richard Haas, "Alliance Problem in European Mediterranean", *Adelphi Paper,* Vol. 229, Spring 1988, pp. 61-71.
48. EC, Commission's Opinion in the Application by the Republic of Cyprus for Membership, Com (93), 313 final, Brussels, 30 June 1993.
49. Cf. C.A. Dodd, *The Cyprus Issue: A Current Perspective* (Cambridge: Eothen, 1995).
50. As Cited in *The Independent,* 23 January 1997.
51. EC, Commission, "EU-Russia Relations", *Press Release,* MEMO/96/26, Brussels, 15 March 1996 pp 3-4.
52. For text see, EC, Commission, Speech by Hans van den Broek,

"EU-Russia: A Challenging Partnership", Carnegie Foundation, Moscow, 18 March 1996, *Press Release,* no. 96/66, 18 Mach 1996. 8pp.

53. R.K. Jain, "Migration in Germany : Issues and Response", *India International Centre Quarterly,* Winter 1993, p.20.
54. Timothy Ash Garton, "Mitteleuropa" in Stephen Granbard (ed.), *Eastern Europe, Central Europe, Europe* (Boulder : West view, 1991), pp. 3-4.
55. Lily Gardner Feldman, "Germany and EC: Realism and Responsibility", *The Annals of the American Academy of Political and Social Science,* vol. 531, January 1994, p.32.
56. Rupnik, n. 15, p. 259.
57. *The Economist Intelligence Unit* (EIU), Country Report: Hungary, 3rd Quarter 1994 (London), p. 23.
58. Pap News Agency (Warsaw), 20 July 1994, in BBC, *SWB,* EEW/2054, 22 July 1994, P.A./10.
59. *EUROSTAT.* no. 7, 1994.
60. As cited in R.K. Jain, "Germany and the EU: Maastricht to the 1996 IGC", Paper presented at the International Seminar on *Germany in the Ninties,* JNU, New Delhi, 4-5 November 1996.
61. Feldman, n. 55, p. 41.
62. *Financial Times* (London), 14 October 1994.
63. *As cited in International Herald Tribune* (Paris), 24 November 1994, p. 7, A similar reference can be seen in an Address by Chancellor Kohl at the Nordic Council in Helsinki, "The Role of Germany in the United Europe" on March 1992, *Press Release,* Embassy of the FRG, New Delhi, 30 March 1992, no. 14, 5pp.
64. As cited in an interview with Chancellor Kohl in *International Herald Tribune,* (Paris), December 1994, p.2.
65. Editorial Report (Prague) in BBC, *SWB,* EE/2089, 24 August 1994, p. A/2.
66. Duna TV Satellite Service, (Budapest), 18 July 1994, in BBC, *SWB,* EE/0343, 28 July 1994, p. A/7.
67. Sylvia P. Forgus, "German Nationality Politics in Poland", *East European Quarterly,* March 1986, p. 262.
68. Timothy Garton Ash, "Germany's Choice", *Foreign Affairs,* vol. 73, no. 4, July-August 1994, p.76.
69. Ole Waever, "Three Competing Europes", *International Affairs,* vol. 66, no. 3, 1990, p. 481.
70. Michael Sutton, "France and EU's Enlargement Eastward",

The World Today, vol. 73, no. 4, July-August 1994, p. 154.

71. For text see, "Inaugural Conference on the Pact for Stability in Europe", Agence Europe, Europe Documents, no. 1887, 31 May 1994.
72. For the Text of Edouard Balladur's Memorandum, see, Agence Europe, *Documents*, no.'1846, 26 June 1993.
73. As cited in Sutton, n. 70, p. 155.
74. Jacques Chirac, *Une nouvelle France: reflexious' 1* (Paris: Nil Editions, 1994) pp. 102-103.
75. Vallerie Guerin Sendelbach and J. Rulkowski, "Euro-trio: France-Germany-Poland", *Aussen Politik*, Vol. 3, 1994, p. 246.
76. Pap News Agency, (Warsaw), 8 September 1994, in BBC, *SWB*, EE/2075, 10 September 1994, p. A/1. Reasons for a high degree of complementarity between France and Poland was also because of the fact that the latter recognises French interest in extending the association of the EU and intensifying cooperation with the Southern-Mediterranean countries. Poland also supports the French argument that the Mediterranean should be considered politically important for the EU because it constitutes an area of close proximity with Europe, though outside the EU. Refer, Hartmut Elsenhans, n. 42.
77. As evident in Prime Minister Balladur's statements in press coverages, Radio Slovakia, 20 August 1994, in BBC, *SWB*, EE/2075, 10 August 1994, p. A/6 and MTI News Agency (Budapest), 27 July 1994, in BBC, *SWB*, EE/2059, 28 July 1994, p. A/7.
78. *Financial Times* (London), December 1994, p. 2.
79. *The Economist* (London), 14 January 1995.
80. R.K. Jain, "The European Muslims", *Asian Affairs*, no. 5, March 1997, p. 29.
81. France has about million Muslim population from Algeria, Tunisia and North Africa. Signs of religious fervour amongst the Muslims have led to various religious organizations. There is a growing fear in France that this could endanger European identity and cultural homogeneity. For details see, Jain, n. 80.
82. Hartmut Elsenhans, "Mission de I'Europe : Complementaries and Rivalries between the two Options and Incompatibilities in the Historically Rooted Collective Memories of Some Actors" in Elsenhans, n. 42, p. 174.
83. The already existing patterns in the legal system of the EU

makes it hugely complex and complicated. For background details see, Daniel Wincott, "Is the Treaty of Maastricht an adequate Constitution for the EU?", *Public Administration,* vol. 72, Winter 1994, pp. 573-590.

84. *Financial Times* (London), 13 December 1994.
85. Martin Holland, "*European Community Integration* (London: Pinter Publishers, 1993), p. 161.
86. *Financial Times* (London), 30 November 1994.
87. *The Economist* (London), 21 January 1994, p. 58.
88. Gerhard Schroeder, "Prioritaeten des deutschen EU-Vorsitzes", *Bulletin,* no. 4, 1999, pp. 33-39.
89. Speech by Rene Steichen on "Outlook for European Agriculture and Agricultural Policy with the Central East European Countries", at Centre for Agricultural Strategy, Agence Europe, *Europe Documents,* n. 1914, 7 December 1994, 8pp.
90. See, E. Baldwin, *Towards an Integrated Europe* (London : CEPR, 1994).
91. Quoted from Agenda 2000, *Commission Opinion on Poland's Application for Membership of the European Union,* http:/ europa.en.int.com/dg 1a/agenda2000/en/opinions/ poland/a.htm.
92. See A. Mayhew, *Recreating Europe: The European Union's Policy towards Central and Eastern Europe* (Cambridge: Cambridge University Press, 1998) p. 323.
93. Barbara Lippert, "From pre-accession to EU Membership-Implementing, Transformation and Integration" in B. Lippert and P. Becker (ed.), *Towards EU Membership: Transformation and Integration in Poland and the Czeck republic* (Bonn: Europa, 1998) p. 28.
94. Michael Kreile, "Federalism Doomed: Institutional Implications of EU Enlargement", Unpublished Article, Institute Fuer Politik Wissenschaft, Humboldt Universitaet, Berlin, 1999, p. 19.
95. Lippert, n. 93, p. 58.
96. See Mayhew, n. 92, p. 22.
97. Michael Dauderstaedt, "European and German Interests in Central and Eastern Europe compared to the Mediterranean", in Elsenhans, n. 42.
98. Christian Deubner, *Deutsche Europa politik : Von Maastricht nach Kerneuropa* (Baden-Baden:Nomos, 1995), p. 124.
99. Michael Dauderstadt, "Can the Democracies of East-Central Europe cope with the Double Impact of Transformation and

Integration", *Conference on Political and Social Change in Central Europe"*, Prague: Friedrich Ebert Foundation, 8 to 10 May 1996, p. 1.

100. *The Economist* (London), 14 January 1995, p. 14.
101. The hijacking of an Air France jet by Algerian extremists in 1994 was a grim reminder to France that their former colony (Algeria) was fighting a civil war that may well spill over France. Spain and Italy too, have already been receiving a steady flow of illegal immigrants from North Africa where poverty and instability combine to make them seek a better life in Europe.
102. *Financial Times* (London), 12 December 1994.
103. For details see, EC, Commission, "Strengthening the Mediterranean Policy of the EU: Establishing a Euro-Mediterranean Partnership", *Bulletin of EC*, Supplement 2 (Luxembourg: Office for Official Publications of the EC, 1995).
104. As cited in *International Herald Tribune* (Paris), 8 December 1994, p. 9.
105. Institute fuer Europaeische Politik, *Enlargement/Agenda 2000-Watch*, Pilot Issue, Bonn, October 1998, p. 36.
106. EC, Commission, "Reflections on European Policy", Paper submitted by the CDU-CSU to the Bundestag, 1 September 1994, Agence Europe, *Europe Documents*, no. 1895/96.

Chapter IV

France, Germany and the Common Foreign and Security Policy

The European Union's (EU) economic weight demands that it play a commensurate political role in world affairs. The end of the Cold War and the emergence of new conflicts in Europe have made it vital for the EU to develop a foreign and security policy identity. The political agenda for Europe adopted by the Madrid European Council in December 1995[1] identified the foreign policy challenges which the EU confronts today: enlargement negotiations with Cyprus, Malta and Eastern Europe (CEEC), cooperation and partnership with the EU's neighbours in particular, Russia, Ukraine, Turkey, the transatlantic cooperation, its traditional relationship with the African Caribbean and Pacific countries, closer relations with Asia, Middle East and Latin America and finally the establishment of a European security system.[2] The foreign policy arm of the EU is significant both for its institutional development and for its impact on world events. The post 1989 changes in the global architecture have heightened the demands on EU to shape its international role independently, assert its identity of the international scene and shoulder their share of global responsibilities. One of the most difficult areas of cooperation in the EU has been in foreign policy matters. Creating a wide-ranging collective unit with a common policy by accommodating a multitude of national units, each with its own identity differing historical traditions and specific sensitivities is an extremely complicated process involving a lot of preconditions.[3]

HISTORICAL OVERVIEW

The various attempts to develop a collective foreign policy in the EU can be traced back to the failing initiatives of creating a European Defence Community in the 1950s, the experience of European Political Cooperation (EPC) in the 1970s and 1980s and the contemporary proclamation of a Common Foreign and Security Policy (CFSP) as proposed in the Maastricht Treaty of 1993.

The origins of European Political Cooperation can be sought in the post-war period when the West European states' decision to replace the faulty political structures which had caused the war, coincided with the necessity to create conditions in which Germany could safely be allowed to rearm. The first move in this direction was the attempt to create a European Defence Community in 1957 which would have attached to it evaluative powers over foreign policy.[4] This step however, failed essentially for french domestic politics.[5] The Treaty of Rome of 1957, which was the first step to European integration stipulated five areas which indicated the need to provide the European Community (EC) with an international political role.[6] The first enlargement of the EC lent impetus to the 'political' content of these areas thereby adding depth and thrust to the integration process. EPC was also facilitated by external factors and inextricably linked with the vagaries of the international environment, in particular the twists and turns in the relations between the super-powers.[7] It was in this connection that at the Hague Summit in 1969, it was agreed between the EC members to set a structure for foreign policy on intergovernmentalist lines.

The origin and history of EPC manifests three intertwining strands which have constantly influenced its development. The first aspect reveals the dichotomy between the integrationists (federalists) and the intergovernmentalists (functionalists).[8] The second strand refers to the influence of the United States (US) on West European foreign policy making.[9] The third is the organisational factor involving the bureaucratic machinery which was set up in a piece-meal way to cope with the challenges facing EPC. There was a lack of a "grand design"; rather the structure of organization depended to a larger extent on the way EPC reacted to certain events.[10] It has been acknowledged that the EPC "has evolved through practice, shared experiences"[11] and not intended as a "legalistic exercise but as a pragmatic enterprise to establish common positions and common actions in foreign policy"[12] which unfortunately lacked an institutional structure and has been versed in intergovernmentalism. The ambitious proclamation of the 1969 Heads of States and Government meeting at the Hague, calling for "a United Europe capable of assuming its responsibilities in the world"[13] was followed by the Luxembourg Report of 1970 where the objectives of EPC were "to ensure greater mutual understanding with respect to major issues of international policies by exchanging information and consulting regularly".[14] The Luxembourg Report established a formal schedule for ministerial meeting to discuss foreign affairs marked the birth of EPC.[15] It reinstated the intergovernmental procedure which kept the European Parliament and the Commission on the fringes of foreign policy. Nevertheless, it also created the practice of working cooperatively which had a strong socializing effect within the Community.[16]

In its first three years, EPC succeeded in forging a united position on the Conference on Security and Cooperation in Europe (CSCE) and at the initiative of France made progress in collaborating diverse national opinions on Middle East.[17] It was still difficult to address the more politically important aspects of the EC's joint foreign policy positions. Therefore, the Copenhagen Report of 1973 updated and codified procedural reforms. The Report clarified the integrationist objective of EPC although political cooperation remained clearly intergovernmental.[18] With the subsequent enlargement of the EC in 1973, the need to redefine the relationship with the US came to the fore. This was thrust upon the EC of Nine by Kissinger's 'Year of Europe' in an attempt to retain the Atlantic leadership in the continent. No Member State could remain indifferent to the position of the US with direct consequence for the positions taken by the EPC. The EC's response during this phase was made complicated by the outbreak of the October War and the Arab oil crisis. During this period external pressures once again compelled the EPC to widen its scope. The invasion in Cyprus in 1974 and the execution of the Basque terrorists in Spain in 1975 forced the EC into action.[19] Their reaction posed the problems of how the EC's trade policy towards these countries should be affected by political judgements. In the same period the EC had to turn its gaze to South Africa following the break-up of Portugal's ex-colonies.[20] The Nine emerged from these ordeals with shared experiences of working jointly. The future was secured by a radical attempt to reform EPC in the Tindemans Report in 1975 which called for a single decision-making structure and the merging of the EC and EPC.[21] Its most ambitious recommendation was that the basis of EPC should be revised from its existing voluntary concentration to legally binding obligation on the Member States to comply with common foreign policy decisions.[22] The Tindemans Report, despite suggesting institutional advances, did not provide the hoped for breakthrough. Once again, it required a series of international crisis to confront the existing inadequate nature of the EPC. The EC's response to the Soviet invasion of Afghanistan in 1979-80 and Polish domestic crisis highlighted the slowness of the EPC to act and also reflected the dichotomy that still existed between the EC and the EPC.[23] With negotiations for enlargement to Greece, Spain and Portugal in 1978, the Nine had to cope with the difficulties of how to organize parallel accession to EPC. In view of this, the EC responded in the London Report of 1981 which began codifying EPC practices. The importance of the European Council was recognized and the Troika arrangement[24] was extended.[25] However, the traditional distinction between the EC's economic and political affairs continued to exist. Intergovernmentalism was embodied as much as possible in the functioning of the EPC.[26] The years that followed the London Report were marked by Europe's increasing uneasiness with President Reagan's administration.[27] This had a noticeable impact on the development of EPC where the EC was torn between lending support to the US and maintaining their independent stance on certain issues. This reflected on their position in Poland, the CSCE and Middle East where the EC could consider using Community instruments to implement policies decided in political cooperation. Sanctions followed the imposition of martial law in Poland, it applied to Argentina after the Falkland crisis[28] and in South Africa. The London Report of 1981 created by the UK since 1978, adopted a tightening procedure but nevertheless, did not appeal to all Member States. There were apprehensions in Germany that international economic and political developments were making the European integration process go through some bumpy stretches. The potential of the EC seemed to be directed to finding solutions to problems caused by the oil crisis, enlargement and the economic hazards. These factors almost made the political goal of the EC recede into the background.[29] A political prospect was incumbent in order to retain the internal cohesion and commitment of the Europeans to the EC. Repeated attempts to achieve institutional progress of EPC during the early 1980s continued with initiatives like the Genscher-Colombo Plan[30], the Solemn Declaration and moves in the European Parliament which led to the setting up of an ad-hoc Committee on Institutional Affairs and later with the decision by the European Council in 1985[31] setting the process till the culmination of the Single European Act (SEA) in 1987[32].

The most significant feature of the SEA was that it combined provisions for political cooperation and amendments to the Community treaties in one legal text. Despite this, the preamble of the SEA reflected more of "integrationist wishful thinking" than the actual political realities. It sought to create a European Union which in relation to the foreign policy will have the "necessary means of action with the purpose of speaking with one voice and to act with consistency and solidarity".[33] The SEA succeeded in blurring the intergovernmental distinction between the EPC and EC activities by connecting EPC directly to the EC treaties.[34] Though SEA provided EPC with a legal basis, both the EC and EPC activities were distinguished by their decision-making structures and by the role of other community institutions. Title III of SEA introduced many innovative procedural reforms:

— it clarified and extended the role of the Commission as fully associated with the proceedings of EPC (Art. 30 3 (b));
— it acknowledged a close association between the European Parliament and the Presidency (At 30.4);
— EPC was entitled to have its own Secretariat (Art. 30.10(e));
— Finally, EPC was entrusted with the task of coordinating positions more cohesively on the political and economic aspects of security (Art. 30.6 (a)).

Such commendable innovations were not enough guarantees for common action. The need to develop an obligatory common foreign policy by Member States by adopting a consensus on foreign affairs were again absent. The step to *communautaurise* EPC was wasted in favour of the same form of intergovernmentalism that previously impeded the development of a common foreign policy.[35]

The first two decades of EPC revealed some drawbacks that jeopardized the development of a more integrated Community. Both necessitated reforms of EPC.[36] In 1990, the EC confronted a precarious imbalance between the achievements of EPC and the greater accomplishment of the Economic and Monetary Union (EMU). With the emergence of the Single Market, equilibrium between the political and economic union was paramount. The external imperatives, like the political changes in Central East European countries, German unification, and the anticipated Nordic enlargement led the EC to reassess its role in Europe. The EC had to use its economic instruments like trade sanction and aid to promote its policy. The joint Franco-German Communique in March 1991 outlined the aims of those Member States committed to an integrated community.[37] The economic momentum generated by the Single Market encouraged the

EC to commence a new Inter-Governmental Conference (IGC) on Political Union which would run parallel with the IGC on Economic and Monetary Union, both commencing on December, 1990 and concluding in the end of 1991. The issues debated within the IGC on Political Union were disparate, ranging from foreign policy, citizenship democracy and institutional reform. During the Luxembourg Presidency, a treaty centered on strengthening common defence policy and a federal objective as common foreign policy was drafted.[38] The draft treaty indicated how the EC had reached a crossroad in making a choice between deeper integration or intergovernmentalism. It also reinstated the principle of unity. (viz. a single institutional framework to ensure consistency and continuity of actions). Nevertheless it remained unsuccessful in the 'federal' debate. Foreign policy was perhaps the most potent area where debate was the fiercest. Vagueness and non-specific alternatives continued to influence the discussion revolving around the concept of CFSP. In keeping with the traditional tussle between the federalists and functionalists, the debate that was carried over the Dutch Presidency draft and Luxembourg draft treaty in 1991 highlighted the incompatibilities between the intergovernmental and federal options of a common foreign policy.

MAASTRICHT TREATY AND CFSP

The most gigantic leap which laid down the foundations for a refined CFSP was taken at the Maastricht Conclusions of the IGC in December, 1991. The Treaty on European Union (TEU) came at a time when the EC found itself facing a new order with the collapse of the socialist regime and a receding influence of the US in the European scene. An extremely uncertain nature of security threat seemed to replace the old concepts. The TEU represented a compromise between the various ambitions of the 12 Member States. Though the TEU established the framework of an all-embracing European Union, it nevertheless involved the continuing distinction between the supranational activities of the EC and the intergovernmental traits within the EPC.[39]

Art 3.1 of the TEU states that the main treaty revisions were designed to "define and implement a CFSP....covering all areas of foreign and security policy". Setting the objectives of the CFSP, it called upon the Member States:

— to safeguard the common values, the fundamental interests and the independence of the Union;
— to strengthen the security of the Union and its Member States;
— to preserve peace and strengthen international security;
— to promote international cooperation, to develop and consolidate democracy and rule of law, respect for human rights and fundamental freedom (Art 3.1.2).

The provisions of CFSP as embodied in the TEU called for states to consult within the Council in order to ensure that their combined influence is executed as effectively as possible by means of concerted and convergent action (Art. J. 2.1.); it required national foreign policies to conform to the EC's common positions (Art. J.2.2.) and instructed the Member States to coordinate their actions and to promote common positions in international organizations (Art. J.2.3.).

A move towards a federalist approach was made in the procedure for attaining and executing common action. This was to be maneouvered through the Council of Ministers. Under Art. C.1, the Council was authorised to determine which foreign policy issues were subject to joint action. The details for implementing joint action were to be taken by majority voting.[40] Once adopted, any joint action could be binding on the Member States in the positions they adopted and in their conduct of their activity (Art. J.3.4). Art J.3.7. further provided for the possibility with the approval of the Council of Member States to exclude themselves from joint action so long as such decisions do not "run counter to the objective of the joint actions nor impair its effectiveness".

Along the lines of the codification of EPC provisions in the SEA, the TEU enhanced some aspects of the CFSP. Art. J.5. confirmed the role of the Presidency and the 'fully associated status of the Commission' (as similar to Art 30.3 (b) and 30.10 (b) of the SEA). A new provision empowered the Troika system with legal recognition. Modifying Art. 30.8 and 30.9 of the SEA, the TEU called for closer diplomatic cooperation and consultation between Member States' missions in other countries. As regards the European Parliament, it was to be kept regularly informed and consulted with its views 'duly taken into consideration' (replicating Art. 30.4 of the SEA). The Treaty only bestowed the Parliament with a limited form of initiative as it did not provide the latter with the ability to shape Community foreign policy. The TEU was concerned with developing a 'common foreign policy' and not a 'single foreign policy'. This difference between such policies is of paramount importance. Member States could on grounds, where it concerned their own geographical, political or economic interest, adopt a national policy provided it did not clash with the aims of any common policy of the EC. Such a provision although allows for progressive development in the implementation of collective Community's foreign policy, also provides the possibility for Member States to abstain or be excluded from a common policy because of specific obligations.

The principle of unanimity which required the EC to commit to joint policy, had the potential of promoting policy sclerosis and thereby lead to decisions based on the lowest common denominator.[41] A consensus rule or unanimity was required for defining the scope of CFSP and once unanimously decided on the issue, majority voting was to be used for the implementation of the policy. The question that arises is what constitutes 'majority decision'. In this context, it would be quite appropriate to mention what Jean Monnet commented "that the member states were entering an unknown world where the veto would be the exception and the rule of the majority would be the law". The issue remains as to what constitutes "majority".[42] In the Maastricht negotiations, weighted majority was adopted. This move towards majority decision was balanced with an 'exception clause' which provides for 'vital national interest'. This implies that the situation of common and bilateral foreign policy existing in tandem would continue in the foreseeable future.[43]

So far as the security dimension of the TEU was concerned the Western European Union (WEU) was to be created as the primary pillar of European defence, either by incorporating it within the EC or as a parallel regime. The problem lay in creating a European pillar within the North Atlantic Treaty Organization (NATO) as it carried the question of an appropriate security architecture for the EC in the post Cold War era. Although the TEU redefined and widened the scope of security by 'including all questions relating to the security of the Union' (Art. J.4.1.), it made the structure of future defence role of the EC more complicated because despite implementing all security matters through the framework of the WEU (Art J.4.2.), it did not rule out the development of other forms of defence cooperation. To give an example, there were signs of the existence of foreign and security policy sub-systems.[44]

Under the TEU there are three centres of foreign policy activity, all loosely connected but fused together by the objective of consistency. The 15 Member States (with the admission of Sweden, Finland and Austria into the EU) still continued to shape and implement their own national foreign and defence policies. Secondly, the CFSP itself is another framework within which the Member States and the EU are expected to coordinate their foreign policy. Finally, the Commission is also a participant in the CFSP process. The CFSP lacks central institutions apart from the Secretariat and depends to a large extent on the Presidency and the Troika for carrying out its tasks.[45] Uncertainties over an appropriate division of work between the COREPER and Political Committees and a massive dispute both inside CFSP and with the European Parliament over the CFSP turned out to be more laborious than expected.

The TEU provided for three new pillars dealing with the EU, the CFSP and a new pillar concerning cooperation in justice and home affairs. The TEU also provided for a common institutional framework which is designed to establish and increase consistency between the three pillars. There remains a problem concerning the overlapping between the external policies of the EU and CFSP. The third pillar entitles the EU to deal with matters like immigration, terrorism, drug trafficking etc., which relate to its internal security but also have a distinct external dimension. Any viable Common Foreign and Security Policy needs the harmonious coordination and joint cooperation in all three pillars. The TEU has entrusted the Commission and the European Parliament with a formal role within the CFSP process. The Commission is to be associated with all aspects of CFSP and shares the right of initiative with the Member States. Despite this shared right, the Commission has never been a very keen actor in dealing with the issues in the CFSP agenda. The European Parliament too lacks any legislative role, which implies that there is no role envisaged for the European Court of Justice. The establishment of a common institutional framework means that the Council of Ministers have become the Council of the Union and considers all aspects of external relations–foreign and security policy within the same form regardless of which pillar they originate.[46]

The performance of CFSP in the period between 1993-1995 reveals many deficiencies much of which can be drawn from EU's international involvement during the early 1990s and its response in particular to the Yugoslavian civil war, which provides a useful case-study for examining the effectiveness and efficiency of CFSP.

YUGOSLAV CRISIS : A CASE STUDY

The origins of the Yugoslav crisis can be traced back to early 1991 with hostilities eventually breaking out at the end of June. After the Second World War, Yugoslavia symbolized a 'third-way' between Soviet communism and Western free-market economy. After emerging a victor out of the conflict with Soviet Union in 1948, Yugoslavia assumed the position of equi-distance in relation to both the super powers. The Federal People's Republic of Yugoslavia consisted six republics and two autonomous provinces which was built on the nationalistic version of communism called 'administrative socialism', which in turn drew its legitimacy and cohesion from its neighbouring nemesis-the Soviet Union. By the late 1950s and the early 1960s, it turned its gaze towards the Third World countries and under Marshall Tito's tutelage it developed a policy of non-alignment. Non-alignment legitimised an independence from the Soviet Union and bestowed some kind of a national identity to Yugoslavia. Coupled with this was the profit and prestige that it derived from bipolarity.[47]

The national problem of Yugoslavia centered on a fundamental conflict between federalism and centralism. The 'Second Yugoslavia' was based on the absolute centralized rule of the Communist Party which served of hold the system together in its grip through the charismatic leader Marshall Tito. The end of the Cold War, and bipolarity reduced the importance of the principle assumptions on which its national and international position was based. The 'artificial constitution', proclaiming the Federal Republic of Yugoslavia a multi-national constitution containing the distinct but latent potentiality for secession broke into a violent ethnic struggle with the death of Marshall Tito. The Serbs who were the dominant group in the government, bureaucracy and secret service realized that they had nothing to maintain their dominance when in 1990 other republics began to strike out for national independence. The Soviet disintegration made them lose their *raison d'etre*, non-alignment become almost irrelevant and the concept of 'administrative socialism' was discredited with the collapse of Eastern Europe. The only weapon left in abundance was resorting to old ethnic classes. As succinctly observed by Josef Joffe, " if Serbia could not dominate all of Yugoslavia, then Greater Serbia was the second best solution".[48]

The idea worsened as centrifugal tensions grew within the state-party. As national and ethnic ambitions revived,

Slovenia and Croatia rose against Serbia over secession. This added new dimension in the clashes with ethnic Albanians in the south when Bosnia-Herzegovina voted for independence in 1992 while the Serbians proceeded to extend the war into that republic. By the end of 1992, the war escalated to the whole of Yugoslavia and 70 per cent of Bosnian territory was under Serbian control.[49]

EU'S RESPONSE TO THE YUGOSLAV CRISIS

The escalation of the Yugoslav crisis coincided with broader geopolitical changes in the continent, including the unification of Germany, disintegration of the Soviet Union and emergence of new states. Against this background, the EU emerged as the undisputed force in European affairs. The outbreak of the Yugoslav civil war also coincided with the European Council Summit in Luxembourg in 1991 which provided the EC to react immediately. With initial statements calling for institutional reform, support for Yugoslavia's territorial unity and integrity and diplomatic appeals for restrain, the EC dispatched a Ministerial Troika on 28 June 1991 to Yugoslavia to assess the situation.[50] During 1991 the EC policy consisted of two broad approaches. In its first phase of solving the crisis, it oriented towards providing 'good services' and other forms of mediation. It sent a team of diplomats to monitor the situation and when this process failed to achieve practical results, the EC began to act from a position of authority and abandoned the role of a mediator and assumed the role of an arbitrator which was manifested in the following activities :

— it began to exert efforts to halt armed conflicts by pressurising the parties concerned to sign cease-fire agreements;
— a peace conference on Yugoslavia was launched at the Hague under the chairmanship of Lord Carrington for the purpose of finding a solution to crisis; and
— an Arbitration Commission was established to "arbitrate" the legal issues regarding the future organization of states and their links in the Yugoslavian territory.[51]

Successful breaches of cease-fire by the Serbian armed forces and rejection of EC proposals formulated federation saw this process derailed. In November at The Hague Conference in 1991, the republics failed to reach a consensus and this gave way to economic sanctions, which included:

- — suspension of the application of the trade and cooperation agreements with Yugoslavia;
- — restoration of quantitative limits for textiles;
- — removal of Yugoslavia from the PHARE Programme; and
- — exclusion from G-24 forum.

These economic measures failed to discriminate between those republics regarded as aggressors (Serbia) and those whose territory was being violated (Croatia, Slovenia). Consequently, a series of compensatory measures for those who had been negotiating in good faith were adopted. These republics were Croatia, Slovenia, Macedonia, Bosnia–Herzegovina. They were reintegrated into the PHARE programme and trade preferential system. While Greece opposed the positive measures, it chose to abstain thereby allowing EPC consensus to be enacted although this consensus was put to test by a German initiative in December, 1991. The lifting of these economic sanctions did not necessarily imply the Community's intention of recognizing these four republics despite German pressures. However, a week after the Maastricht meeting, the Community's collective policy was jeopardized by Germany's unilateral recognition of Croatia and Slovenia. To avoid the EPC from being derailed, the EC adopted a dual strategy: a general policy on the recognition of new states and a set of conditions which had to be met before any Yugoslavian republic would be recognized. These conditions emphasized the rule of law, democracy and respect for human rights with the commitment to the protection of ethnic minorities and national self determination as stipulated within the CSCE framework. On 11 May 1992, the EC on a Declaration on Bosnia–Herzegovina restated its faith on the principles established in the constitutional talks between Serbs and Croats and Muslims sponsored by the Peace Conference in order to bring a political solution to the crisis.[52] This was followed by the European Council Declaration at Lisbon on 27 June 1992, which reaffirmed the application of sanctions as stipulated by the UN Security Council. It also called upon the CSCE of take necessary steps to restore its confidence by not recognizing Serbia and Montenegro as a successor state of former Yugoslavia.[53]

Though the political involvement affected the development of the Yugoslav crisis, it did not succeed in halting the conflicts. The involvement of the EC was appraised as positive in the republics which had taken steps to recede from Yugoslavia, but on the other hand, it was appraised as one-sided and biased in political circles which opted in favour of remaining in Yugoslavia.[54] In any case the continuation of "ethnic cleansing" in Yugoslavia made the EC aware that its possibilities were almost exhausted in halting the civil war. This prompted the UN to appear on the scene and find means of solving the crisis.

CRITICAL ANALYSIS OF EU'S ROLE

The Yugoslav conflict entered its fourth year in 1995 with renewed encounters in Croatia and a deteriorated situation in Bosnia-Herzegovina followed by a worsening condition in Kosovo in 1997-98.

The ongoing stalemate and the rejection of all peace plans by Bosnian Serbs calls for a re-examination of objectives and assumptions. The Yugoslav crisis gave the EU its first chance to prove that it could settle a problem in its own backyard especially after the formulation of CFSP on the Maastricht Treaty. The activities of the EU in this civil war revealed that the Member States were ill-prepared to deal with such forms of conflict. The process of coordination between EU mechanisms and EPC mechanism, as well as within these respective political systems proved inadequate in several aspects.[55] The threatened break-up of Yugoslavia highlighted the tensions of hitherto latent dangers that were surfacing in Eastern Europe. At the outset any ethnic dimension was played down by the EC-Twelve in the interests of encouraging democracy and liberation within the territory. There was hardly any move towards allowing the minorities to take a centre-stage given the overlapping of ethnic identities and boundaries.[56] With the primary responsibility assigned to the EU by CSCE, there was a belief that the coincidence of the IGC on Political Union would likely reinforce the EU's influence since the assumptions of a greater security identity was a core matter.

By the year's end the new Europe which was confident about mastering its own future in early 1992 proved unable to coalesce into a single purpose. The Yugoslav crisis underscored the limits of the capabilities of the budding EU as a political institution and raised questions about the aim of establishing a true system for European security. The policies of EU revealed the limits of CFSP and the institutions of the Union and the divergence of approaches and interests among the Member Sates highlighted the shortcomings of the EU in times of crisis. The fact that after six months of fruitless attempts to find a solution, the EU was forced to hand the question over to the United Nations revealed the continued dependence in the involvement of other institutions. The EU's policy of pursuing traditional and restrictive measures of introducing economic sanctions were not particularly effective, for as Lawrence Feedman put it:

> The economy was in a ruinous state before the fighting and will be in an even more watched condition now. Sanctions are unlikely to be persuasive when the fundamentals of national identity are believed to be at stake.[57]

With the continuation of the conflict, the EU like other Western democracies could not cross the gap between preventive diplomacy and military interest and there was little consensus amongst the Member States on what should follow when preventive diplomacy failed. As Nicolle Gnesotto suggested :

> Having been unduly virtuous at the outset of the conflict—refusing to back the redrawing of frontiers which were previously internal—the democracies now run the risk of an

> ultimate moral indignity by accepting the *fait accompli* achieved by violent means.[58]

The EU's failure to act in a timely and decisive fashion on the Balkan crisis had a dismaying outcome. Its aspirations to act as a political entity on security matters was not matched by the authority and institutions a true sovereign requires.[59] The EU's principal deficiency was in the political will needed to overcome divisions on the hardest decisions. They revealed deep divisions between the Member States and their incapacity to agree on how to handle the break-up of the Yugoslav federation. They also highlighted the fragility of the Franco-German axis. Since the beginning of the crisis, the EU Member States particularly Britain and France upholded their claim for a united Yugoslavia (implicitly supporting Serbia) while the Germans wanted to recognize the independence of Slovenia and Croatia. For France, Yugoslavia was still a recognized legal entity and it did not favour the idea of recognizing the dissident republics as long as the question of the rights of the different minorities in Yugoslavia could not be settled. Behind these legal considerations lay concerns about the political fall-out of any hasty recognition of Croatia and Slovenia. This had an impact on other Yugoslavian republics which were getting ready to proclaim their independence. As the pace of recognition was rushed by Germany, it widened the division especially within France and Germany. The French could spot a "Teutonic bloc" with long-term designs on CEEC.[60]

German leaders sought to rationalize their pressure for recognition through their own exercise in self-determination. To quote Volker Ruehe, former German Defence Minister, "we have no moral or political credibility if (we) did not recognize Croatia and Slovenia".[61] The German stance, while sought to balance its domestic pressures ended up in a mockery of both the aspirations to a common policy and the principles on which it was meant to be based. As Lord Owen remarked:

> The EC....recognized those republics against the judgement of France and Britain in the mistaken belief that the hallmark of

> a future Maastricht–type European foreign policy was simultaneous recognition.[62]

Prior to unification, Germany had an impeccable EPC record. Its break with the principles of consensus underlined the weakness of foreign policy coordination based on unanimity. Ironically enough, Germany was one of the strong advocates of CFSP which aimed to prevent intra-community divisions. Though the Franco-German axis played an important role in unifying the European position on the Yugoslav conflict, it was not without conflictual differences as was evident in the Copenhagen Summit of June 1993, when Kohl's proposal of lifting embargo on arms in former Yugoslavia faced strong opposition from the French (and also the British). Similarly, during the Geneva Agreement of 8 September 1995, French suggestions that the Franco-German Eurocorps should play a major part of a multi-lateral intervention force to enforce eventual peace was rejected by German Defence Minister, Volker Ruehe.[63] After overcoming their initial disagreement over the recognition of separate republics, Germany took a significant initiative in the 'global concept' which lay the foundations of EU's peace plan in November 1993.

The conflict in Yugoslavia transformed the traditional perceptions of European security. Not only did it become essential to broaden the old concepts of security but also redefine the existing security institutions. The CSCE despite being the organization concerned with the preservation of peace and security in Europe, did not prove particularly effective in the Yugoslav crisis primarily as all decisions in the CSCE had to be based on unanimity and the CSCE did not dispose of a system of collective security like the UN. The WEU was relegated to overseeing sanctions against Serbia and the EU was reduced to administering Mostar. The NATO assumed the dominant role, given its structure and resources and the Yugoslav crisis once again confirmed the continuity of the role of the US in managing any crisis in Europe.[64]

The Yugoslav conflict also revealed the uncertainties of the EU's institutional structure. The heavy burden on the

Presidency was also coupled with the lack of expertise within one foreign ministry. What came as a relief to some Member States were the negotiations which moved gradually to form a Contact Group. Nevertheless, this too reflected the reservations of Germany until it was included in the group and Italy whose presence in the negotiations depended largely on its internal political situation. Perhaps a paradoxical situation arose with the Member States' commitment to act together within a CFSP, on the one hand, and ensuring legitimation for going beyond political and economic institutions to involve intervention from the UN, on the other. By seeking authorization from the UN Security Council, the EU had to reduce its autonomy as its policy had to be based on the agreement of the other members of the Security Council, namely, the US, China and Russia. This highlighted the unequal balance between the role of Britain and France who are permanent members of the UN Security Council and the other Member States of the EU. Such a tendency in future strengthened Germany's claims to be a permanent member of the Security Council.[65] A more general problem of inequality and efficacy in decision-making of the EU during the Balkan conflict brings us to the question whether the Presidency should remain the primary interlocuter for the EU or whether the Commission should be entrusted with a more viable role. To make up for the shortcomings, the French proposal for a Stability Pact was signed in 1995 which laid down mechanisms for settling problems of ethnic minorities and border issues.

The events in Yugoslavia revealed not only the weakness of the institutions but also the absence of any effective institutions for ensuring preventive security. Despite the declarations for CFSP, the Member States failed to create a system readily able to meet non-traditional security challenges. What the Yugoslav conflict offered was both the opportunities for innovative policies in a changed scenario and also revealed the limits to common action. The crisis which presented the Member States with a challenge to commit themselves to common action brought to the fore their own national concerns and highlighted the absence of an overall coherent policy that encapsulated the "common European interest". Jacques Delors' suggestion that "the lesson to be learned here is that a strategic planning and analysis capability is needed at a European level."[66], could form the basis of a future viable CFSP of the EU.

WESTERN EUROPEAN UNION : PROSPECTS AND ROLE FOR EUROPEAN DEFENCE

In so far as there is an attempt to identify and develop common West European security interests outside the NATO structure, it is the WEU which has provided the most convenient institutional umbrella for those Member States wishing to participate in it. The WEU owes its origin to the Brussels Treaty of 1948. As a stepping stone for Germany to enter the NATO, seeking to lock the UK into a significant political and military framework to European defence, and committing to a mutual military assistance clause, the WEU offers enigmatic but intriguing prospects for working towards a European security order.

With the initial failure of the European Defence Community in 1954, European security and defence were mainly organized within the NATO and the WEU. After three decades of virtual inaction, the WEU—"a Sleeping Beauty kissed awake by the Maastricht agreements"[67] received a fresh impetus when the Treaty called upon the WEU "to elaborate and implement decisions and actions of the Union which have defence implications". During the drafting of the TEU, there were significant differences between those Members States who favoured the US stronghold in European defence affairs (and feared that a total European defence arm would weaken the NATO) and those who supported the development of an exclusive European defence (to replace the NATO). Therefore, the WEU which was relegated by the TEU, formed the nucleus of a compromise between Member States like Great Britain, the Netherlands, Denmark and Portugal, who feared anything that could weaken NATO, and other Member States like France, Germany, Belgium and Spain, who wanted a more 'Europeanist' responsibility for European defence.[68] This was reinstated in the Declaration on WEU attached to the TEU where the WEU is referred to as "the defence component of the EU and as a means to strengthen the European pillar of the Atlantic alliance". The TEU relegated the WEU to the status of the defence arm of the EU and sought to strengthen the European pillar of the NATO. The Petersburg Declaration of WEU in June 1992 attempted to strengthen the WEU's operational role by incorporating peace-keeping, peace-making and humanitarian operations at the request of the UN or the CSCE.[69] The ascendance of the UN in European security constrained the authority of the WEU in crisis-management due to the provisions of the UN Charter and a relatively more effective decision-making process. In November 1992, the WEU expanded its domain to include Greece, and offered membership to Iceland, Norway and Turkey. Denmark and Ireland agreed to the status of observers. The fact that the WEU shifted its headquarters from London to Brussels in 1993 reflects the need to facilitate closer cooperation between the European Commission, the WEU and NATO.[70] Soon after the ratification of the TEU, there was a confusion in the EU over the extent to which the European Commission could involve itself in WEU meetings. Britain and France were reluctant to allow the Commission access to the WEU. However, a consensus was reached to allow the Commission to participate in and obtain information from the WEU meetings as part of the delegation of the Member States holding the EU presidency.

The WEU has often been regarded as the "second pillar of NATO, as its rival, as a bridgehead between the Alliance and the EU".[71] Nevertheless, these aspects did not prevent tensed relations between both these organizations in recent times.[72] This came under strain in 1992 due to the duplicate assignments of the WEU and NATO ships in the Adriatic to monitor the UN embargo. The two organizations also experienced mutual clashes over their role in the peacekeeping and crisis-management activities of the UN and CSCE. Pro-Atlantist Member States like the UK and the Netherlands preferred NATO's primacy over the WEU while France favoured the WEU. This had to be resolved by seeking mandate from the Member States of both the organizations. Relations improved in 1993 when France adopted a softer attitude towards the NATO and when the US under President Clinton appeared more relaxed about the development of a European defence identity. A joint NATO/WEU command had been formed for the Adriatic operations.[73]

Although several Member States of NATO (like Germany and France) support an independent European defence mechanism, others still prefer interlocking the WEU into NATO. Britain still continues to stress the need of NATO as the most suitable device for European defence. In order to retain is cooperation with the WEU, NATO allies agreed in a Summit in January 1994 to allow WEU to use the collective assets of NATO and also develop a Combined Joint Task Force (CJTF) as a means to improve cooperation between the two organizations.[74] To what extent the CJTF could be successfully implemented is still uncertain as France still is not too keen on NATO's involvement in crisis management. French and German dissatisfaction with some of the defence provisions of the TEU prompted them to develop a "Euro-Corps"—a bilateral military organization, subordinate to NATO, on the insistence of the US. Members of the WEU who favour the role of the US in European defence seek to guarantee that the WEU is not opposed to NATO, on the contrary, it ensured that it (WEU) acts as a supplement to and strengthen cooperation.[75]

Despite the deficiencies, the WEU faces in so far as its functioning capabilities are concerned, it has extended its arms to nine Central East European Countries (Bulgaria, Czech Republic, Estonia, Hungary, Latvia, Lithuania, Poland, Romania, Slovakia) in 1994 offering them the status of associate partners. This relation did not serve as a security guarantee but it gave these countries the opportunity to acquaint themselves with the security and defence of the EU through its participation in WEU meetings and peacekeeping activities. This initiative for introducing the status of associate partner was launched by France and Germany with Britain joining later. A problem arises with the distinction between the associate partners of the WEU and the associate members which are also the members of NATO. Secondly, there are overlapping of membership since some countries are members of the NATO and the WEU but not of the EU (like Turkey) or those who are members of the NATO and EU but not of the WEU (Denmark, for instance).

WEU's performance and institutional build-up does not offer ground for much optimism. Its activities in the Adriatic and on the Danube have revealed certain potential problems. In the Adriatic, WEU's independent operation was followed by cooperative action with the NATO. However, the situation changed when the UN Security Council expanded its mandate from monitoring to enforcing the embargo. This necessitated the introduction of a joint-command between NATO and WEU due to the former's superior military assets and command facilities while the latter remained subservient to NATO. On the Danube too, the WEU supports Hungary, Romania and Bulgaria in order to ensure the effectiveness of the embargo against Serbia and Montenegro. Germany, a strong supporter of the Danube mission was constitutionally constrained to participate in the WEU or NATO or the UN. On the other hand, the permanent members of the Security Council, like France and Britain, in view of NATO and UN's role in the Yugoslav crisis expressed their doubts on the capability of WEU's a-typical operations in the Danube. The question remains that as long as most of the EU Member States show a preference for the UN or NATO in cases of operational capabilities, WEU's role will only remain in the fringes.

Given the fact that WEU is only a nascent defence organization with regard to its operational development, its institutional structure still needs to be modified to a large extent. Its planning cell which was set up in April 1993. lacks support by the Member States, the satellite centre, aimed to incorporate a space-based observation system, needs to develop its operational capacity. Finally, bodies like Eurocorps are not fully operational and the problem of political and military management structures of WEU still need to be addressed. There is also a problem of compartmentalization of policy-making in security matters at the level of the WEU, CFSP, the Commission and the EU itself.

Another problem which the WEU is likely to confront with further enlargement of the EU is the idea of 'second-class members' which would hamper the political cohesion of an enlarged EU especially with respect to the development of an effective CFSP. An issue that could be on the agenda in the IGC, 1996 is concerning the development of a common defence policy. As long as there is no unanimity amongst Member States on Europe's role in international security, it would be difficult to define Europe's military needs and capabilities. This leads to the need for appropriate institutional set-ups and decision-making procedures. There is a further problem arising from the shift of the US in relevant aspects of European security.[76] As West Europeans are confronted with the task of a credible leadership capacity in certain circumstances, it remains uncertain as to whether this can be carried out with purely intergovernmental procedures, *i.e.* on the basis of unanimity. In view of the anticipated enlargement of the EU, greater efficiency in decision–making would require the application of majority-voting in CFSP matters. It is not just WEU's military capacity that requires improvement but also a political will and consensus amongst Member States to use WEU in crisis management tasks that would enable it to emerge as 'Europe's defence arm'.

GERMANY AND CFSP

The search for domestic and international accord and recognition in the post-war years was one of the primary reasons behind Germany's commitment in shaping the content and framework of European political cooperation. The most viable demonstrations were the Genscher-Colombo Initiative in 1981, the Stuttgart Solemn Declaration in 1983 and the

Kohl-Mitterrand proposals at Milan in 1985 which contributed to the Single European Act and set EU's agenda for the 1990s through the Treaty on European Union. Germany's active pursuit of EPC and political union reflected the dual goals of national political and economic interest, satisfied through an "internally coherent and externally assertive EC and an idealistic conviction, based on German history that the EC represented an antidote to excessive nationalism".[77]

The unification of Germany rendered it with a dynamism that required it to accelerate European integration which as Chancellor Kohl stated was the 'absolute priority' of unified Germany. This was demonstrated with Germany's push at Maastricht for a federal Europe, for increased powers of the Parliament and the Commission and for CFSP. Germany viewed political union as a necessary fore-runner of the Economic and Monetary Union. Political union represents the "enshrinement of Germany's post-war ideal of muted national power and the opportunity to exert international influence. "[78]

The EU's activities during the Gulf War and the Yugoslav crisis indicated that Germany would define the parameter of CFSP through its political reluctance and constitutional limitation to use military force. Although Germany declined military action in the Balkan conflict, it failed to dominate the political action through its decision of granting recognition to Slovenia and Croatia in December, 1991. Unified Germany's geo-strategic location in the centre of Europe has added a new thrust in its security perceptions in Europe. This perception has led Germany to seek to meet its security concerns through the full participation in the political and economic reconstruction of CEEC and the simultaneous integration of West Europe. The presentation of collective security in terms of Western Alliance and extending it either through the North Atlantic Cooperation Council or the Partnership for Peace of Eastern Europe and Russia, form the basis of Germany's security policy.[79]

One persistent element of German policies has been its pursuit of balance along the East-West axis in Europe. From the German perspective, a security vacuum in Central Europe also makes Germany vulnerable to the diverse threats emerging in that region. This makes it important to bring the area between united Germany and former USSR into a close security relation with Germany. Consequently there has been a German security drive to the east to extend the NATO security umbrella over the Visegrad countries. This security logic has implications for Germany's role in NATO. Germany sought NATO to provide membership and security guarantees and perhaps deployment to the Visegrad Four. Germany also views NATO as a way to contain nationalist extremes and political instability. Nevertheless, the whole question of NATO's eastward enlargement gives rise to new versions of old problems regarding commitment and credibility. Coupled with this security dimension is the economic-logic, which is driving Germany to create a Central European realm. This has been an underlying theme in Germany's interest in building CFSP and has created a double tension between Germany's eastern necessities and its Western rigidities.[80]

Germany resides at the pivotal point between the designs for European security that emphasize European institutions and those that emhasize NATO. It is largely due to German mediation that a fundamental contradiction between the development of a 'European security and defence identity' and the maintenance of a strong US connection has reduced. It is still not clear as to where the European identity should be built–in NATO, in the WEU or in the EU itself for it would have major implications for the membership policies of each organization. German leaders have devised a formula for answering such questions with the acronym of 'final congruence'. Under this policy the EU would set a time-table to take over the responsibility for European defence while the EU and NATO would agree to make their membership congruent within the next decade. Advocates of this approach vary in their degree of rigidity but its application in any form would make it difficult for the EU to extend membership to a country that was not a near-term candidate for NATO membership. NATO would face the same constraints with respect to a prospective members' EU candidacy.[81]

The real basis of German security lies in its relation *vis-a-vis* the US. Germany's efforts towards forming a Franco-German defence umbrella would only mean another attempt to strengthen is Atlantic Alliance through NATO. Germany has been one of the strongest advocates in identifying the need and the instruments for a EU-US partnership in responding to all regional challenges. This pre-requisite is a revised transatlantic relationship that has unfolded in a number of cases, whether in a "close and confidence-based partnership" as propounded by Klaus Kinkel or a "strengthened and expanded alliance" by Helmut Kohl, a "NATO-plus-partnership-of-responsibility" coined by foreign minister Hans-Dietrich Genscher, or "Trans-atlantic structures" by Edzard Reuter.

The Federal Republic of Germany's approach to international issues was dominated by is twin concerns for security and for the maintenance of the principle of a united Germany. Therefore, relations with the US was paramount. Prior to unification FRG needed US protection and support—protection against the Soviet threat and support for reunification. As far as its relation with the US is concerned, German leadership occupied a position between the confident partnership "to which the British declared their commitment and the combative competitiveness of the French".[82] Germany's special relation with the US in security matters sometimes came in conflict with its relation with France. At one level, Germany teamed up with France in the 1980s through its active commitment to European integration but it never relinquished its attachment to the US. Perhaps Germany faces a constraint in its efforts to "ensure that greater defence integration with France does not weaken its defence link with the US".[83]

German foreign policy experts continue to stress the fact that European integration is the only way of preventing a denationalization of German foreign-policy. The latter could be fraught with dangerous consequences resulting in increasing alienation from its neighbours as its geographical position has strong political under-pinning. The policy initiatives formally to establish CFSP in the EU and to link the WEU with the CFSP so that it becomes the operational arm of the EU in defence-related matters, and the creation of Eurocorps are consistent with a determination to give European cooperation in foreign and security policy more substance.[84]

In view of the IGC 1996, Germany sought to lend greater momentum to the CFSP and prepare the basis for a European defence identity. According to the Christian Democratic Union (CDU) member Wolfgang Schaeuble, Germany intended to make all foreign policy decisions, except those with direct military implications subject to majority-voting amongst EU members. That would do away with national vetoes in the policy domain.[85] On 20 September 1996, former Foreign Minister, Klaus Kinkel proposed the setting up of the office of a EU Secretary-General for foreign and security policy who would be accountable to the European Council. A Planning and Analysis unit under the chairmanship of a new Secretary General would prepare the European Council's foreign policy decisions, define long-term interests and help in crisis-management.[86] In a paper published by the Committee on Foreign and Security policy of the CDU, the party expressed its reservations regarding the solution of a high representative for CFSP as proposed by France during the IGC 1996. According to the paper the increased CFSP visibility which would arise would not reduce the risk of "later complications regarding the institutional matters and the breakdown of tasks". The CDU also distanced itself from the French position when insisting on the significance of the participation by the European Commission personnel in the future Planning and Analysis unit to be set up for CFSP. By doing so, the EU could ensure to carry its foreign policy activities on the basis of "common interests" and not on that of "evaluations by Member States competing amongst themselves by using the smallest common denominator" as a base. On the other hand, the CDU endorses the French proposal of a "new form of Troika" formed by the Council President, the Secretary–General of the Council and the European Commissioner responsible for foreign policy. The CDU expressed its support for the principle of majority-voting by double-majority (of states and populations) in order to prevent the "inflexibility of the consensus principle".[87]

As regards European defence, proposals show a strong German desire for a common European defence where an essential step during the IGC, 1996 would be to fix a time-table for integrating WEU with the EU which would compliment NATO. This could be done by including in the EU treaty all the West European Union tasks including the 'Petersburg tasks'. In view of the varying members and 'neutrals' of the EU, Art. 5 of the WEU treaty, dealing with territorial defence on the one hand, and humanitarian assistance on the other, would have to be excluded or attached in a Protocol to the EU treaty.[88] The former German Defence Minister, Volker Ruehe, suggested that the IGC, 1996, "should not preclude the higher aim of a political union and the development of a European defence". According to Volker Ruehe, the IGC should "provide a mandate for making defence policy which should become part of the Union's responsibilities on an intergovernmental basis". Any decision that was backed by a majority within the EU should not be blocked by a veto. A "positive abstention" could allow countries ready to make a commitment to act legitimately in the name of the EU. Moreover, he proposed closer links between the Commission and CFSP. On matters concerning EU and WEU, Ruehe suggested that the European Council should be the only body to take decisions concerning CFSP and defence policy, the decision-taking would be up to the Union and their implementation up to the WEU.[89]

FRANCE AND CFSP

Since the mid-sixties, France has been pursuing the goal of establishing a 'special status' within the Western alliance. It was not easy to disentangle French policy towards European political integration between 1958 to 1963 from the personal strategy of General Charles de Gaulle, the President of the Fifth Republic. De Gaulle who opposed the Jean Monnet vision of European supranational institutions and an Atlanticist Europe, believed that the basic unit in politics is the nation. Thus, he refused to subjugate France to any supranational authority.[90] The US provided the standard against which to measure France's status, the foil for French efforts to demonstrate the status, and the most immediately visible threat to the independence and autonomy which de Gaulle considered intrinsic to the preservation of French status and power.[91] Till the Algerian Crisis, the strength of the French challenge to US domination was moderated to an extent by a cautious acceptance of loading itself with too many foreign policy tasks. The development of 1963-66, from the veto on British entry to the EC in 1963, to the withdrawal from the NATO in July 1966 all reflected French preoccupation with international prestige and status.

The French idea of a European Political Union was encapsulated in the Fouchet Plan in 1962 which aimed to build a "European Europe" capable of dealing with the US on an equal footing.[92] The Fouchet Plan provided a model for European collaboration in foreign policy in deliberate contrast to the Atlantic collaboration enshrined in the NATO. De Gaulle's efforts to create through a mechanism of state consultations through the Fouchet Plan European unity was rejected by the Benelux countries who felt it would undermine the EC.

The failure of the two Fouchet Plans at the beginning of the sixties allowed the antagonism with the US to surface more clearly. When the foundations of EPC were laid at The Hague Summit in 1969, defence policy was tacitly excluded.[93] French keenness to have an independent CFSP was never clearly defined by the other Member States of the EU since they feared that this might strain the European–American relation.

The French need to bridge the gap between their wide

foreign policy objectives and the resources available to them required them to find partners in their endeavours. The Treaty of Rome which had successfully harnessed German economic resources to French political objectives in Africa through the creation of the European Development Fund made France seek the cooperation of West Germany. The FRG appeared more easily as a partner because of its limited international acceptability and its limited foreign policy objectives made it a potential auxiliary rather than a rival.[94] This relation was sealed with the Elysee Treaty in 1963 providing for foreign policy and defence collaboration. After de Gaulle, on President Pompidou's insistence at The Hague Summit of 1969, on reviving the Fouchet proposals of 1961 for consultations between European governments on foreign policy, was a reminder of the Gaullist legacy. The French proposals at The Hague Summit included the completion of the CAP, through agreement on common funding and proposals for EMU through which some hoped to lock the French economy with its German counterpart and its commitment to accept Britain as a member of the EU. Political cooperation would thus serve as a framework for balancing Britain against Germany as foreign policy priorities shifted, provided that Britain's priorities were shifting towards a course convergent with that of France.[95] On French insistence, EPC was exclusively intergovernmental and not accessible to the Commission and the European Parliament. The institution of the EU Council as the highest decision-making body following the initiatives of Giscard d' Estaing gave EU's foreign policy greater clout. This gave the Member States an excellent platform for the management and co-ordination of foreign policy with a 'nation-state accountability'. Despite its considerable interest in CFSP, France obstructed a further development of EPC for many years through its resolve to leave it intergovernmental. President Mitterrand, for instance, rejected the proposal of the Genscher-Colombo Initiative of 1981 which wanted to dovetail the EU Council with the EPC.

It was only in the SEA that Mitterrand's policies towards

political union underwent changes. He agreed to transfer the external competence of the nation-state within the framework of the EU.[96] President Mitterrand brought in a sea-change in the French policies towards European political development.[97] In 1984, declaring himself a 'federalist' which was a great departure from his predecessors, Mitterrand affirmed that a federal Europe was desirable as a long-term objective and the EU's economic entity would be destroyed if it had no political entity.[98] Commenting on European political authority he stated:

> I am utterly convinced that quarrels will not be resolved and there will be no further progress if Europe fails or fears to provide itself with a political policy. The time has come to provide our institutions with the coherence they lack.[99]

The emergence of German unification in 1989 accelerated French efforts to bind Germany to Europe by deepening the EU. On 19 April, 1990, in a joint letter, President Mitterrand and Chancellor Kohl advocated a European political and security union. French designs for a political Europe was different from German proposals. While Germany wanted the European Parliament to be given a much greater role, France preferred the Council with more extensive powers on CFSP. During the Maastricht referendum debate, President Mitterrand stated:

> I like federalism as a concept very much but I believe the introduction of a federalist structure would be precipitate step for Europe at this juncture and if... such a step never becomes necessary for Community development well then! It would be useless to attempt it.[100]

The French attitude can be explained for two reasons: first, the weak role of the French National Assembly is perhaps not the right model for a strong European Parliament and second, the size and population of a united Germany entitles it to a greater number of members than any other Member State. Enhanced power would thus imply German dominance in political and monetary issues.[101]

Although President Mitterrand was willing to contribute

towards the breakthrough of the majority rule to share foreign policy competence with partner states to a much larger extent than before, he categorically rejected 'supranationalism' with rights of co-determination for the Commission and the Parliament. French Minister for European Affairs, Elizabeth Guigou stated that sovereignty should not simply be ceded but that it should be shared and not only in fields in which further progress was impossible on one's own.[102] There was a continuity in President Mitterrand's policy with regard to a deprivation of the power of nation-state in favour of the EU, even though it allowed for change in certain respects especially with regard to the perception of external competence of the nation-state. Whereas his predecessors would have aspired for an independent role for France, Mitterrand realized that France can play a part together with European partners, particularly Germany.

As far as security questions were concerned it was intertwined with French inhibitions around their continuing ambivalence towards Germany's international role and their uncomfortable awareness of their dependence on German cooperation. The certainties of Gaullist foreign policy had rested upon the assumptions of an American commitment to European security and German acceptance of the American security guarantee, both of which were weakening. The painful reconstruction of French priorities which this situation necessitated erupted from time to time outbursts of French hysteria about the direction of German policy. During 1979-80 and in 1981-82, the French elites were preoccupied with the 'German problem' and with the FRG turning to the East. French attacks on the FRG for its failure to support the US sufficiently firmly under conditions of East-West tension repeated from 1981-83 reflected their perceived dependence on Germany for their security. This relationship did not, however, fail to go through spells of shot-lived crisis owing to the lack of congruence between the two states on international issues.[103] Eventually French willingness to reopen a dialogue on defence policy between the two countries in

1982 and President Mitterrand's vigorous support to Chancellor Helmut Schmidt on the need to accept the US intermediate nuclear missiles in Germany were indicative of French adjustment to a more assertive and self-confident Germany.[104]

In 1983, under French insistence the Elysee Treaty of 1963 with Germany was reactivated, a moribund WEU was revived and in 1991, the French desire for European identity in the fields of defence led France to set up a Franco-German Eurocorps around the WEU.[105] Some reports suggest that the Franco-German proposals stem primarily from French initiatives and Germany's support is based on a desire to maintain positive relations with France.[106] Germany shares the long term French aspirations for a political union but has concerns similar to those of the UK regarding the risk of weakening NATO.[107]

German unification brought in France an array of contradictory anxieties regarding EU's defence implications. A substantive concern was the fear of a strategic vacuum in Central Europe and that Germany might follow an independent course in its relation with Russia,[108] which France alluded as characteristic of historical pattern in German-Russian relations. It became imperative "to organize Europe so that it escapes the two perils of hegemony or explosion.... (with) a better assured security and a will to solidarity ".[109] In institutional terms, the movement of the EU towards Political Union should include 'European identity' in the domain of security but within the Atlantic Alliance.[110] Therefore, moving closer to NATO and accepting the American nuclear umbrella as compatible with an independent French defence policy became visible by early 1990s and this was a marked change from the Gaullist stance.[111] On 5 December 1995, in the North Atlantic Council Meeting, the French Foreign Minister announced that France would resume full participation in the NATO military committee which do not encroach with its independent nuclear planning.[112] This was followed with its suggestion to establish a 'concerted deterrence' in Europe. In February 1996, President Jacques

Chirac proposed to overhaul its defence mechanism which can be seen as a step to joint action through CJTF in future.[113] Germany as the main ally of France expressed it reservations fearing that this 'contagion of professionalism' might spread to its own guarded "citizens' army", and due to its (German) 'historical baggage' would not follow the French desire for a stronger international defence role.[114] The political scheme for European integration for France means that security and defence matters would be dealt at EU level, but at the same time it would be a means to consolidate the Alliance. To quote French Defence Minister, Charles Million:

> There can be no European defence policy that does not take account of the Atlantic dimension, there can be no lasting Alliance without the affirmation of a strong European pillar. The purpose is to arrive at a form of collaboration between Europe and North America within NATO.[115]

Recognizing the WEU as 'natural tool for the development of the European defence identity', the French Foreign Minister stated on 5 December 1995, that it needs to become the consultive body for European cooperation on defence matters, both as the defence component of the Union and the European pillar of the Alliance.[116] French defence policy thus conceived embedded in a broader framework that of a foreign policy designed to reassert French presence in South Africa, Asia and Middle East or by its attempt at mediating between Israel and the Arabs in April 1996.

In view of the IGC 1996, the proposals made by France with regard to CFSP differed substantially with those of Germany. The two governments did not concur in their view on majority voting in CFSP although Germany was more keen on it than France. Unlike Germany, France sought to limit the role of the Commission while enhancing that of the Council.[117] The French government supported the role of a High Representative–'Monsieur Pesc', in charge of CFSP. French proposal to marginalise the European Parliament's role while strengthening the National Parliament,[118] was in tune with its earlier preference for intergovernmentalism. De Gaulle sought to devise a political union based on intergovernmental procedures, Giscard d' Estaing initiated the European Council and Francois Mitterrand suggested the creation of the 'second' and 'third' intergovernmental pillars at Maastricht.

PROSPECTS FOR CFSP

In spite of an expected *rapprochement* between France and Germany over the proposed structure of CFSP in the IGC, 1996, it might prove difficult to bring out a position of convergence on foreign policy matters with regard to the other 15 Member States. Britain, in particular is opposed to the strengthening of CFSP and a close relationship between the EU and WEU.

Since the inception of the CFSP pillar in the TEU, it has become quite clear that the Treaty is an insufficient basis for the EU to meet the mountain pressures of external challenges. The Yugoslav crisis and recent incidents highlighting deep divisions in the EU on China's record on human rights and over the issues on Middle East crisis where Britain and France came under sharp divisions[119] all indicate that the EU has not been able to meet the challenges as an effective international actor in terms of both capacity to produce collective decisions and its impact on events.

The EU also did not fail to witness constant wrangles over the legal base and budgetary aspects of CFSP. There has been a lack of strategic planning, an almost disregard for EU procedures complete with loopholes in the Council Presidency system.[120] The inception of CFSP heightened the capabilities of EU but a significant capability–expectation gap exists and this is already presenting the EU with difficult choices and experiences.[121] This also poses a serious challenge to EU in terms of its ability to reach a consensus in terms of its resources and the instruments at its disposal. An element of 'collectivity' present in the functioning of CFSP varies in its degree and extent due to the differing levels of commitment of the Member States to cooperate in a consistent and cohesive manner. This has been perhaps aggravated with the presence of the 'variable geometry' pattern in foreign policy matters with some states heading towards *communautarization* and others concerned with 'national sovereignty' or 'special status'.[122] When 'variable geometry' tends to undermine EU solidarity, as was the case during the Yugoslav crisis (with German recognition of Croatia and Slovenia), then the question arises whether collective action can be sustained over time without a leap into federalist structures.[123] The earlier performance of EPC and later of CFSP reveal increasing difference between the expectations and the actual capability. The gap can only be narrowed through coordination and harmonization of views and strengthening the institutional set-up like the decision-making procedure and the role of the Commission and by evolving common defence structure. The 'consensus principle' which has been the defining characteristic of the first two decades of EPC has promoted policy sclerosis and led to decisions based on the lowest common denominator. This rule if applied in a wider Union could "bring the embryonic CFSP to a grinding halt".[124]

In post-communist Europe, CFSP is confronted with a formidable challenge and an opportunity to derive strength and motivation by providing the CEEC with an anchor of stability. As the EU is preparing the ground for negotiation strategies with some of the East European countries, the issues related to national and ethnic minorities and bilateral disputes involving the applicant states, could run the risk of burdening the cohesion of the EU. A geographically expanded EU would be more heterogeneous in its foreign and security interests and perceptions.[125] Although the applicant countries in all probability could adopt the EU *acquis* but the CFSP needs to emphasize collectivity in order to ensure that the new entrants find the *acquis politique* more binding upon them.[126]

During EU's Nordic enlargement the candidate countries like Austria, Sweden and Finland managed to enter the EU without changing their foreign policy traditions and their status as 'neutrals'. This probably reflects a sign of light constraints imposed by CFSP or confirms the need to re-emphasize the *acquis politique.* An effective and consistent CFSP comprising elements of preventive diplomacy and reinstating 'collectivity' would be necessary if the EU is to successfully tackle the impending challenges with which it is confronted. As a matter of fact, ensuring a strong commitment to reinforce CFSP did not seem to be too easy to achieve in the IGC, 1996. The weight of national history, national administration and most of all national interest may again prove stronger against an effective CFSP.

NOTES

1. Also see, EC, "The Political Agenda for Europe", Presidency Conclusions, 15/16 December 1995, Agence Europe, *Europe Documents,* 17 December 1995.
2. EC, *The European Union's Common Foreign and Security Policy* (Luxembourg: Office for the Official Publications of the EC, 1996), p. 1.
3. For a critical analysis of the problems associated with European integration see, Richard Muench, "Between Nation State, Regionalism and World Society", *Journal of Common Market Studies,* vol. 34, No. 3, September 1996, pp. 379-399.
4. For a detailed background on the initial performances of EPC see, Simon Nutall, *European Political Cooperation* (Oxford: Clarendon Press, 1992), pp. 30-50.
5. See, H. S. Chopra, *De Gaulle and European Unity* (New Delhi: Abhinav, 1974).
6. This refers to the provisions for Common Trade Policy (Art. 113), the association with Overseas Territory (Art, 132), association agreements with the countries (Art. 238), power to conclude international treaties (Art. 228) and the ability to receive and establish diplomatic missions.
7. P. Tsakaloyannis, "The EC, EPC and the decline of Political Cooperation" in M. Holland (ed.), *The Future of European Political Cooperation: Essays on Theory and Practice* (London: Macmillan, 1991), p. 36. P. Tsakaloyannis attributes the development of EPC to superpower crisis of 1960s, Soviet invasion in Czechoslovakia and American offensive in Vietnam in 1962.
8. For a critical appraisal of the models of political develop-

ment see Paul Taylor, *The Limits of European Integration,* (Kent: Croom Helm, 1983), pp. 118-160 and also M. Holland, *European Community Integration* (London: Pinter, 1993), pp. 117-143.

9. See, Robert. S. Jordan (ed.), *Europe and the Superpowers: Perception of European International Politics* (Boston: All You & Bacon, 1971).
10. Cf. Nutall, n. 4, p. 4.
11. Cf. M. Holland, *The EC and South Africa: European Political Cooperation under Strain* (London: Pinter, 1988) p. 1.
12. E. Regelsbeger, P. de Schoutheete, S. Nutall and G. Edwards, *The External Relations of EPC and the future of EPC,* EUI, Florence Working Paper. n. 172, 1985, p. 41, as cited in M. Holland, n. 8, p. 118.
13. EC ,"Final Communique of the Conference, The Hague, 2 December 1969", *Bulletin of the EC,* n. 6 (Luxembourg : Office for the Official Publications of the EC, December 1969) p. 11.
14. See, "First Report of the Foreign Ministers to the Heads of Sate and Government of Member States of EC, 27 October, 1970", Luxembourg Report, *European Political Cooperation* (Bonn: Press and Information Service, 1988) pp. 24-30.
15. For a Summary on the Luxembourg Report, See Nutall, n. 4, pp. 50-60.
16. Cf, Holland, n. 11, p. 3. For a critical evaluation of the Luxembourg Report and its impact on EPC in 1970 see W. Wallance, "Political Cooperation Integration through Intergovernmentalism" in W. Wallace and H. Wallace (ed.), *Policy-making in the EC* (London: John Wiley, 1983a), pp. 373-402.
17. Simon Nutall, "Two Decades of EPC Performance" in E. Regelsberger, G. Edwards (ed.), *From EPC to CFSP and Beyond* (London: Lynne Riener, 1997), pp. 16-39.
18. "EC Second Report on EPC and Foreign Policy, Copenhagen, 23 July 1973" *Bulletin of the EC,* Supplement (Luxembourg: Office for the Official Publications of the EC, 1973), pp. 14-21, Also Embassy of FRG, Communique of Conference of the Heads of State and Government of the Member States, Copenhagen, 15 December 1973, *European Political Cooperation* (Bonn: Press and Information Service, 1988) pp. 54-55.
19. See Nutall, n. 4, p.6.
20. For EPC relations on South Africa see M. Holland, "Three

approaches for understanding EPC : A Case Study of the EC-South African Policy", *Journal of Common Market Studies,* vol. 25, 1987, pp. 295-314.

21. L. Tindemans, "EU: Report to the European Council", *Bulletin of the EC,* Supplement (Luxembourg: Office for Official Publications of EC, 1976,) pp. 14-15.
22. Holland, n. 8, p. 120.
23. For details on EPC's a activities during the late 1970s and early 1980s see, Nutall, n. 4, pp. 149-181.
24. 'Troika' refers to the arrangement where the current, preceding and succeeding presidencies operate collectively.
25. For excerpts see, "Report on EPC issued by the Foreign Ministers of the Ten, London, 13 October 1981", *European Political Cooperation* (Boon : Press and Information Service, 1988) pp. 61-69.
26. See, Holland, n. 8, p. 121.
27. See, E. Regelsberger (ed.), n. 17.
28. For EPC reaction to Falkland crisis, see G. Edwards, "Europe and the Falkland Crisis", *Journal of Common Market Studies,* vol. 22, 1984, pp. 295-313.
29. See, Nutall, n. 4, p. 183.
30. See, in this connection, "Statement by Hans Dietrich Genscher, Federal Minister for Foreign Affairs to European Parliament, 29 June 1983", in *European Political Cooperation (EPC),* n. 14, pp. 326-337.
31. For excerpts see, "Conclusions of the 32nd European Council on EC-COMECON relations, Milan, 28/29 June 1985", in *EPC,* n. 14, p. 200.
32. For background see, "Resolution adopted by European Parliament on SEA, 11 December 1986", in *EPC,* n. 14, pp. 39-18.
33. Cf. Holland, n. 8, p. 121.
34. The Common Provisions of Title I state that "The EC and the EPC shall have as their objective to contribute together to making concrete progress towards European unity." Title III envisages the replacement of 'national foreign policy autonomy' by 'constant development of EPC'.
35. W. Nicoll and T.C. Salmon, *Understanding the European Community* (Maryland: Barnes and Noble Savage, 1990) p. 117.
36. The constraints of the "consensus principle" imposed on EPC had become apparent in EC's policy in Gulf War, South Africa and Eastern Europe. See M. Holland, n. 20 and E.

Regelsberger, "The Twelve's Dialogues with Third Countries" in Holland, n. 7, pp. 143-160.

37. See in this connection, "The Kohl-Mitterrand Letter", Agence Europe, *Europe Documents*, no. 5238, 20 April 1990.
38. EC, Draft Treaty of Luxembourg Presidency, Agence Europe, *Europe Documents*, no. 1722/23, 5 July 1991.
39. For more details see, Phillipe de Schoutheete Terverant, "The Creation of CFSP", in Regelsberger, n. 17, pp. 41-63.
40. See, David Allen, "The CFSP of the EU" in Phillipe Barbour (ed.), *The EU Handbook* (Illinois: Fitzroy Dearbon, 1996) pp. 44-52 and also, C. Hill, "The EC towards a CFSP", *The World Today*, no. 71, 1991, pp. 189-193.
41. See, C. Hill, "Research into EPC : Tasks for the Future", in A. Pijpers, R. Regelsberger (ed.), *European Political Cooperation in the 1980s* (Dordrecht: Nijhoff/TEPSA, 1988) & W. Wallace, *The Dynamics of European Integration* (London : Pinter/RIIA, 1990).
42. Monnet, *Memoirs* (translated R. Mayne) (New York : Doubleday and Company, 1978) p. 353, as cited in Holland, n. 8, p. 126.
43. Holland, n. 8, p. 80 and p. 126.
44. See, P. de Schoutheete Terverant, "The EC and its Subsystems" in Wallace, n. 41.
45. Cf. Allen, n. 40, p. 47.
46. Ibid.
47. This was also largely due to the strategic interest of the West to preserve Yugoslavian stability in times of crisis in the 1970s and 1980s, as the country was a buffer-zone between the Warsaw countries and NATO members in Europe. Any instability in Yugoslavia, as was the case during the economic crisis of 1980s, brought in all kinds of economic measures by the West to support its economy.
48. Josef Joffe, "The New Europe: Yesterday's Ghosts", *Foreign Affairs*, 1993, p 31
49. For details see, Paul Lendavai, "Yugoslavia without Yugoslavs", *International Affairs*, 1991, pp. 251-261 and L. Cohen, "Disintegration of Yugoslavia", *Current History*, vol. 91, no. 568, November 1992, pp. 369-375.
50. Cf. Holland, n. 8, p. 136.
51. Ranko Petkovic, "Role of the EC and the UN in Solving the Yugoslavian Crisis", *Review of International Affairs*, Vol. 43, no. 1002, 1992, p. 4.

52. "Declaration on Bosnia – Herzegovina, 11 May 1992, Documents on Yugoslavian Crisis", *Review of International Affairs,* vol. XLIII, no. 10005-6, 1 July 1992, p. 23.
53. "European Council Declaration on Former Yugoslavia", Lisbon, 27 June 1992, Documents on Yugoslavian Crisis, *Review of International Affairs,* n. 52, p. 26.
54. Petkovic, n. 51, p. 5.
55. Gerhard Wettig, "Security in Europe: A Challenging Task", *Aussen Politik,* vol. 1, 1992, p. 20.
56. G. Edwards, "The Potential and Limits of CFSP: The Yugoslav Example", in E. Regelsberger, (ed.) n. 17, p. 174.
57. *The Independent,* 12 September 1991.
58. N. Gnesotto, "Lessons of Yugoslavia", *Challiot Papers,* No. 14, (Paris : WEU, Institute for Security Studies, 1994) p. 11, as cited in Edwards, n. 56, p. 190.
59. Michael, J. Brenner, "EC; Confidence Lost", *Foreign Policy,* no. 91, Summer 1993, p.31.
60 Alex Macleod, "French policy towards the war in the former Yugoslavia", *International Journal,* Vol. LII, no. 2, April 1997, p. 246. The declaration of Germany to recognise Croatia and Slovenia was the outcome of two declarations on Yugoslavia and recognition of new states which were adopted upon the joint initiative of France and Germany at the meeting of the EU Council of Ministers on 16 December, 1991. Contrary to these, Germany recognized the two republics which were interpreted by the other EU Member States as a demonstration of newly acquired strength of a united Germany.
61. Cf. *Financial Times,* 4 July 1991. To German policy makers, Western countries were prepared to accept the new role of Germany and Europe and the fact that Yugoslavia was the first testing ground for this was only an unfortunate coincidence which probably created obstacles for German participation in UN peace-keeping forces in Yugoslavia.
62. Cf. Edwards, n. 56, p. 177.
63. *Le Monde,* 25 October 1995.
64. Marie J. Calic, "Bosnia-Herzegovina after Dayton: Opportunities and Risks for Peace", *Aussen Politik,* vol. 47, no. 2, 1996, pp. 127-135.
65. See, G. Edwards, "European Responses to the Yugoslavia Crisis : An interim Assessment" in R. Rummel (ed.), *Toward Political Union: Planning CFSP in the EC* (Baden-Baden, Nomos, 1992) pp. 165-190.

66. Jacques Delors, "European Unification and European Security", Conference Papers: *European Security after the Cold War* (London : ISS/Adelphi Paper, 1992), p.5.
67. Dominique Moisi & M. Mertes, "Europe's Map, Compass and Horizon", *Foreign Affairs,* January/February 1995, p. 125.
68. Mathius Jopp, "The Defence Dimension of the EU" in R. Regelsberger (ed.), n. 7, p. 155. For background, see, W. Wallace and Anand Menon, "A Common European Defence?", *Survival,* no. 3, Autumn 1992, pp. 98-118.
69. EC, "Petersburg Declaration of the WEU, Ministerial Council, 19 June, 1992", *Europe Documents,* Part II. par. 4, no. 1787, 20- June 1992, p.23.
70. EC, "Conclusions of the Presidency, European Council of Edinburg, 11-12 December 1992", Agence Europe, *Europe Documents* (special edition), 13 December 1992, pp. 9-11.
71. Cf. R.K. Jain, "European Security after the Cold War", *International Studies,* vol. 31, no. 4, 1994, p. 405.
72. See F. Heisboug, "The European-US Alliance: Valedictory Reflections on Continental Drift in Post Cold-War Era", *International Affairs,* vol. 4, 1992, pp. 665-678.
73. For further details see, Mathius Jopp, "The Strategic Implications of European Integration", *Adelphi Paper,* no. 290, (London : ISS, 1994), p. 31.
74. See, "Declaration of the Heads of State and Government a the North Atlantic Council Meeting, Brussels, 10-11 January, 1994", *Atlantic Document,* no. 83, 12 January 1994, par. 6, 9.
75. Cf. Jain, n. 71, p. 406.
76. See in this context, Nanette Ganz and John Roper (ed.), *Towards a New Partnership: US- European Relations in the post Cold-War era* (Paris: WEU/IISS, 1993).
77. Roger Morgan, "Federal Republic of Germany" in Carl Twitchett (ed.), *Building Europe : Britain's Partners in the EEC* (London : Europa, 1981) pp. 61-66.
78. Lily Gardner Feldman, "Germany and the European Community: Realism and Responsibility", *Annals of the American Academy of Political and Social Sciences,* vol. 531, January 1994, p. 37.
79. For background see, C. Bluth, "Germany: Defining the National Interest", *The World Today,* Vol. 51 no. 3, March 1995, pp. 51-65.
80. James Kurth, "Germany and the Re-emergence of

Mitteleuropa", *Current History,* vol. 94, no. 55, November 1995, pp. 384-385.

81. Gary L. Geipel, "Germany and the Burden of Choice", *Current History,* vol. 94 no. 595, November 1995, p. 377.
82. W. Wallace, "Foreign Policy: the Management of Distinct Interest" in Roger Morgan (ed.), *Partners and Rivals in West Europe* (Aldershot : Gower, 1986), pp. 268-209.
83. Cf. Jain, n. 71, p. 411.
84. Bluth, n. 79, p. 54. Also see, Timothy Garton Ash, "Germany's Choices", *Foreign Affairs,* vol. 73, no. 4, July-August 1994, pp. 65-81.
85. *The Economist,* 17 June 1995.
86. R. K. Jain, "Germany and the EU", International Seminar on *Germany in the Nineties,* School of International Studies, Jawarharlal Nehru University, 4-5, November 1996, p. 21.
87. *Europe-Hebdo Overseas Selection,* No. 792, 24 September 1996, p. 4.
88. Ibid.
89. *Europe-Hebdo Overseas Selection,* No. 732, 13 June 1996, p. 8.
90. See Paul Godt (ed.), *Policy-making in France: From de Gaulle to Mitterrand* (London: Pinter, 1989).
91. Wallace, n. 82, p. 206.
92. See Elie Kedourie, "De Gaulle", *Commentary,* vol. 95, no. 1, January 1993, pp. 43-49.
93. Gisela Mueller-Brandeck Bocquet "French Policy on Europe during the Mitterrand Era", *Aussen Politik* vol. 4, 1995, p. 335. Also see, W.W. Kulski, *De Gaulle and the World* (New York : Syracuse University Press, 1966).
94. Wallace, n. 82 p. 210, Also for background see, R. Cobb, *French and Germans, Germans and French* (London: Branders University Press, 1983).
95. See Edward A. Kolodziej, *French International Policy under de Gaulle ad Pompidou,* (New York : Cornell University Press, 1974) pp. 90-92.
96. For details see, G. Ross and S. Hoffman (ed.), *The Mitterrand Experiment* (Cambridge: Polity Press, 1987).
97. See for details, Sonia Mazey and M. Newman (ed.), *Mitterrand's France* (London: Croom Helm, 1987).
98. Mitterrand's Interview in *Agence Europe,* no. 3782, February 1984.
99. Mitterrand, *Relexions sur la politique exteieure la France* (Paris: Fay 1986), p. 278, Cf. E. Haywood, "The European Policy of

F. Mitterrand," *Journal of Common Market Studies,* vol. 31, no. 2, June 1993, p. 276.
100. *Le Monde,* 22 September 1992.
101. Haywood, n. 99, p. 277.
102. *Le Monde,* 23/24 June 1991.
103. This refers to the less well-established relations between President Mitterrand's government and its German counterpart over the imposition of martial law in Poland in 1981 with accusations about German 'designs' being voiced in *Le Monde* and in French circle.
104. Cf. Wallace, n. 82, p. 220.
105. Steven P. Kramer, "France faces the new Europe" *Current History,* vol. 89, no. 550, November 1990, pp. 365-386.
106. N. Doughty, "Secret Memorandum Reveals Deep Divisions on NATO Role", *Financial Times,* 8 February 1991.
107. *The Economist,* 2 February 1991, p. 30.
108. See Chevenement Interview, *Le Monde,* 13 July 1990.
109. Speech of Roland Dumas, French Foreign Minister to French Senate, 27 June 1990, Cf. *Bulletin d'Information,* Paris, Foreign Ministry, 28 June 1990.
110. Dumas Interview in *Le Figaro,* 25 July 1990, reproduced in *Bulletin d'Information,* Foreign Ministry, Paris, 25 July 1990, cited in David Yost, "France in New Europe", *Foreign Affairs,* vol. 69, no. 5, Winter 1990-91, pp. 107-28.
111. Anand Menon, "NATO: the French way: From independence to Cooperation? France, NATO and European Security", *International Affairs,* vol. 71, no. 1, January 1995, pp. 19-34.
112. Anna Marie Le Gloanmec "Europe by other means?", *International Affairs,* vol. 73, no. 1, January 1997, pp. 83-98.
113. Some analysts agree that the new structure of French nuclear force will be parallel to that of Britain's especially at a time when two countries are exchanging information on defence strategies with a view to creating common policies. See for details, Stuart Croft, "European Integration, Nuclear Deterrence and Franco-British Nuclear Cooperation", *International Affairs,* vol. 72, no. 4, October 1996, pp. 1-17.
114. *The Economist,* 12 March 1996.
115. Charles Million, "France and the Atlantic Alliance, "*NATO Review,* vol. 4, no. 3 May 1996, p.15.
116. Excerpts from Herve De Charette, French Foreign Ministers' address at the North Atlantic Council Meeting, Brussels, 5 December 1995, as reproduced in *NATO Review,* vol. 44, no. 1,

January, 1996. For background see, Jean Marie Guehenno, "France and the WEU," *NATO Review*, vol. 42, no. 5, October 1994, pp. 10-12.

117. *The Times*, 1 March 1996.
118. *The Independent*, 14 March 1996.
119. *The Guardian Weekly*, I February 1998, Also L. Barber, "EU fails to build Common Foreign Policy", *Financial Times*, 7 April 1997.
120. Gunter Burgardt, "The Potential Limits of CFSP" in Regelsberger, (ed.), n. 17, p. 321.
121. Christopher Hill, "The Capability-Expectation Gap or Conceptualizing Europe's International Role", *Journal of Common Market Studies*, vol. 31, n. 3, September 1993.
122. To give an example, Franco-German close bilateral relations have often been rivalled by the Benelux countries. Britain too makes no mystery about its 'special relations' with the US. South African issues which keep France preoccupied does not exist for the other EU members. Italy's interest in developing a Central European policy through the Pentagonal or Hexagonal initiatives often raises questions about the presence of a "foreign policy sub-system". For details see, P. de Schoutheete, "The EC and its Subsystems" in W. Wallace (ed.), *The Dynamics of European Integration* (London : Pinter, 1990).
123. See Hill, n. 121, p. 325. For an analysis on 'variable geometry', see Helen Wallace & A. Ridley (ed.), *Europe : The Challenge of Diversity* (London: Routledge, 1985).
124. Burghardt, n. 120, p. 331. Also see R. Rummel, "The IGC 1996 : How to Reform CFSP" in Regelsberger, (ed.), n. 17.
125. C. Hill, "The Actors Involved: National Perspectives", in Regelsberger, (ed.), n. 17, p. 88.
126. EC, "Widening and Deepening of the EU: Economic and Political Challenges", Address by M.B. McGeever, Ambassador, Head of the Delegation of European Commission in India, *Europe Forum*, Jawaharlal Nehru University, New Delhi, 24 February 1998, p. 13.

Chapter V

Amsterdam Treaty: Issues, Options and Responses

After adopting the Single Act in 1985 and negotiating the Maastricht Treaty in 1990-92, West Europeans once again found themselves confronting the unending task of re-examining the institutions, reviewing the existing structure that holds the existing 15 Member States together and seeking to find answers to the unresolved issues and challenges of the 1990s. The years following the signing of the Treaty on European Union revealed how bright promises gave way to apprehensions in face of new threats. The Maastricht Treaty after completing its hazardous journey towards ratification exposed its deficiencies as a blue print for a federal community. The Treaty resulted in an elaborate compromise between the United Kingdom, France, and Germany. A fixed timetable was agreed for the Economic and Monetary Union (EMU) by 1999 and the European Parliament extended its powers to block or amend EU laws. But at Anglo-French insistence, matters of internal and external security remained subject to loose cooperation between national governments. The only ambitious design was to build a federal Europe, with a Common Foreign and Security Policy (CFSP) and this rendered a political dimension to the EU. Combining the political and economic dimension of the EU was a gamble and a hope.[1] The hope was that the methods of integration that formed the basis of economic harmonization could be applied to political unification. The gamble was "making West Europe's huge stake in both its own solidarity and conciliation with the East hostage to that hope".[2] The gamble gradually seemed to fail due to the contradiction between the attitudes that made economic integration possible and those needed of forge a legitimate political union. The strategy laid down at Maastricht was bold in its goal but fearful in its method for attaining that goal.[3] The leaders of the 12 Member States committed their people to a plan for relocating the sovereign authority that governs them without serious public debate about either the aims of this exercise in constitution-building or the basis for its legitimacy. It was perhaps rightly pointed out by Jacques Santer when he said:

> It is not the willingness of political leaders to find satisfactory answers to many of these questions. But I am concerned about our ability to involve the citizens in our project... We must clarify what we are upto and why we believe it is in their long-term interest. We must listen to their reactions and concerns....we cannot make progress if we have two agendas-one for the citizens and one for the political leaders.[4]

The sovereignty gap lay at the heart of the debate over Maastsricht and the EU's crisis over democratic legitimacy was accentuated by the Member States that were no longer able to employ standard powers of the state.[5] Supranational institutions in Brussels continued to lack independent sources of authority. The TEU which promised greater privileges to a sceptical citizenry symbolized how a EU so conceived cannot authoritatively resolve interest disputes above a certain level of intensity.[6] Mounting popular scepticism about the Maastricht mission of the EU owed much to the economic downturn in the early 1990s. Of the one hand, political elites viewed the supranational organisations like the European Central Bank as a necessary step towards political union, while the citizens, on the other hand, were concerned with the immediate economic hardship. The French legislative elections in March 1993 that forced the ruling Socialists to take a back seat were the most significant signs of a political mood which was also evident in Germany, Great Britain and Italy. That disillusionment revealed the fragility of the foundation for the Maastricht design for a fully integrated

West European economy.[7] The economic and financial issues came into the forefront with some of the Member State's reluctance to increase the budget (Germany) and reform the CAP (France). The EU also witnessed fractious disputes over how to fulfil its collective needs by the changing direction to aid to assist the fledging democracies in Eastern Europe.[8] The strains placed on the economic fabric of the EU by such contentious issues highlighted both the strengths of parochial interest and weaknesses of governments.[9]

IGC 1996: AGENDA AND ISSUES

The Intergovernmental Conference (IGC) 1996, which was conceived as far back as 1991 was intended to assess the functioning of the TEU and to address the institutional changes necessary for further enlargement.[10] A number of key issues were likely to emerge after the IGC, for example, decisions concerning moves towards the EMU, enlargement negotiations with the applicant countries and proposals for the EU budget. In addition, the CAP and the Structural Funds, which were not part of the IGC agenda were recognized as two main policy areas that needed to be revised with successive enlargements.[11] The EMU formed one of the basis of the context of IGC. Although it was not on the IGC agenda itself, yet it had a strong background presence and influenced negotiations between France and Germany, both of which have been crucial actors in shaping the EMU and in particular with regard to their positions in the IGC.[12] The issue of EMU determined the pace of progress at the IGC, on the one hand and affected the pace and attitude towards enlargement.[13] The progress of EMU could also bring in questions of an inner-core and outer-core with only some of the Member States joining it and others opting out if EMU goes ahead on schedule. In view of this, the IGC would directly or indirectly address the issues of a "multi-speed" Europe and "variable geometry".[14]

The question of successive enlargement of the EU to the CEEC presented major institutional challenges to the plethora of problems ranging from budgetary arrangement to the balance between commonality and flexibility, from operational capacity of an enlarged EU to the role of unanimity in decision-making which were some of the vital questions that IGC, 1996 sought to answer.[15] Monetary union alongside enlargement was likely to dramatically sharpen the sense of diversity of the EU. There have been urgent calls for new and more flexible forms of integration as the EU's structure have undergone very little change since its inception in 1957. Two issues were the focus of discussions at the IGC, 1996. The first was whether to anticipate the impact of monetary union and enlargement by planning far-reaching changes in decision-making and the institutions. The other was how to effect any changes that are necessary without damaging the interests and rights of the existing Member States of the EU.

Issues

The issues discussed in the context of 1996 were matters which struck at the root of national sovereignty and went well beyond national interests. One crucial question which aroused differing opinions from different Member States was regarding the areas whose jurisdiction could not be transferred to the EU and what powers were to be placed under the domain of the Union.[16] The main institutional reforms targeted in the IGC 1996 dealt with problems of democratic deficit, voting procedure, decision-making, role of the Parliament, Council and the Commission, Justice and Home Affairs, and the CFSP.

One of the major deficiencies in TEU was the *democratic deficit* where the national governments (represented by the Council of Ministers) and a Community executive body (the Commission) stand against a weak Parliament. The question of democratic deficit arises in view of the absence of any democratic legitimation of the sovereignty of the EU which must emanate from the citizens of the Member States-via the national parliaments–a goal the TEU failed to achieve.[17] As was observed by the Federal Constitutional Court of

Germany during the Maastricht Treaty ratification, the democratic legitimation of the EU is provided by the European Parliament which is elected by the citizens of the Member States. In order to overcome the democratic deficit, it is essential to bring the EU closer to the citizens and closely associating the national Parliaments and the European Parliament.[18] All aspects of subsidiarity also play an important role. A primary task for the 1996 IGC was to find out the level at which political tasks could be carried out more efficiently and to delineate the powers at the various levels more clearly. This would bring in the basic question of whether the EU should be organized on an intergovernmental basis or whether a federalist approach would be required to define the policies of the EU. Institutional questions are of paramount importance in view of the problem of creating greater legitimacy for the process of European unity. This includes the task of finding means to incorporate national parliaments into the process of integration and simplifying the much complex decision-making process and positions regarding majority-voting.

The view that the EU's *decision-making process* needs a fundamental overhaul has been broadly accepted. The system was originally designed for the EC of Six. It needs to be streamlined now with the expansion of EU membership. The TEU aimed at making the system more efficient. For instance, the areas where a 'qualified majority' was required had been expanded. This also implied that the national veto had been restricted in certain areas. Nevertheless, the system has become even more complex due to the piecemeal granting of powers to the European Parliament. In some fields, especially the budget, the Parliament is the most crucial actor.[19] In other matters, the Parliament and the Commission can overrule the Council of Ministers. But overall the Council retains the key legislative powers and the Commission has the "power of initiative" but burgeoning the legislative powers reduced the effective workability of the system. Although, the system of legislative and implementing procedures have functioned relatively well, it has three major weaknesses:

- — the continuing divergence between the legislative and budget procedure;
- — the complexly of the decision-making system; and
- — the lack of logic in the choice of the various procedures and the different fields of activity where they apply.[20]

A linked question was how to *redistribute voting weights* in favour of countries with large population such as the UK, France, Germany, Italy and Spain. The voting powers are roughly calculated according to the size of a country's population. Smaller Member States have a disproportionately higher number of votes in the Council of Ministers, for instance, Luxembourg with a population of 450,000 has 2 votes while Germany with 80 million population has 10 votes. Larger Member States are pressing for the balance to be reweighted according to the size and population. They point out that under the present system a coalition could outvote big countries representing 40 per cent of EU population. In a EU of 28-30 members, a qualified majority could outvote Britain, France, Germany and Italy while former communist states of CEEC could be enough to form a blocking minority.[21] In view of future enlargements, where Poland is the only applicant country with a large population, the bigger Member States want the voting weights adjusted lest the "smaller members gang up on them".[22] This would strengthen the bigger countries' ability to block decisions but smaller countries such as the Benelux are insisting that a shift in voting weights must be accompanied by more majority-voting.[23]

A decision-making mechanism used in the Council of Ministers in certain fields allow laws to be passed without the need for complete unanimity. But unanimity is still required in many important areas, thus enabling a single Member State to block an important decision. It is argued that more majority-voting is needed to prevent institutional paralysis.[24] The system of *Qualified Majority Voting* (QMV) can be implemented only if supported by around 70 per cent of the votes which means 62 out of 87 votes. It follows that

26 votes against the motion means a 'blocking minority'. The large Member States note that Germany, the UK, and the Netherlands together make up two-fifths of EU's population but it cannot block a decision. By contrast, Ireland, Luxembourg, Sweden, Greece, Austria and Finland can block and with only 12.5 per cent of the EU's population. There fore, the 'imbalance' is likely to aggravate as the EU expands.[25] Hence, the larger Member States feel that decisions should need 'double majority' (in terms of the Union's population and votes in the Council) or even 'super-qualified-majorities' with higher percentages both ways. The smaller Member States agree to QMV only if it is included in areas like social and environmental matters.[26] However, some Member States wish to preserve their 'veto'. The IGC has the task of defining those areas where majority-voting should be applied in future.

A major issue confronting the IGC is the size and composition of the *Commission.* Smaller Member States like the Benelux countries, Ireland and Portugal retain the right to appoint a EU Commissioner and to take their turn on the rotating EU Presidency for six months. If there is no change in the principle that each Member State provides at least one Commissioner, then one day the Commission will have more than 30 members. It remains to be seen whether the larger states would forego their right to have two Commissioners and the smaller states agree to be represented in groups or by rotation. The smaller states are apprehensive of the domination by the larger states in foreign policy matters and in the political union. There is no doubt a case for reducing the number of Commissioners but in a manner that would alleviate the fears of the smaller states in relation to the Big Four.

An important issue in the IGC was to review and modify the role of the *European Parliament* with a view to enhance transparency and democracy in the EU.[27] Some proposals suggest a demolition of the Maastricht architecture which implies introducing more qualified voting, a simple system of legislation and an equal status with the Council of

Ministers.[28] The European Parliament has a weak legislative authority and exerts very little influence on the executive function of the EU. If there is more majority-voting in the decision-making body, *i.e.* Council of Ministers, some national governments argue that there is a need for a democratic counterweight in Brussels. The European Parliament is the natural choice, despite the dissatisfaction with its performance. The broader point is that decision-making in the EU is complex with more than 20 procedures leaving ample scope for streamlining. The Parliament with some support in the Member States argue that these could be nationalised in three categories in EU legislation-extending the 'co-decision' co-procedure with the Council for all normal legislation where the Council decides by majority; giving the Parliament the power of assent where the Council decides by unanimity and reserving consultation mainly in areas of foreign affairs and intergovernmental cooperation.[29]

The need for stronger policies on *justice and home affairs* have been under-estimated so far. Here, the agenda has been set by certain facts; migration, increasing crime, terrorism, drug-trafficking resulting to the need for internal security and external border controls. There is an urgent need to incorporate certain fields of internal affairs and legal-policy-making step-by-step into community processes. At present, the 'third-pillar' is a matter for intergovernmental cooperation and the results of which have proved inefficient and very time consuming. The consensus is that the EU needs to overhaul its decision-making in internal security matters also.[30]

The conflict in Yugoslavia demonstrated that viable security structures within the EU are more necessary than ever before.[31] A CFSP enshrined in the TEU is more than just a 'second pillar', achieved in the field of European political co-operation, as it institutionalises a role for the Commission. The common framework aimed at in the TEU supposed to become a reality through the CFSP, but unfortunately the Member States have tended to take foreign policy initiatives either alone or in small groupings, thus side-stepping joint action.[32] The CFSP has suffered among other things, from a 'lack of political will', difficulties with the decision-making system and crippling budgetary procedure.[33] To establish a firm basis for the EU's CFSP was an important agenda in the IGC, 1996.[34] This would mean increased efficiency and solidarity, more continuity and transparency which would necessiate the extension of majority-voting in this field. In the field of defence, a step-by-step integration of the WEU into the EU within the framework of the Atlantic Alliance has been suggested.[35]

Given that the institutional issues took a centre-stage in the 1996 IGC, it was hardly surprising to note that the Commission's main recommendations were for the reformation of the legislative system. The two main elements of the Commission's opinion were the replacement of the unanimity principle by Qualified-Majority-Voting as a general rule and the introduction of the streamlined decision-making process. The Commission also advocated pushing forward the subsidiarity principle and involving national parliaments more closely in Union business. It also stressed on the essential point that deepening and widening are inter-twined and urged the Union to be closer to its citizens. To achieve this, it advocated the integration of the Social Protocol to the Treaty. The Commission also proposed a transfer of Justice and Home Affairs of the Community framework in order to attain the objectives relating to the problem of cross-border immigration and drug-trafficking problem. Following this logic, it also proposed that the Schengen Agreement be incorporated into the Treaty. Most significant was its opinion restating a "multi speed Europe" when it opined that the "EU must not forever be bound to advance at the speed of its slowest members."[36] It also emphasised the need of having an institutional system which will work in an expanded Europe. For this to succeed, the President of the Commission, Jacques Santer urged that the IGC process has to be backed by a 'clear political will'.[37]

The Commission's opinion on the IGC, 1996 offered reason for hope since the national positions of the core-group of countries–France Germany and the Benelux countries, seemed to coagulate around the fundamental principles and guidelines which were at the basis of the Commission's opinion. However, it also offered reason for doubt as some of the suggestions of the Commission appeared unconvincing on further analysis. The Commission's proposal concerning the improvement of the visibility of CFSP does not meet a major objective. The Commission's solution based on the strengthening of the Presidency along with the Commission, itself raises the question as to how the larger members who play a major role in world affairs be convinced with an EU President with increased power especially when he might belong to a smaller Member State (like Greece, Portugal, or in future Slovenia) whose foreign policy has not always been on the same wave length as some of the larger countries. Another aspect that was avoided in the Commission's agenda was how to reconcile the radical divergences between the participant states at the IGC and to what extent should compromises be sought without jeopardising the essential goals.

On 20 March 1996, the 15 Member States gathered in Turin, Italy for the ceremonial launch of the negotiations of the IGC. The main conclusions of the Turin European Council summarised the aims of the IGC as follows:

- — bringing the union closer to its citizens in particular by the fulfillment of the objective of a high level of employment and ensuring social protection among other things; providing transparency and strengthening European citizenship;
- — strengthening and enlarging the scope of CFSP by addressing the decision-making process;
- — problems of CFSP budget and effective interplay of the various institutions of the EU, corresponding to the links between the EU and WEU;
- — and finally, assuming the proper functioning of the institutions in view of enlargement which includes the scope of Qualified-Majority-Voting, weighting of votes, composition of the Commission and the role of European Parliament and the European Court of Justice and proper application of the principle of subsidiarity.[38]

The agenda that the IGC set for itself were bound to prove controversial. Despite current widespread opinion that the EU suffers from a 'democratic deficit' even a modest enhancement of the Parliament's role would likely be resisted by certain Member States. Restraining the veto power was a pragmatic proposal to ensure that an enlarged EU does not suffer from operational paralysis. Nonetheless, it touched a sensitive national nerve in some Member States. The essential problem was that there are competing and apparently irreconcilable visions of what the EU ought to be. One view is Germany's campaign for further integration which is driven by fears of it being drifted at the centre of the continent. At this point, German governments have also pressed its EU partners to be more flexible with their respective national sovereignty to compensate for the sacrifice of the D-Mark for a single currency in 1999. The other vision of EU is backed by the UK which rests on looser form of integration in which the Member States can still select areas of cooperation while resisting further transfer of sovereignty in Brussels. The British are also joined to some extent by the Nordic Member States in their scepticism towards the EU.[39] The position of France remains a crucial deciding factor. Whether France would tilt towards the German approach or repeat the experience of Maastricht would shape the outcome of the IGC.[40]

It was anticipated that the IGC would introduce major policy competence into the EU. As the Reflection Group stated, the Community should try to do not more but better.[41] One view expressed was that the IGC should make only a number of small changes. This cautious approach was driven by worries about public opinion in the 15 Member States and problems of public dissatisfaction over the Treaty ratification and lack of agreement on major changes–notably by the UK.[42] The outcome of the IGC would act to improve the existing EU but was unlikely to bring about a resolution of major challenges caused by future enlargement. This depended largely on the attitude of the agenda of different Member States. Since the EU has always shown a remarkable capacity for achieving compromises between ostensibly irreconcilable positions, the IGC too would see a lot of hard inter-state bargaining in order to reach a certain level of harmony. One possible scenario likely to emerge out of the IGC was a multi-layered system with Member States choosing whether or not to participate in certain aspects of the integration process.

If the EU is to achieve its goal of moving towards an "even closer union", the emergence of some sort of federal system would become incumbent–a structure not supported by some 'Eurosceptic' Member States. On the other hand, reverting to a traditional intergovernmental structure would contradict the very ideal of the Treaty preamble to which all Member States are committed.

NATIONAL POSITIONS

The key actors in the IGC, 1996 were the Member States whose positions and agenda underlined the diversity of views about the direction in which the EU is heading. The IGC faced divisions over the methods and political philosophy along much the same lines as in the Maastricht negotiations.

Germany

For the German government, the IGC held both promises and threats. The hope stemmed from Germany's belief that the IGC would be able to advance integration in areas neglected in the Maastricht Treaty and close to Germany's desire of an 'even closer Union'. The threat lay in its domestic politics, in view of the German general elections in September 1998, as the IGC would have a bearing on a series of European issues that would dominate the election with unpredictable effects. While issues like enlargement, reform of the CAP and a potentially acrimonious debate over the EU budget could see Germany pushing for a more equitable burden-sharing with the risk of reducing support for the EU among German voters.[43]

The German government proceeded slowly in developing

its aims and strategies for the IGC, 1996. An additional problem that influenced Germany's position was the unpredictability of French cooperation under Jacques Chirac, when some of the assumptions based on Franco-German relations had been upset.[44] The formal goals for the IGC were decided by Germany after the Reflection Group of Member States senior Foreign Ministry officials reported on the prospects of the conference in late 1995.[45] The main purpose of the IGC was to look at the possibilities for deepening the EU in four main areas: foreign and security policy, internal and judicial affairs, reform of the EU institutions and making the EU more democratic and transparent. In all these areas Germany's proposals revealed a strong federal tilt. The German government proposed the majority-voting principle to be applied as a rule for Community legislation.[46] The Council of Ministers already decides in many issues on the majority basis with weighted votes and it is bindingly committed to certain precisely laid down forms of cooperation with the Commission and the European Parliament. According to the German proposal, the Council resolutions should be bound to the majority of the weighted votes and to a sufficient majority of the population represented by the voting states. The German government favoured the introduction of 'double majority' which would ensure a maximum degree of democratic legitimacy so that the number of decisions lack the approval of one or two of the bigger Member States. The German government has proposed the application of QMV on all Council decisions. The German Foreign Office Minister Werner Hoyer argued that the pressure of possible outvoting would increase the willingness of Member States to compromise on certain decisions.[47] This would prevent cases of "hostage taking" where a Member State blocks a required consensus-based-decision until it has been given concessions in a parallel required majority-voting. Inspite of Chancellor Kohl's efforts to quicken deeper integration, several German government ministers rejected a quick move towards majority-voting in sensitive areas like taxation, finance, social security and industrial policy decisions.[48] German Interior Minister Manfred Kanther and Agriculture Minister Joachem Borchert expressed their reservations towards majority-voting. Kanther especially opposed the concept of security and asylum policies while Borchert feared that such a move could dilute Germany's regulation of small business, such as bakeries, opening them to competition from the less regulated foreign competitors.[49] The German government proposed an enhancement of the Parliament's role in EU legislation as a counterweight to the decision-making Council of Ministers. The German position argued for the renewed powers of equal rights and equal co-decision of the Parliament alongside the Council. According to the German view, such reform would counteract Euroscepticism in the German population (which sees the decision-making process as incomprehensible) notwithstanding the problem that such an upgrading of the Parliament would inevitably delay and impede legislative process. In order to ensure the efficiency of legislative process, Germany suggested the reduction of decision-making procedures to three types instead of the existing twelve. Accordingly, there would be only consultation, assessment and co-decision by the European Parliament in future.[50] In its efforts to increase the role of the Parliament, the German government's initiative had been limited by the federal Constitutional Court during the Maastricht ratification that the national parliaments must retain competence for tasks of local and substantial significance. The German government also favoured an extension of the Commission's right of initiative.[51]

A key German desire has been the introduction of the 'flexibility clause'. This is intended to ensure that those willing and able to proceed are not excluded from any common policy while those outside, cannot exercise their right to veto and thereby block the integration.[52] It is for this reason to deepen cooperation in certain areas that Germany is a strong advocate of majority-voting so that certain issues do not face any hindrance from uninterested members. The 'flexibility clause', so strongly favoured by Germany stems from their much controversial 'hard-core' concept.[53] According to Karl Lamers, the author of this controversial paper[54]:

> The core Europe idea is now accepted by the key countries with the exception of Britain....there has to be a core to hold the whole thing together.[55]

Pursuing the 'flexibility clause' in the 1996 IGC, arises from German fears that the proposed enlargement of the EU would dilute the EU's capacity for concerted action and policy making. Axiomatic to the German case is the determination to enable the EU to have a more viable CFSP. The inauspicious state of cooperation in foreign policy matters within the EU and the Bosnian disaster have added thrust to the German resolve.[56] A major objective of Germany was to extend the competence of EU in CFSP by changing the voting structures and foregoing the veto. Werner Hoyer and the members of the Free Democratic Party proposed Qualified-Majority-Voting in this area in order to avoid the lowest common denominator decisions of blocking EU actions by a single Member State. However, in cases where an EU member feels a vital security interest is involved, there should be scope for 'constructive abstention'. A Member State would not be able to hinder an agreed EU policy but it would be able to abstain from its implementation. Germany favoured building of the WEU to become the defence policy arm of the EU. Former Foreign Minister Klaus Kinkel proposed the appointment of a single person as a Secretary-General of the EU's Council of Ministers and the Secretary General of the WEU.[57] Contrary to this, the Christian Democratic Union (CDU) ruled out the idea of a 'Mr. Europe' or an appointed official for EU's external affairs.[58] According to German Defence Minister, Volker Ruehe, the IGC, 1996 should retain the veto power in defence matters.

On internal security, Germany proposed a "single integrated space" which would guarantee the movement of EU citizens while forging a joint approach among Member States on asylum, visa and immigration matters. Greater integration of internal and judicial matters is necessary in view of the problems concerning terrorism, organised crime and drug trafficking. Germany's desire to push ahead this issue is understandable for Germany is the only country that has absorbed more asylum seekers and refugees from problem-ridden states like Bosnia. Measure to achieve an overhaul in this internal security structure included a reduction of national veto rights and entrusted the Commission with the right to initiate policies. The free democrats went as far as to demand a European constitution with a bill of basic rights.

With regard to EMU, Germany proposed to achieve the EMU through the strict observance of the convergence criteria. It has always stressed on the feasibility of a monetary union dependent on a political union. However, Finance Minister Theo Waigel softened Germany's stance on EMU rules by adopting a more flexible approaching a meeting at Noordwijk in April 1997.[59] On German insistence EU members agreed on a Stability Pact to reinforce fiscal discipline amongst members of the single currency on Euro zone. In order to clinch a deal on a watertight pact to enforce budgetary discipline in a single currency zone, Chancellor Helmut Kohl stressed on an "effective pact to show that the governments are committed to a forward-looking and permanent stability".[60] Under the Stability Pact, governments should keep their budget deficits within right confines and failure to do so would inevitably trigger punitive fines. Germany held the whip hand on two of the most contentious issues facing the heads of EU members—how to achieve a stable currency and how to streamline EU's decision–making process. Franco-German calls for a flexible-cooperation to build a 'core Europe' which could relegate Britain of a second division appear to be more elusive than the Stability Pact.[61]

In view of predictable differences between the Euro-enthusiasts and the Euro-sceptics, the German government was in favour of a lean agenda. Outlining a 21-points list of specific reform proposals, Foreign Minister Klaus Kinkel warned the EU partners that the IGC goals should not be too ambitious. The main objective was to concentrate on key issues of making the EU more effected in common action in foreign policy and internal security. Institutional reforms should make it more able to absorb new members while action should be taken to overcome 'Euro-fatigue' among voters by making the EU more open and transparent. In particular, the subsidiarity principle should be spelled out in a protocol to the EU Treaty to enable the policy-makers with more transparency in any policy. Kinkel underlined that the IGC was "a step, not a final stage" in European integration. It was important not to set goals that were too low. But equally unrealistically ambitious objectives could jeopardise other parts of the EU's agenda for the end of this century.[62]

France

The objectives favoured by France were less far-reaching than the German government. Since President de Gaulle, France preferred intergovernmentalism to supranationality when any reform of the EU was initiated. At the same time, France sought to agree to intensify integration on the basis of national coordination if it expected its own room for manouevre.[63] With respect to internal reforms targeted at the IGC, the French government and the French President favoured far-reaching reforms in terms of the structure of decision-making co-decision of the EU Council. During the election campaign, President Chirac stated that he was willing to strengthen the role of the Council-which meant extending the term of office of the Council President and the Council's right of initiative. This implied a corresponding weakening of the Commission's legislative process. As regards the Council voting, the French government, like its German counterpart supported a 'double-majority'.[64] Both the governments believe that though 'double majority', several smaller countries would be unable to make decisions with one large country which would then be binding for the other members of the EU.

According to France, the role of the European Commission should be scaled down to those responsibilities and powers with which it was expressly vested by the Treaty.

Although it should exercise initiative and executive powers, it should be accountable to the Council. Accordingly the Council would issues mandates with precisely specified content to the Commission which would thus be reduced to being the executive organ of the Council.[65] There is a clear reflection of French tendency towards intergovernmentalism. Like Germany, France proposed that the Commission's role should have greater accountability to the organs of the EU than before and unlike Germany, bind the Commission to the directives of the Council. Moreover, the number of Commissioners should be reduced from 12 to 10. Scaling down the role of Commission was one common objective to which both France and Germany agreed upon. Whereas the German government combined this goal with a status of enhancing the powers of European Parliament, the French rejected any upgrading of the same. According to the French position, the distribution of power between the Council and the Parliament should on no account be shifted in the Parliament's favour, (something the German government support). The French intention seemed to change the existing institutions as little as possible and without strengthening the supranational organs. As far as the intergovernmentalist bodies of the EU are concerned, France suggested the need for a reweighting of votes. This proposal arises from the realisation that reweighted votes in the EU Council would make it difficult for other countries (namely Britain) to block resolutions for which a qualified majority was obtained. France also favoured an increase in the number of votes for the larger Member States from 10 to 11 or 12 to make it easy in future to reach the qualified majority of 63.

In a policy statement before the IGC in Turin, French Prime Minister Alain Juppe called for the reform of EU institutions and ruled out the creation of a 'European super-state'. Outlining his belief in a "two-speed" or "multi-speed" Europe, Juppe said there should be a 'second circle' within the existing one, around France and Germany which wanted to move further or more quickly than the others on subjects such as defence and single currency.[66] To quote Prime Minister

Juppe:

> There will be a Union made up of the 15 present members and those who want to join. In the centre of this first circle, there would be another much smaller and changeable one, composed of few states around Germany and France—countries ready to go further and faster than the others on subjects like currency and defence.[67]

On the questions of reforming the institutions, French position appeared close to that of Britain. Limiting the role of the Commission to issues such as external trade and single market, France proposed a minimal role for the European Parliament, which should 'monitor' the implementation of policies rather than make it. Emphasizing the role of the national parliaments, French proposed the formation of a new body – a "higher parliamentary council", made up of deputies from national parliaments that would review legislation to judge whether it confirmed to the principle of subsidiarity.[68] In an address to the European Democratic Union (the group comprising right of centre parties from Western Europe), Alain Juppe stated:

> For us Gaullists, nation-state remains more than ever the place that is both essential and central for realizing the democratic contract, the social and political link between the citizens and those who represent them.[69]

Summing up the French position, Juppe said that the expectations of the IGC in France tended to be either too fatalistic or too ambitious. France expected the IGC to achieve three objectives—"a more prosperous Europe, a more secure Europe and a Europe closer to the citizens".[70] This reflects French aspirations for sharp and firm decisions on reforming the institutions before accession negotiations begin. The broad lines of French proposals for the Turin conference were outlined by French Minister for European Affairs. Michel Barnier who said a common foreign and security strategy was urgently required and this could be brought about by changing the voting structures to avoid immobility in the EU after more countries had joined. To Barnier, voting power in the Council of Ministers had to be changed to take into account the real weight of Member States while the use of QMV had to be enhanced. France also proposed the creation of a 'super Secretary-General of the Council' in charge of CFSP, who would be 'the official face and voice of Europe". The formal statement presented by Barnier to the National Assembly placed France between the Euro-federalism favoured by Germany and the more Euro-sceptical path taken by Britain. The French argument in favour of a "multi-speed Europe" around a Franco-German core brings close to German desire for a "hard-core" Europe. The French proposal for the appointment of a 'Monsieur Pesc' (Mr. CFSP) was opposed by the Christian Democratic Union (CDU) of Germany which feared that France had former President Valery Giscard d'Estaing in mind for the role. The CDU conceded in a policy paper on 16 September 1996 that the appointment of a 'high representative' for foreign affairs would make the EU decision-making even more complicated.[71] As against Germany's proposal for QMV in all areas, France put forward the proposal for 'constructive abstention' on foreign and security matters allowing those EU members unwilling to take part in a particular European operation to abstain rather than block the whole venture.[72] In matters of defence, there was a convergence between the Franco-German proposal *vis-a-vis* the role of the WEU. France too favoured the membership of WEU as a pre-condition of EU membership and the former should form the executive arm of a European defence policy. It is in matters of defence that France differed most from the British position.

The Single European market has, on the one hand, opened France to foreign investments and has enabled it to compete in the European and world markets. On the other hand, the EU has made it difficult for France to continue with its policies of state subsidies and anti-competitive regulation. The proposed reforms of the CAP could prove detrimental to an agriculture-sensitive France. Regarding a proposal by Jacques Santer concerning the introduction of co-decision for the CAP, Michel Barnier expressed 'serious reservations' adding: "{This} is the least one can say... The French government's position has not changed for 15 or 16 years and I do not think it will change".[73]

There seemed to be a broad consensus among French political parties regarding the objectives it had set for the IGC, 1996. The only divergence visible amongst the main parties was over the EMU. As regards EMU, it had been posing problems for France. Faced with soaring unemployment and budget deficits, France began to realise the pitfalls of being inside a currency zone designed and likely to run along the lines of the Bundesbank.[74] France was likely to suffer from more unemployment and dislocation and restricted market-access than Germany.[75] During the French Parliamentary elections in 1997, French political scene was dominated by fine divisions amongst French political parties. To Jacques Delors of the Socialist Party, a currency union would establish an "economic government to coordinate macroeconomic policies to support monetary policies". Meanwhile amongst the Gaullists, Phillipe Seguin favoured the idea of Europe dropping "its monetary obsession and tackle more pertinent issues like unemployment". Meanwhile Jean-Marie Le Pen of National Front, denounced the idea of Europe "dominated by Germany and organised into Laender-like provinces ignoring existing nations which would make Hitler's dream come true".[76]

Britain

Britain, often labeled as the 'reluctant European', treats the EU with healthy scepticism. It takes a fundamentally different view of European integration. The British government's White Paper on 'European Policy': 'A Partnership of Nations', presented to the Parliament in March 1996 pointed out the British aims and objectives targeted for the IGC, 1996. The British attitude towards reforming the institutions were minimalist. It did not favour QMV, since Britain would lose the veto power-one of the most vital instrument in the EU.[77] This argument was justified by British

Foreign secretary Malcolm Rifkind on the grounds that the democratic legitimacy of decisions had to be guaranteed. Every decision in EU agreed upon by a majority accounted to outvoting a democratically elected government. In the long term this would undermine the legitimacy of the EU.[78] At the same time, Britain expressed reservations to the introduction of 'double majority' with regard to institutional reforms. Like France, it favoured a containment of the role of the Commission. The White Paper suggested that the Commission's proposal should be declared null and void if it is not accepted by the Council within a certain period. Similar to the French proposal, the British government sought to enhance the importance of the national parliaments as the main agencies of European legislation. The national parliaments should be consulted before the Commission initiated a law, and integration of the former in the work of the European Parliament should be bindingly specified in the revised treaty. Along the lines similar to the French government, the British government also rejected any extension of powers of the European Parliament. A persistent problem for Britain had been the historic tendency of the European Court of Justice to augment its own federal powers. In view of this, it proposed to curb the 'retrospective judgement' from the European Court of Justice. The British government also took a cautious approach in reforming the decision-making process of the EU. While supporting a reweighting of votes in the Council, the British government suggested that the larger Member States should continue to have the same share of votes and the smaller members should be given a more appropriate influence'.[79]

At a meeting of the European Foreign Ministers, Malcolm Rifkind stated that Britain would oppose most of the plans in connection with establishing a common home affairs and justice policy. Entrusting the EU with powers over immigration and asylum would be positively damaging. This view is shared by France, which also confirmed its reticence towards the Commission's idea of a Community competence to justice and home affairs.[80] Rifkind also reaffirmed British opposition to give the Commission the power to make common policies on job-creation. Calls for the WEU to become part of the EU had been opposed by Britain.

Italy

Setting its objectives for the IGC, 1996 Italy proposed measures which were firmly federalist in nature. Italy sought to introduce QMV especially in foreign policy matters unlike the proposals by France and Britain. Contrary to Franco-British proposals and similar to the German proposal, Italy proposed an enhancement of the powers of the European Parliament. As far as defence was concerned, Italy endorsed the Franco-German proposal supporting the merger of the WEU with the EU itself, which would place the Euro-army at the disposal of Brussels. Boris Biancheri, the head of Italian Foreign Ministry, reinstating that the federalist moves were indispensable for the EU, said : "If we fail, we go back to a medieval system where there are no rules and disorder will reign".[81] Italy's objectives showed a strong support for an extension of the powers of the European Parliament and the European Court of Justice (as opposed to the proposals made by France and Britain). Italy's position was justified by Italian Foreign Minister, Susanna Agnelli when she said:

> The work of the Parliament and the European Court of Justice is inadequate as far as the freedom of the citizen is concerned....we have to simplify the way we work, introducing decisions by majority.[82]

In another statement, Agnelli added that majority-voting in the Council should become the general rule except for issues of a constitutional character and suggested that different degrees of integration were possible—an 'avant garde' of Member States moving quickly towards integration would be a "logical" part of the process.

Southern Member States

For the Southern Mediterranean Member States like Spain, Portugal and Greece, membership in the EU made them net beneficiaries.[83] Moreover, their commitment to their national democratic institutions are not as strong as that of Britain. Against this background, the South Europeans have generally been slow to distinguish between the enthusiasm for membership in the EU and a commitment to the course set out in the TEU and this became clearer and critical during the IGC 1996.[84]

In Portugal, the main political parties remained committed to meeting the criteria for EMU but their right-wing party (PP-CAS) which made a significant entry in the parliament in October 1995 questioned the cost in jobs and bankruptcies to a weak economy. The Spanish Popular Party leader, Jose Maria Aznar categorically stated their desire to take a more 'Gaullist' line which implied more intergovernmentalism than the stance taken earlier by Felipe Gonsalez and the Socialists. In Greece, there was a growing scepticism and little conviction regarding its joining the single currency in 1999. Greece is the only Mediterranean country which has taken a firm line on a specific issue in a way that could jeopardize the outcome of CFSP in the IGC. Although CFSP remains a priority to Greece[85], its outgoing dispute with Turkey over Cyprus prompted Prime Minister Costas Simitis to say:

> As long as our vital national interests are not safeguarded by the EU commitments, Greece will always keep its right of veto active.[86]

Rejecting the "multi-speed Europe" and pressure for creating a "hard-core" EU, Greece affirmed that unanimity cannot be dropped on CFSP when national interest of Member States are concerned.[87] The clout of the Southern Member States could most likely be curbed by their overwhelming dependence on the EU and by the dominance of the larger states.

Nordic Member States

A tide of Euro-scepticism in the Nordic Member States of the EU amid public discontent over the Union's perceived failure to solve economic problems like unemployment, failed to capture attention of the Scandinavians. In Sweden, the issue of common currency replacing the Krona aroused deep antipathy as many Swedes felt duped by the pro-EU campaign which promised lower interest rates and more jobs if Sweden joined the EU. Finland, on the other hand, whose food prices fell by 10 per cent, saw this as a reason for EU's popularity and its positive attitude towards the EMU. Opposition to EMU was deep-rooted in Sweden where the ruling Social Democrats were largely divided over the issue. In Denmark, EMU participation was one of the several opt-outs engineered to persuade the Danes to ratify the TEU in 1993. Some Danish Ministers believed that EMU could confer important economic advantages but were concerned by public opinion. An official echoed Denmark's Euro-scepticism by saying, "the problem for Social Democrats and for Denmark as a whole is that we are split down the middle on Europe and have been ever since we decided to join in 1972.[88] Sweden's economic problems led it to organise a concerted action before the Turin Conference, to force the inclusion of employment policy into the EU and tackle unemployment affecting 18 million people. Sweden's representative on the Reference Group which prepared the IGC agenda, Gunnar Lund said:

> There is clear support in this group for amending the (Maastricht) Treaty (to include employment provisions) and a dominant view is that a separate chapter on employment would be the best way for achieving it.[89]

As far as CFSP is concerned, the 'neutral' Member States have not signalled a clear commitment of joining the EU defence initiative.

A CRITIQUE OF NATIONAL POSITIONS

The IGC was perceived as a political climax which would decisively shape and remake the EU. The principal problem for the IGC was to find a workable EU-wide compromise in view of the wide divergences of objectives and proposals suggested by the Member States. While Germany and the Benelux countries hoped it would press on from the TEU towards an "ever closer union", Britain, Denmark, Sweden and Spain expressed their reservations towards deeper integration. France, on the other hand, found itself a balance between the two opposite positions. The institutional reforms designed to make the organs of the EU more efficient turned out to be the most tricky problems confronting the IGC. As the national proposals suggested, there was hardly any agreement between Germany, France, and Britain the key actors in the IGC, over the most important aspects. There was neither a consensus nor a compromise between the 'big three' over questions relating to the status of the European Parliament or reweighting of votes in the Council. In so far as the role of the Commission and the Parliament was concerned, French and British position appeared closer than that of the French and Germans. Jacques Santer's allegation that "states are using the conference to restate their old proposals",[90] leading to internal squabbles, became clear when France and Britain tried to block the European Parliament's presence at one of the conferences, causing a deadlock of action between Britain and France on the one hand, and a firmly integrationist Italy, on the other.[91]

A very fundamental dilemma which had existed since the creation of the EU has been the balance between the large and small Member States. Even during the IGC, whenever the larger Member States proposed reforms in the Council, or the composition of the Commission or a reweighted voting pattern, they found themselves facing the smaller Member States who rightly fear that they would be deprived of influence and powers of co-decision with respect to further EU integration. A meeting organized in Sweden by the smaller Member States to force the inclusion of a separate employment policy[92] in the IGC highlighted their inherent doubts about the attitude of big members on issues confronting the smaller states over which the former had been hesitant to take any initiative. Secondly, the fact that the 'big four' were excluded from this meeting revealed the underlying fears of the smaller states whose role have always been to "trail along to the conferences hoping the big boys will take notice of their sensible but 'self-interested' pleas for a community of action".[93]

The most important changes that the EU needed to incorporate were with regard to its institutions to enable it to cope with future enlargement. The primary institutional change was the modest extension of QMV to certain issues keeping unanimity only for matters as tax and social security. A second priority was to give the Commission powers for tackling negotiations on trade-in services which are the biggest sectors in most European economies. The third objective was to redress the balance between the smaller and bigger Member States.[94] The French, German and British ideas would accentuate the differences between the Member States more strongly. A unanimous decision to change certain provisions like increasing QMV, enhanced power to the Commission and European Parliament and merger of the WEU, could become an obstacle as Britain's veto was impregnable. Although ways had been found to circumvent individual obstinacy through the opt-out clause rendered to Britain and Denmark on the creation of a single currency or protocols attached to the TEU (like Social Policy, defence etc.), the challenge was to reconcile Britain's aim of a larger and looser EU with the goal shared by Germany and the Benelux of a larger and more federal Union while a vacillating position of France would become crucial between these two extremes. UK's intransigence triggered the campaign by Germany and France for more flexibility.

The anxiety that a prolonged IGC might have disastrous knockout effects on an enlarged EU compelled states like Germany to drop the early ambitions of the conference. The German government which once stressed on 'political union as pre-condition for monetary union' reversed its view that a monetary union would enable is partners to push for political integration and greater powers for the European Parliament. Chancellor Kohl suggested deferring the task of creating institutions for an enlarged EU to a 'Maastricht Three'.[95]

In view of this scenario, three main elements appeared significant in shaping the outcome of the final treaty. The first was the attitude of the UK. With a change of government, the UK gave the impression of shedding the conservative rigidity on EU but during the IGC, participant states were still split between those who consider having modified its basic positions and willing to reach a compromise and those, on the other hand, who consider that it is firmly anchored to its traditional position. The second was Italy's position which was based on a 'minimum threshold' below which the outcome of the IGC would be unacceptable.[96] The problem arose in view of an impending clash between Italy's minimum objectives and Britain's position. What could be a minimum requirement for Italy could also be rejected by the UK. For example, the transfer of justice and home affairs falling under the 'third pillar' (intergovernmental cooperation) to the 'first pillar' (supranationalism) was rejected by the UK. The third was represented by the Franco-German compromises on several aspects of negotiations which could lead to solutions. One of the compromises concerned the composition of the Commission (20 members each after enlargement), role of the Presidency and the role of the European Parliament.

AMSTERDAM TREATY 1997–A CRITIQUE

The European Council meeting in Amsterdam in June 1997 concluded the IGC with an agreement on a draft treaty. This meeting revealed how internal bickering among Member States could not give way to more concrete policies. The Summit also saw national interest clashing with the federalist's vision of a Europe with that of the inter-governmentalists. The result was a treaty, which although is another step down the road to integration, was not a great leap forward as many countries had hoped for. The points of agreement in Amsterdam were with regard to the following aspects:

- zone of freedom, security and justice to come into force for the EU citizens within five years of Treaty ratification,
- Member States which violate the basic freedom would face

suspension of voting rights in the Council of Ministers;
- immigration, visas, political asylum, civil and judicial co-operation will become common policies. Unanimity is required for at least five years in decisions on immigration, visa policy and asylum;
- free movement of persons throughout EU would be ensured but Britain and Ireland would retain border controls;
- the Stability Pact will regulate the participating states' budgetary deficits once the single currency is introduced;
- a new chapter in the treaty has been included which deals with an employment strategy between the Member States;
- the Social Charter would be integrated into the treaty following Britain's agreement to sign it;
- the CFSP of the EU is to be represented by the Council's Secretary-General rather than a high-ranking politician;
- any state which believes its vital interests are at stake can block majority votes on implementing foreign policy;
- the merger of WEU into EU would be possible in future but NATO would remain central to European defence;
- the Commission would have only 20 members after enlargement, with one member per state;
- there was no agreement on how to re-weight votes of Member States in the Council;
- the authority of the President of the Commission has been strengthened by introducing a requirement that his/her nomination be approved by the EU Parliament;
- QMV would enable some EU states to move together without waiting for others, but only in limited policy areas.[97]

The Treaty spelt out for the first time that the Community will have massive powers over policies on borders, asylum and immigration with all internal frontier checks being dismantled within five years of the Treaty coming into force. Britain secured an opt-out from the policy. The European Parliament also won new powers on co-decision, the system by which it has a joint role in the legislative process with the Council of Ministers. Co-decision would apply to all areas covered by QMV. But the decision-making procedures used by the Parliament so far have been cut from over 20 to just three.

The Conference failed to reach an agreement on the most vital agenda—reform of institutions.[98] There were three core changes sought and there has been a virtual failure on all three. The federalists' ambition to make decision-making swifter through QMV and reduction of vetoes were thwarted by disagreement among the 15 Member States over where unanimity should be dropped. Germany blocked QMV in industrial and environmental policy, transfer of pension and social security right.[99] QMV was extended in social and research policy and in foreign policy to some extent.

In the most politically sensitive argument of the Summit, the smaller nations resisted pressure from Britain, Germany and France to change the EU voting rules. This was aimed at ensuring that the big states retain their clout when the EU opens itself to East Europe. A specific Dutch Presidency proposal which would give the four largest states 25 votes compared with six each to Denmark and Ireland, was not agreed upon. The smaller states feared their national interests would be threatened by the reweighting of votes.

As regards the size of the Commission, Ireland and the smaller states retained their right to nominate a member of the Commission despite pressures from the larger states to curtail that right. They agreed that in a Union of 25 or more, a Commission of this size may prove unworkable. The five large states have agreed to give up one Commissioner each upon enlargement. However this issue is to be reopened with enlargement.[100]

In view of the fact that the Treaty did not achieve the institutional changes, it remains unclear whether inviting new members into an unreformed EU would be to invite paralysis of function. The Member States agreed to limit the number of Commissioners to 20, thereby protecting each country's right to nominate a representative to the executive body. When the first wave of enlargement occurs, the large Member States will have to give up their right to have two Commissioners in exchange for added voting power. But the decision is likely to pose problems, once more than five states join the EU. As Werner Hoyer remarked, "over time we have to find a solution where as the EU grows, the Commission doesn't grow with it". That should pave the way for the enlargement process to begin with and for the first wave of members to join.

In response to the Amsterdam Treaty, many candidate countries of East Europe, especially Poland restated the need for enlargement process to continue irrespective of the success of reforms in the EU.[101] This implicitly showed that even the applicant states, waiting to join the EU, recognise the fact that institutional reforms have been insufficient in order to enable the EU to cope with enlargement. However, among the second group of candidates for membership, there is a growing unease. There is a concern that by failing to restructure the EU's institutions to accommodate more than 20 members, the leaders are sending negative signals. "Its not very good for us. There is almost a pre-judgement that they (EU) will enlarge to include only four or five countries",[102] stated Rytis Martikonis, a Lithuanian diplomat echoing their fears of being left out. By paving the way for just a few new members to join, the road to EU may prove to be even more difficult for future applicants. An EU of 15, which is already struggling to resolve their differences over the balance of power, may find it even more difficult to function in a wider EU.

An important issue in the IGC, 1996 was reforming CFSP. By common consent CFSP lacks credibility, coherence and 'political will'. In the revised Treaty, some degree of QMV has been introduced in CFSP with a corresponding change in the definition of CFSP. But Franco-German plans to incorporate WEU as the defence arm of EU has been rejected by Britain. An attempt to create a common enterprise in defence have been resisted by Ireland and the 'neutral' Member States. NATO still remains the cornerstone of European defence but the Treaty has included a defence of the possibility of eventual integration of WEU into the EU. While most decisions will still be taken by unanimity in order to bypass the veto, the Treaty nevertheless provides a new decision-making mechanism. Unanimity will be used for agreeing to common strategies whose implementation in detail can be carried out by QMV by the Council of Ministers. At the same time, the Member States can retain an "emergency brake" and veto on the implementation of joint actions for 'important or stated reasons of national policy'. The overall result is a formula which can appear to satisfy both the veto and the QMV lobbies. However, Eurosceptics like the Irish representative on the IGC, Noel Door suggested that the definition of a strategic decision may be seen as leaving too much scope for later decisions by QMV. Since decisions are taken by traditional consensus, the Treaty provides the possibility of 'constructive abstention'. This will allow states who do not wish to participate in an action but are also reluctant to veto it, to abstain while the action proceeds. If abstentions amount to more than a third of the weighted votes of the Council, a decision will deemed not to have passed. The only significant change in CFSP has been the appointment of the Secretary-General of the Council as the "Mr. CFSP".[103]

The most significant outcome of the Summit was in terms of the EMU. Nevertheless, the road to single currency generated divisive tensions between France and Germany. Their differences over the fiscal discipline sharpened with Germany's refusal of accede to French demands of including a social clause on investments in jobs and fight against unemployment in the Stability Pact which sets out a framework for macro-economic policy in the EU.[104] The French Socialist Party's pledge to find a solution of the unemployment problems[105] came into direct collision with Germany's resistance to any further public spending that would weaken the Euro's economic criteria.[106]

Germany was determined that a single currency be accompanied by a Stability Pact which would prevent Member States running deficits of more than three per cent of their GDP. French too was sanguine not to proceed with EMU if doing so would mean spending cuts and job losses.[107] In view of the fact that a Franco-German discord carries the potential of destabilising the European integration process, a consensus was reached between the two states in order to prevent the EMU from getting off the track. The deal enabled Germany to retain the Stability Pact without modifying it and as per French demands, the Treaty agreed to include a new chapter on employment strategy and hold a Summit on jobs.[108]

Both France and Germany can legitimately claim victory for their positions in the European Monetary Union. The French claim that the single currency has now a "human face" with a commitment to helping the unemployed, while the Germans can point to a Stability Pact which has been left untouched. On the one hand, this demonstrates the political commitment of both France and Germany to EMU, on the other hand, this has made their divisions more apparent. There are clear indications that the rules for qualifying for the single currency will be interpreted in a loose manner.[109] On balance it could mean that upto 11-13 Member States could belong to the new Euro-zone with the exception being Greece which cannot conceivably quantify the rules. Britain and Denmark have opted out and Sweden announced its will not to join it in the first wave. Once EMU has begun, the politics are likely to change. The fines laid down by governments for excessive deficits will be difficult to implement since they require a QMV in their favour. Meanwhile, the Member States will be under strong pressure to raise public spending notably on pensions while states like France seem likely to find unemployment rising further. Without a strong economic recovery, higher fiscal deficits are in prospect along with an unbalanced fiscal and a monetary policy. This could easily irrate an externally strong but internally weak Euro.[110]

The skirmish over the single currency reveals the continuation of Franco-German struggle over the contours of EMU. While the compromise helps to bury the tensions between the two states, analysts say that the compromise also marks little more than an uneasy truce between two driving forces of EU. The core conflict between the two countries remain unresolved as an economist in Bonn, Adrian Ottrad said, "there is a fundamental conflict between the monetary philosophy of France and Germany".[111] The agreement that sought to strike a compromise between France and Germany also reflects a means of building a convergence from positions that may be diametrically opposed in order to overcome splits between Europe's twin driving forces. This point was best summed up in the words of a Dutch spokesman that the Summit's single biggest success was something that wasn't even on the original agenda and had nothing to do with constitutional reform–healing a Franco-German rift over how of manage a common currency once it arrives.[112] Despite the success in EMU, strains between France and Germany subjected to an exposure during the Summit, signalled increasing French frustration. French Foreign Minister, Hubert Vedrine said, "it is more complicated than it was before to find convergence (between Europe's Member States)". He described French relations with Germany as neither hot nor cold. "The alliance between France and Germany," he said, "had never been pre-established harmony" but "a system for building convergence from positions that may be different". Former President Valery Giscard d'Estaing remarked, "the first time we have witnessed a deterioration in the Franco-German partnership".[113]

Inspite of reaching a compromising position in EMU, doubts about Paris being a 'reliable partner' in EU began to loom in Bonn as Gerhard Schroeder signalled a dramatic shift in alliances arguing that the Franco-German marriage was now over. Instead he argued in favour of a new 'menage a trios' involving Germany, Britain and France.[114]

CONCLUSION

The IGC was taking place at a time when any attempt to restructure institutional arrangements would be under circumstances dominated by internal struggle or adjusted by compromises amongst the Member States. The national differences among the Member States surfaced with Germany's refusal to accept majority-voting in matters relating to immigration controls and asylum.[115] This move marked a shift from Germany's original position of a vanguard of integrating the EU policies on justice and home affairs.[116]

Britain's reservation against the WEU becoming the main arm of European defence and retaining control over its own border and national veto was according to Italian Foreign Minister, Lamberto Dini, a "dampner on the whole treaty negotiations". The Amsterdam Treaty confirms that once again the EU, after trying on many occasions has failed in its attempt to produce an agile, simple text. In the words of Marcelino Oreja:

> The complexity of the different questions, the need to respond to the specific demands of each state and the negotiating technique strictly speaking, resulted in a text that is extraordinarily difficult to understand and to explain to citizens. The hoped-for simplification has been put off till a later date.[117]

The disappointment with the Treaty which emerged from nearly two years of negotiations at the IGC was hinted by President Jacques Santer in his statement when he said, "I would have liked it to have been more adventurous in one or two areas". He also spoke of the "inflation of protocols and declarations. 14 protocols and 46 declarations–a record that adds nothing to the legibility of the treaty".[118]

There was a disparity of judgements amongst the European citizens who qualified the Treaty as either a considerable progress in matters of economic affairs or a resounding failure in matters concerning institutional construction.[119] Belgium, France and Italy noted that the Treaty did not respond to the need reaffirmed by the European Council of Madrid for substantial progress in institutions. These Member States stated the need for institutional reinforcement as indispensable conditions for concluding the first accession negotiations. Admitting that the Summit was "frustrating in relation to our ambitions which remain vast",[120] French Foreign Minster, Hubert Vedrine remarked:

> We have not worked, Italy and ourselves for 40 years to take the risk of this European construction dissolve. We want an institutional reform that puts Europe in a position to decide, to act and to remain strong.[121]

The IGC, 1996 was faced with several interrelated challenges. The key areas dominating the agenda included enlargement, EMU and future budget package. Major issues concerning enlargement included remission of the CAP and Structural Funds, institutional questions, of balancing commonality and diversity in the EU. The outcome of the IGC would appeal to the Eurosceptics, like Britain who claimed it to be "excellent". Germany which had earlier stressed on a 'political union as a precursor to monetary union', abandoned this ambition and instead settled for a reversal of intentions.[122] Perhaps it is the small states, who have so long been the loudest advocates of a quasi-federal Europe, have successfully blocked any development in this direction. They were unwilling to renounce their right to national representation in the Commission whose very *raison d'étre* is to represent the union as a whole, or to accept a redistribution of voting weights that would make the Council more representative of people as opposed to states. The deeply contentions issues concerning CAP and Structural Funds (which has been a constant rift between the richer 'North' and a poorer 'South') too were left to be settled in tandem with the enlargement negotiations. Perhaps the most significant achievement of the Amsterdam Treaty was bringing the EU closer to the citizens, calling for a Social Europe, by incorporating an employment strategy and citizen's rights at the heart of the Union.

NOTES

1. See M. Brenner, "EC-Confidence Lost", *Foreign Policy*, no. 91, Summer 1993, p. 23.
2. Ibid.
3. See, W. Sandholtz, "Choosing Union: Monetary Politics and Maastricht", *International Organisation*, vol. 47, no. 1, Winter 1993, p. 41.

4. EC., Jacques Delors, "The Economic and Political Challenges facing Europe", Speech in the Conference on Economic and Political Perspectives, Copenhagen, 11 April 1996", Speech 96/83, *Press release,* p. 3.
5. For background analysis ad theoretical perspectives on political legitimacy and public opinion see, Daniela Obdradovic, "Political Legitimacy and the EU", *Journal of Common Market Studies,* vol. 34, no. 2, June 1996, pp. 191-216.
6. For instance, in the post Maastricht period, the farmers, fishermen and steel workers saw their respective economic position threatened from new sources. This also holds for a large mass, who for a long time did not show much inclination to embrace their neighbours of the erstwhile communist states.
7. See for e.g., H. Rathinger, "Public attitudes toward European integration in Germany after Maastricht : Inventory and Typology", *Journal of Common Market Studies,* vol. 32, no. 4, December 1994, pp. 525-540.
8. See D. Nuti, "European Community; Responses to the Transition", *Economies of Transition,* vol. 4, no. 2, October 1996, p. 404.
9. Also see EC, *Commission Export for the Reflection Group, IGC, 1996* (Luxembourg: Official Publications of the European Communities, 1995) pp. 3-4
10. See EC, *Background Report, IGC, 1996.* No. B/2/97, London, January 1997.
11. For a detailed and critical analysis on the complications arising in the EU as a result of enlargement see, M. Haynes and K. Pinnock, "Towards a Deeper and Wider EU", *Economic and Political Weekly,* vol. 33, no. 8, 22 February 1998, pp. 415-430.
12. For background details, see, Niels Thygesen, "Towards Monetary Union in Europe", *Journal of Common Market Studies,* vol. 31, no. 4, December 1993, pp. 447-472 and Louis W. Pauly, "Politics of EMU: National Strategies, International Implications", *International Journal,* vol. 47, no. 1, Winter 1991-92, pp. 93-111.
13. EU Commissioner Hans van der Broeck has said that without progress on EMU or on political union, enlargement is unlikely. See, Hans van der Broeck, "Briefing at the European Commission, Representation in the UK, 17 November 1995",

Press Release, Also see, EC, "The Issues as The Amsterdam Summit Approaches", Speech by Padraig Flynn, Commissioner for Employment and Social Affairs, Institute of Economic Affairs, Dublin, 18 April 1997. According to Flynn, IGC is a "window of opportunity through which the EU can pass before it plunges into the EMU".

14. "Multi-speed" denotes common commitments to policies but differing timing of implementation and "variable geometry" refers to the possibility of some countries not participating on the basis of opt-outs in a policy. For a more detailed discussion, see, Helen Wallace, "Flying together in a larger and more diverse EU", (Netherlands Scientific Council : Working Document, W 87, 1995).
15. For a discussion on the institutional challenges that eastward enlargement would entail see, C. Haepfer and R. Rose, "Democracy and Enlarging the EU Eastwards", *Journal of Common Market Studies,* vol. 33, no. 3, September 1995, pp. 427-450. Also see, L. Barber, "Hopes of a Wider Union turn to fear of no Union", *Financial Times,* 9 December 1994 and *Europe Documents,* no. 1879, 14 April 1994.
16. For theoretical perspectives on European integration process see, Richard Muench, "Between Nation-State, Regionalism and World Society", *Journal of Common Market Studies,* vol. 34, no. 3, September 1996, pp. 379-399.
17. See G. Ross, "The Constitution and the Maastricht Treaty: Between Cooperation and Conflict", *German politics,* vol. 3, 1994, pp. 55-68.
18. See Klaus Haensch, "The Relations between the European Parliament and National Parliaments," Speech at European Policy Forum, 23 January 1995, *Europe Documents,* no. 1920, 27 January 1995, p. 6. Haensch stressed the need to develop these relations but rejected a number of proposals which in his opinion would make the system less transparent and more complicated.
19. Alan Osborn, "Like no other Parliament on Earth" and L. Barber, "European Parliament: A power to be reckoned with", *Europe,* April 1996, pp. 20-21.
20. EC, n. 9, pp. 28-31.
21. *The Economist* (London), 13 May 1995.
22. See, *The Economist,* 30 March 1996, p. 49, Also, Lionel Barber, "IGC: What it means?", *Europe,* March 1996, p. 23.
23. The introduction of Qualified-Majority-Voting in the Coun-

cil of Ministers in matters relating to the internal market as a result of reforms of the Single European Act reduced the capacity of smaller members to block certain measures which are more often pushed by the big members. See, A. Moravcsik, "Negotiating the SEA: National Interests and Conventional Statecraft in the EC", *International Organisation,* vol. 45, no. 1 Winter 1991, pp. 19-56.

24. For views on EU institutions and IGC, 1996, see, Errkki Likkanen, "The Challenges of the IGC", Speech at the Nordic Council Conference on European Questions, Copenhagen, 4 March 1996, *Press Release.*
25. To understand how individual Member States can safeguard their influence in a larger EU, see. Torsten Peters, "Quantifying Influence in the EU", *Aussen Politik,* vol. 47, no. 2, 1996, pp. 117-126.
26. *The Economist,* 30 March 1996, pp. 49-50.
27. It was stated by Klaus Haensch, President of the European Parliament that "what EU needs is more parliamentary democracy, rather than greater powers". This implies that the Parliament must have a share in the decision-making along with the Council. All European decisions must have a two-fold legitimacy and the Parliament should not be the sole decision-making authority. See Klaus Haensch, "The EU needs more Democracy", DG-Information Culture and Audio Visual, *Europe* (Monthly Newsletter), November-December 1994.
28. *The Economist* (London), 20 May 1995, p. 50.
29. See Barber, n. 22, pp. 23-24.
30. EC, 1996 IGC: *Reflection Group Report and other references for Documentary Purposes,* (Brussels; General Secretariat of Council of EU, December 1995).
31. See for background details, David Owen, *Balkan Odyssey,* (New York: Harvest, 1995).
32. Examples of this are the Contact Group for Bosnia, preparations by the larger EU states for the CSCE Summit in Budapest on 5-6 December 1994, Greece's unilateral embargo on Macedonia and the incoordinated French initiative in Rwanda.
33. For details on problems concerning CFSP budget see *Agence Europe,* no. 6345, 27 October 1994.
34. Goals defined by the European Council in IGC, *Europe-Hebdo Overseas Selection,* no. 771, 2 April 1996, pp. 2-3.

35. See Jacques Santer, "The EU's Security and Defence Policy", *NATO Review,* vol. 6, no. 43, November 1995, pp. 3-9.
36. *Europe-Hebdo Overseas Selection,* no. 768, 11 March 1996.
37. EC, "Commission presents opinion on IGC", *Press Release,* Brussels, IP/96/179, 28 February 1996.
38. EC, *Turin European Council Presidency Conclusion,* 29 March 1996.
39. EC, "Commission sets out its stall for the IGC", *Europe,* no. 157, May-June, 1995, pp. 38-39.
40. Franco-German relations appeared to be unpredictable with the coming to the power of President Jacques Chirac, especially in matters relating to the EMU and Germany's concept of a federal Europe. See *The Economist* (London), 27 May 1995, pp. 51-52.
41. EC, "1996 IGC: Reflection Group Report and other reference for Documentary Purposes", *General Secretariat of the Council,* Brussels, December 1995.
42. See L. Barber, "Drive for radical EU reforms falters", *Financial Times,* 5 November 1995.
43. See for background, Gary Geipel, "Germany and the Burden of Choice", *Current History,* vol. 94, no. 595, November 1995, p. 380.
44. Refer footnote no. 40. Also see, CIRAC-DFI-DGAP-IFRI (ed.), *Handeln fuer Europa: Deutsch-franzoesisch zusammenarbeit in einer veranderten Welt* (Opladen: Leske and Budrich, 1995).
45. See, EC, *Reflection Group's Report, Messina 2 June 1995",* SN 520/95 (Reflex 21), Brussels, 5 December 1995.
46. Interview of Helmut Kohl. *Time,* 30 September 1996, p. 41.
47. Werner Hoyer, "Perspektiven fuer die Regierungskonferenz 1996 und die europapolitische Agenda" *Integration,* vol. 4, April 1997, pp. 189-196.
48. Matt Marshall, "German Ministers reject EU majority voting", *The Wall Street Journal,* 30 March 1996.
49. *Der Spiegel,* 30 March 1996, p. 55.
50. Carlo Masala, "Institutional Reform of the EU", *Aussen Politik,* vol. 48, no. 3, 3rd Quarterly 1997, p. 230.
51. Cf. Joint letter by Klaus Kinkel to Italian Foreign Minister Lamberto Dini, *Frankfurter Allgemeine Zeitung,* 27 February 1997.
52. Flexibility should be an option when other options fail in order to preserve the *acquis communautaire.* See W. Hoyer, *Weekly Information Service,* no. 8, 26 March 1996, pp. 18-19.

53. See, Christian Deubner, *Deutsche Europa Politik, Von Maastricht nach Kern Europa* (Baden-Baden: Nomos, 1995). Also see A. Shrivastava, "Uncertain future for the hard-core", *The Wall Street Journal,* 8 December 1995.
54. For text see, "Agence Europe", *Europe Documents,* no. 1895/96, 7 September 1994.
55. Cf. lan Traynor, "Leading Europe's fast track", *The Guardian,* 21 September 1996.
56. See B. Crawford, "German Foreign Policy and EPC: The Diplomatic Recognition of Croatia in 1991", *German Politics and Society,* vol. 13, Summer 1995, pp. 1-34.
57. *Europe Hebdo Overseas Selection,* no. 732, 13 June 1996.
58. Ibid, no. 792, 24 September 1996.
59. L. Barber, "Germany softens stance on EMU," *Financial Times,* 7 April 1997.
60. Tim Jones, "Kohl talks tough on Stability Pact goals", *European Voice,* 19 September 1996.
61. Imre Karacs, "Briton smoothes way for Kohl". *The Independent,* 7 December 1996.
62. Peter Norman, "Bonn proposes lean agenda for IGC", *Financial Times,* 27 March 1996.
63. Phillipe Moreau Defarges, "La France, province de l'union europeene", *Politique Etrangere,* vol. 1, 1996, pp. 37-48.
64. It is still unclear between Germany and France whether the second majority on the basis of Council voting with weighed votes should relate to the population or the level of national Gross Domestic Product.
65. Joint. Communique by Jacques Chirac and Helmut Kohl in 6 December 1995 in Europaeisches Parliament (ed.), *Weissbuch zur Regierungskonferenz.* vol. II, Brussels, 1996, p. 95.
66. Andrew Jack, "France affirms its belief in a two-speed EU", *Financial Times,* 14 March 1995.
67. Paul Webster, "France threatens to isolate Britain in two-tier Europe" *The Guardian,* 14 March 1996.
68. Mary Dejevsky, "France shifts EU stance closer to UK", *The Independent,* 14 March 1996.
69. Ben Macintyre, "Paris puts limit on power of Brussels", The *Times,* 14 March 1996. Also see *The Economist,* 14 January 1995, p. 47 for former Prime Minister Giscard d' Estaing's references to a Europe of concentric circles around a 'European space of nation-states'.
70. Dejevsky, n. 68.

71. *Europe-Hebdo Overseas Selection,* No. 792, 24 September 1996.
72. See, *The Economist,* 11 May 1994, p. 53.
73. *Europe-Hebdo Overseas Selection,* No. 813, 24 February 1997.
74. *The Economist,* 20 January 1996, also see, Adam Zagorin, "The Big Bad Bundesbank" *Time,* 28 September 1992, pp. 22-23.
75. *The Economist,* 15 July 1995. France put emphasis on jobs in a memorandum of EU members preparing to make employment its determining criteria. *Financial Times,* 28 March 1996.
76. David Buchan, "Europe at heart of French politics", *Financial Times,* 16 June 1997.
77. Masala, n. 50.
78. Speech by British Foreign Secretary, M. Rifkind to Konrad Adenauer Foundation, Sant Augustin, 19 December 1997 reproduced in *International Politik,* 1997, pp. 120-124.
79. See, J. Laughland, "Britain still lacks a policy on Europe", *The Wall Street Journal,* 14 March 1996.
80. *Europe-Hebdo Overseas Selection,* No. 748, 23 October 1998, p. 11
81. Bruce Johnston & C. Lockwood, "Italians put on a show of Euro-enthusiasm", *The Daily Telegraph,* 27 March 1996.
82. Cf. Webster, n. 67.
83. For background see, EC, "Commission's opinion on the Southern Enlargement of the EC", *Bulletin of the European Communities* (Luxembourg : Office for the Official Publications of the EC, 1978) Supplement 1, p. 55.
84. John Hooper, "South glimpses hidden costs of EU benefits", *The Guardian,* 28 March 1996.
85. *Europe-Hebdo Overseas Selection,* no. 748, 23 October 1995.
86. Hooper, n. 84.
87. *Europe-Hebdo Overseas Selection,* no. 731, *7 June 1995.*
88. Greg Mclvor, "Europe's Scandinavian new dawn fades", *The Guardian,* 27 March 1996.
89. Hugh Carnegie, "Pressure to remove IGC block", *Financial Times,* 14 March 1996.
90. Cf. A.E. Moute and P. Buonadonna, "France sets the IGC pace", *The European,* 19 September 1996.
91. Neil Buckley, "Pressure to remove IGC Block", *Financial Times,* 14 March 1996.
92. See, Carnegie, n. 89.
93. Michael Hindley, "Back to nation-state", *Frontline,* 19 April 1996.
94. *The Economist,* 16 June 1997.
95. Editorial, "Too many Maastrichts", *Financial Times,* 7 October

1996.

96. The Italian doctrine of a "minimum threshold" outlined by the Foreign Minister to the European Parliamentary Committee on Institutional Affairs gained considerable importance due to the support of Parliament and certain other Member States, like Belgium. See *Europe-Hebdo Overseas Selection,* no. 828, 9 June 1997.
97. Treaty provisions cited from EC, Treaty *of Amsterdam* (Luxembourg: Official Publications of the EC, 1997) 144 p. Also EC, *Presidency Conclusions of Amsterdam European Council, 16-17 June 1997, Brussels,* DOC/97/2, 18 June 1997,
98. For a critical assessment see *Europe-Hebdo Overseas Selection,* no. 831, 1 July 1997.
99. Lionel Barber, "Enlargement may test EU's treaty", *Financial Times,* 19 June 1997.
100. Mark Brennock, "Conference fails to retain agreement on essential reforms of institution", *The Irish Times,* 19 June 1997.
101. Daniel Michaels, "EU Leaders Scale down Expectations". *The Wall Street Journal,* 18 June 1997.
102. Ibid.
103. Patrick Smyth, "Struggling to achieve foothold on the world's political stage", *Irish Times,* 12 June 1997.
104. See for comments on Stability Pact, *Europe-Hebdo Overseas Selection,* No. 829, 17 June 1997. Also J. Nundy, "Kohl and Chirac still divided on Stability Pact", *The Daily Telegraph,* 14 June 1997.
105. French Prime Minister, Lionel Jospin was elected on a plea to create 700,000 jobs in France and to rebalance the single currency rules in order to promote greater emphasis on 'Social Europe' See Sarah Helm, "Germany and France settle row over jobs", *The Independent,* 16 June 1997.
106. Germany believes that interest rates, exchange rates, fiscal policies do not cause unemployment. These macro-economic policies can do nothing to reduce unemployment, they should be devoted entirely to keeping inflation under control. That is why, to Germany, the Stability Pact shculd not contain any references to employment.
107. John Lichfield, "France and Germany divided on jobs," *The Independent,* 14 June 1997.
108. Charles Bremner, "Job pact buries Franco-German monetary row", *The Times,* 17 June 1997. Critics point out that employment issues came at a time when the EU Member

States were grappling with 18 million jobless and growing scepticism about the virtues of the political and economic integration. Financial analysts say simply aiming to meet a strict monetary criteria cannot ensure the success of EMU. It is not the financial markets that is the best barometer for EMU but the people whose anxiety are to be addressed. See, *The Wall Street Journal*, 17 June 1997.

109. Under strict interpretation of the rules, countries must have low inflation and interest rates and budget deficit of 3 per cent or less and debt ratios falling to 60 per cent. However, the French Finance Minister insist that these figures be seen as trends and not targets as the stated, "countries must come as close as three per cent....even if they have not achieved it". Germany, too, has weakened its earlier stance on EMU and the Dublin Summit. See, *Irish times*, 16 June 1997.
110. Editorial, *Financial Times*, 17 June 1997.
111. Cf. Brian Coleman, "Victory to both sides on EMU may spell trouble down the road", *The Wall Street Journal*, 17 June 1997.
112. Editorial, *The Wall Street Journal*, 19 June 1977.
113. Sussanah Herbert, "The French show their frustration", *The Daily Telegraph*, 18 June 1997.
114. Anthony Bevins, "A Triple Alliance for European Jobs", *The Independent*, 17 June 1997.
115. To Edmund Stoiber, Minister CDU, the Bavarian Germans would not accept a revised version of the TEU which allows refugees to move from one EU Member State to another. See, Denis Staunton, "Furious EU heads cave in to Kohl's insistence on immigration control", *Irish Times*, 18 June 1997.
116. Owing to pressures from the 16 *Laender* which share responsibility for asylum seekers, Chancellor Kohl had to insist on retaining the veto. Statistics reveal Germany accepted more than half of EU's asylum seekers in 1985.
117. *Europe-Hebdo Overseas Selection*, no. 832, 7 July 1997, p. 3.
118. Ibid.
119. *Europe-Hebdo Overseas Selection*, no. 831, 1 July 1997, p. 3.
120. Toby Helm, "A few small steps but no great leap for federalists", *The Daily Telegraph*, 19 June 1997.
121. *Europe-Hebdo Overseas Selection*, no. 839, 2 September 1997, p. 5.
122. Editorial, *Financial Times*, 19 June 1997.

Chapter VI

Conclusion

The Member States of the European Union (EU) are the key actors who determine the shape and the pace of integration through a bargaining process designed to serve national objectives and interests. Stanley Hoffman and Robert Keohane argue that beyond these inter-state bargains, it is domestic politics and constraints of international institutions, which explain an intergovernmental approach.[1] Andrew Moravcsik, on the other hand, offers a "liberal intergovernmentalist approach that includes the theory of national preference formation to provide a theoretical explanation for the bargains reached in the inter-governmentalist process."[2] France and Germany are the two most powerful Member States of the EU who have greatly influenced the shape and direction of the European integration. The relationship between these two countries has not always been harmonious but they were able to solve their differences through integrational cooperation that was built on a larger balance of power framework. The carefully negotiated bargains and compromise between these two governments were intended to protect each country's perceived national interest and had profoundly affected the process of European integration. Decisions were considerably facilitated by a close personal relationship between the leaders of the two countries.

In the 1950s Germany and France struck a bargain to support the European Coal and Steel Community (ECSC) which enabled France to gain control over Germany's coal and steel and Germany gained greater international acceptance by entering into an economic and political relationship with France. With the signing of the Treaty of Rome in 1957, France agreed to open her markets to German industry in exchange for the Common Agricultural Policy (CAP), which would provide subsidies for French agricultural products. The 1970s witnessed additional ups and downs in the Franco-German relationship as France agreed to British membership on the one hand, but, on the other hand, was concerned with Germany's *Ostpolitik.* However, in 1978 Chancellor Helmut Schmidt and President Giscard d'Estaing's endeavours led to a major initiative towards European Monetary Union. The European Monetary System (EMS) protected the competitiveness of the German products in the European Community (EC) market and President Giscard imposed a politically difficult monetary discipline on the French economy, which allowed France to resist Germany's economic domination. In the early 1980s, the Franco-German relationship was plagued by disputes over deployment of NATO missiles in Germany, the British contribution to the budget and French reluctance to endorse Spanish and Portuguese membership. By 1985, President Francois Mitterrand and Chancellor Helmut Kohl reinvigorated the partnership by signing the Single European Act. In President Mitterrand's view, France would be strengthened by building a strong Europe in which Germany would be closely bound, while for Germany, the Single European Act would help German industry and reassure France of Germany's continuing commitment to West Europe. The unification of Germany in 1989-1990 upset the entente between Bonn and Paris. There were growing strains in the relation. In the past, they were held together by a common threat—the Soviet empire, though it had a delicate equilibrium. With the unification of Germany, the fragile balance saw some shifts in the Franco-German relations. A more secure Germany was facing a France that was less secure in its ability to balance Germany within Europe.[3] Accepting the unification as a *fait accompli,* France and European support for German unification was informally traded for German acceptance of a deepening of the European integration process.[4] The German government also recognized the need for integration to reassure its neighbours that the reemergence of an assertive Germany was not imminent. The Maastricht Treaty came as a response to the concerns of both the countries. The agreement on monetary union and common defence policy during the Maastricht Treaty negotiations involved a concession and a bargain between France and Germany. The bargain led to German sacrifice of monetary sovereignty for French sacrifice of military sovereignty. In the 1990s, institutional issue, such as the accession negotiations with Sweden, Finland and Austria, the voting reform in the Council of Ministers, choosing a new President to the Commission, the General Agreement on Tariffs and Trade (GATT) negotiations and the currency crisis in the Exchange Rate Mechanism (ERM) dominated the agenda where Franco-German cooperation and clout remained immitable. Even in post-Maastricht Europe, Franco-German relations remain at the core and the shape of the EU continues to bear the imprint of bargains and trade-offs rooted in perceptions of national interest. What was more important to the final agreements was the value each country assigned to the outcomes. Thus, Germany found itself in a weaker bargaining position vis-a-vis French struggle in the GATT negotiations over agriculture. In contrast, the German Bundesbank's decision to maintain higher interest rates despite French objections, reflected both the high value it placed on fighting inflation and its ability to assert its greater economic power. The outcomes of specific bargains reached in 1993-94 by the French and German governments were often governed by domestic politics. However, the level of domestic politics is also contingent on the nature of the issue. In the GATT negotiations, for instance, the French farmers and German industries played an important role in shaping their governments' bargaining positions. This was due to the fact that these groups had a direct interest in the outcome of the negotiations. In the currency crisis, on the other hand, domestic politics was more diffused and less constraining.[5] Franco-German agreements were essential but not always sufficient to solve EU conflicts, as was during the British veto of Belgium's Jean-Luc Dehaene for President of the Commission which forced France and Germany to change a previously agreed upon bargain.[6]

Towards the late 1990s the Franco-German relationship underwent strains in their alliance. Recent Franco-German skirmishes over the budgetary issues (mostly related to CAP) and the Economic Monetary Union (during the 1996 Intergovernmental Conference) have led critics to term the relationship as an 'uneasy-truce'.[7] The EU budget continues to be a sensitive issue for Germany, which is a net contributor and the CAP takes more than half of the budget. In 1998, Chancellor Gerhard Schroeder suggested the Member States could begin paying from their national budgets part of the expenditure related to direct agricultural income subsidies. In doing so, Schroeder attacked the principle-defended by France—that the cost of the CAP are to be financed entirely from the EU budget. In response, President Chirac announced his reluctance in reducing the German contribution as this would mean the French contribution would have to be increased.[8] The growing strains in the Franco-German relation have been attributed to the changes in their respective governments (especially in Germany, which has a Chancellor belonging to the post-war generation). Following this, there has been a shift from the traditional patterns of German foreign policy[9] and therefore a subsequent change in the dimension of Franco-German relationship.[10]

In the second half of the 1990s the EU faced a number of major inter-related challenges. The key areas dominating the agenda included the EU budget, enlargement and EMU. Major issues concerning enlargement include the revision of the CAP, Structural Funds, the institutional issues regarding the structure of a EU of 20-25 or more Member States, including the questions of commonality and diversity with the growing heterogeneity within the EU.

The collapse of communism and the dissolution and the

Eastern bloc have altered the basic parameters of European integration. This made the Europeans aware of priorities which have become increasingly divergent. The key question in the early 1990's was whether or not the EC could amass sufficient political and economic capacity to tackle the multiple challenges facing it. The Maastricht Treaty was intended to capitalize upon the triumph of the Single Market by opening the way to a political union that would complement the economic union. Though the Treaty on European Union (TEU) propelled of take the EC to a Union, yet it resulted in an elaborate compromise between the major Member States. The only ambitious design was to build a federal Europe with a Common Foreign and Security Policy (CFSP) and it lent a thrust to EMU through three stages, which would culminate to a Single Currency. The Treaty, instead of resolving, intensified the debate between the federalists and the intergovernmentalists. The opt-outs which Britain and Denmark pushed for during the Treaty negotiations and the expected inability of some of the Member States to meet the convergence criteria signalled the possibility of a Europe of different speeds. The Treaty also revealed the divergence between the views of the leaders and the masses. The narrowness of French approval of the Treaty reinforced the belief that before taking bold integrationist leaps, it would be essential to first seek the voter's mandate.[11] Mounting scepticism about the Treaty owed much to the economic downturn in the early 1990s. The political fall-out of the elections in France, Germany, UK and Italy in 1993-94 revealed the disillusionment of the people and the fragility of the Maastricht design. This also led to fractious disputes over how to fulfil the collective needs to assist the nascent democracies of the Central and East European Countries (CEECs). The strains placed on the structure of an integrated West European economy highlighted both the strength of national and parochial interests and the weaknesses of both governments. On the one hand, political elites viewed the supranational organisation as a necessary step towards political union, while the citizens on the other hand, were concerned with issues of democratic deficit and lack of transparency in the EU. It is probably due to this realisation that bringing the EU closer to the citizens and building a 'common European identity' has become a prime objective in the EU agenda. The EU's credibility as model of peace, security and prosperity drew the attention of the East European countries whose aspirations to belong to this order brought in a new challenge of enlargement at a time when the EU was concentrating on its internal integration. The enormity of problems at its own backyard made the EU deal with the challenge of 'widening' with few hesitations and indecision. In the 1990s membership application came from the CEEC, Cyprus, Malta, as well as Russia and the Baltic States. The challenge of enlargement not only raised issues but also created conditions in which their resolution became difficult. As and when the EU expands its membership to new states, conflicting interests among the Member States as well as between the Member States and the applicant states will become more apparent. Large scale flows of migration from the new eastern members to the EU, due to wage differentials could be a problem in this context. The EU budget would increase substantially if certain policies like the CAP is not reformed. The new members would be net recipients of the budget and there could be a wide discrepancy between the net recipients and the conributors. The old Member States benefitting from the Structural Fund will lose transfers as the thresholds will increase with the entry of poorer regions into the EU.[12] The eastward enlargement of the EU will make the CAP more market sensitive. Extending the CAP in its present form to the acceding countries would create serious difficulties. This would entail a direct budgetary change estimated around 11 billion ECU per year, with direct payment to farmers representing close to two-thirds of this sum. Any reform of the CAP would inevitably be subject to resistance from France and the UK.[13]

Any widening of the EU would imply a restructuring of the EU institutions. The existing institutional structure of the

EU were designed for an EU of Six and then accommodated to an EU of Twelve. Subsequent enlargement of the EU to 20-25 Member states would imply an 'external shock', which would carry the risk of institutional paralysis. Without changes in the composition and working methods of the Commission, the Council, the Parliament, the increase in membership threatens to undermine the decision-making capacity of the main EU bodies. Any politics of institutional reforms would be marked by the struggle between those Member States who would fear a dilution of power and status especially in matters which affect the distribution of power among the big and small Member States.

Enlargement would also change the EU's geopolitical situation by extending its borders in Eastern and South-Eastern Europe. Membership for Hungary and the South-East European candidates, like Romania and Bulgaria, would make Serbia confront it with minority problems including those of the ethnic Hungarians in Romania, Serbia and Slovakia.[14] Bilateral disputes could, therefore, burden the EU's cohesion and its CFSP. An enlarged EU would also be more heterogeneous in its foreign and security interests and perceptions.[15]

Extending the EU eastwards would shift its political and economic weight to Germany. This could, in the perceptions of countries like France, give rise to problems in the 'balance of the European architecture'.[16] Fears of being marginalised by Germany has made France envisage a 'Mediterranean-Latin arc' to maintain an appropriate balance in the geographical commitment. France has urged the necessity to promote a Euro-Mediterranean zone through trade concessions and aid from the EU.[17] Israel, Morocco and Tunisia have already signed association agreements with the EU. It remains to be seen to what extent these countries would be integrated in the EU' to which it has its (geographical) proximity but no great affinity.'[18]

Although the Luxembourg Council in December 1997 clearly proposed enlargement negotiations with five CEEC (Poland, Hungary, Czech Republic, Slovakia and Estonia) and

Cyprus, yet very little progress was made on the issues of internal policy reform. This went against the thrust of the Commission's *Agenda 2000* strategy, where the selection of candidates was tied to agreement on overall guidelines for the future of CAP and EU finances. Those Member States which had a high stake in maintaining existing arrangements for the CAP opposed the CAP guidelines, while the net recipients of EU cohesion funds resisted proposals which would reduce their benefits (Spain, Portugal, Greece, Ireland). In addition, Germany, Sweden and Austria, who are strong advocates of EU's enlargement voiced their opposition to any increase in their budget contribution.[19]

The EU's economic weight coupled with the end of the Cold War and the emergence of new conflicts in Europe made it vital to develop a foreign and security policy. The Maastricht Treaty gave a new dimension to European political co-operation by defining it as a Common Foreign and Security Policy (CFSP) as one of the three pillars of the EU. Eight years after the Maastricht Treaty, the performance of CFSP has not been very promising. The Yugoslav crisis demonstrated that decisive conflict-resolution activities have not been achieved by CFSP. One prime reason is that the CFSP often duplicates functions better accomplished by NATO, the United States (US) or the United Nations.[20] The CFSP is an intergovernmental mechanism controlled by the governments of the Member States in the European Council and the Council of Ministers. The Commission only has the right to propose initiatives to the Council in CFSP matters and decisions on CFSP are based on unanimity, while operational implementation requires a majority-voting. Therefore the coordination of national interests become important to avoid a veto. This often leads to decisions based on the lowest common denominator. The performance of CFSP appears disappointing especially in view of the expectations created by the Maastricht Treaty declarations. The reasons for the weak functioning of CFSP can be traced to three factors, first, national interests of the main EU Member States are not unanimous on how "common" a foreign and security policy should be. Germany is the strongest advocate of a Community approach toward CFSP while France and Britain are reluctant to give up their control over foreign and security matters. Moreover there is a lack of 'political will' to act decisively as a Union and this reduces the element of "collectivity" in EU foreign policy. Due to divergent national interests among some Member States (like Greece) to cooperate in an all-encompassing and uniform CFSP, there has been an existence of foreign policy 'sub-systems' within the EU. Given an increased heterogeneity in the EU with future enlargements, a "coregroup CFSP" seems to be a possible option. This would give impetus to the 'variable-geometry' pattern or a EU of 'multi-speed'. A second reason for the weakness of CFSP is a lack of strategic clarity of common interests and precise goals that could prevail over specific national attitudes. The third factor is related to institutional problems concerning budgetary issues and lack of a firm legal base.

The Maastricht Treaty also declared the Western European Union (WEU) as the defence arm of the EU. The weakness of the WEU has led to arguments in favour of strengthening a European Security and Defence Identity (ESDI) by a military capacity to be built within the framework of the WEU.[21] One of the basic tenets of European security has been its links with the United States. The relevant question today is whether the United States still continues to remain a formidable factor for European security. Nato's role in the Yugoslav conflict and the involvement of the United States re-emphasised the importance of the US in the security policy of the EU.

With the end of the Cold War, European security perceptions have undergone significant change. The political and economic instability in the erst-while Iron Curtain countries, Russia's political and economic instability and the domestic cleavages as a result of socio-economic disparities in the countries of Northern Africa, imply that these challenges need not be addressed by military means. Moreover, with future enlargements of the EU, internal divergences will probably become more accentuated with diverse national interests and distributional disputes which have given a multifaceted approach to European security which can be addressed by non-military means, through viable socio-economic and foreign policies.[22]

EU's endeavours to adapt to post-Cold War challenges and at the same time seek solutions to the unsettled issues that the Maastricht Treaty failed to resolve, led to the which Intergovernmental Conference in 1996 which culminated with the Amsterdam Council Summit in June 1998. The Amsterdam Treaty did not mark a watershed in the history of European integration for the simple reason that despite setting very high objectives, it did not achieve any major goals. Perhaps the•most important issues obtained were—the Community was assigned massive powers over immigration and asylum policies, the European Parliament won new powers of co-decision and a chapter on employment was also incorporated in the Treaty. There were three core changes, which were sought but there was a virtual failure on all three. The IGC witnessed squabbles amongst the Member States over the introduction of Qualified Majority Voting (QMV) and reducing votes to make decision-making swifter. There was partial introduction of QMV in foreign policy matters although with the retention of the 'emergency brake' and the possibility of 'constructive abstention'. In the most sensitive argument of the Summit, the smaller states resisted pressure from Great Britain, Germany and France to change the EU voting rules and the size of the Commission. The most significant outcome of the Summit was in terms of the EMU. Although originally not a part of the IGC agenda, the EMU had a strong background presence. The road to single currency went through divisive tensions between France and Germany over their respective fiscal discipline. Inspite of reaching a convergence from diametrically opposite positions, there are clear indications that the rules to qualify for the single currency will be interpreted in a loose manner, with perhaps 11 to 13 Member States belonging to the new Euro-zone. Once EMU begins, the politics are likely to change. In this aspect, the EU will have an inner-core and an outer-core, with the outer-core reflecting in part a "multi-speed EU" (with some countries wishing to join once ready) and in part a "variable geometry" (with some countries exercising their opt-out rights).[23] Nevertheless, it is generally believed that the EMU would enhance the international role of EU and strengthen European Political Union.[24]

The fact that the Treaty failed to reach an agreement on the most vital agendas—reform of institutions gave rise to doubts to the second group of candidate countries that they might not be accommodated in the EU. In view of this, it remains unclear whether inviting new members into an unreformed EU would be to invite paralysis of function.

The IGC took place under circumstances which were dominated by internal struggle or adjusted by compromise among the Member States. The fact that national interests still dominate all attempts at "community building" was evident from Germany's refusal to accept majority-voting and Britain's reservations against the WEU becoming the defence arm of the EU. The Treaty was categorized either as a leap forward in matters of economic affairs or a resounding failure in matters concerning institutional construction.[25] The contentious issues concerning CAP and Structural Funds have not been settled. The failure of the Treaty to address questions that are likely to arise with subsequent enlargement leaves many of the enlargement-related issues still unresolved. In an expanded EU, the problem of achieving an appropriate balance between 'commonality' and 'flexibility' is still unclear. The EU has already embarked on a number of actions concerning future enlargement and it has also acknowledged the need to address the issues of Structural Funds and the CAP, but balancing in the case of Structural Funds, the varying interests of the Southern and the potential East European Member States continue to pose a problem. The lack of progress on institutional reform highlighted the inherent tension between maintaining the present system of governance and extending it to the east. The IGC was deliberately insulated from the politics of enlargement and internal adjustments. States like France and Germany feared that issue linkage could see trade-offs between institutional change and reform of CAP. It was precisely in order to avoid such trade-offs that the IGC did not discuss policy reforms.[26]

Against the backdrop of prevailing diversity and heterogeneity and given the degree of integration already reached after Amsterdam, each step towards deepening is actually a step towards differentiation. The debate about how to reconcile and manage heterogeneity within the EU-with a view to the dual challenge of "deepening" and "widening" traces its lineage to the seventies with the publication of the Tindemans Report in 1975.[27] Until the early 1990, it became a part of the European political debate only after the famous Schaeuble-Lamers document of 1994.[28] It gave rise to an avalanche of new ideas and concepts about EU going "multi-speed" or "two-tier", "multi-track", or "a la carte" or "variable geometry", whether it should be built around a "hard-core", or take the form of "concentric circles".[29]

Even before enlargement, the EU is not a homogeneous area for integration.[30] Differentiation would be further intensified by EU enlargement, economic divergence, and variable membership of and participation in regimes or groups outside the EU. In view of this, the Amsterdam Treaty included a chapter on "flexibility" as the only way out of the institutional paralysis a single government proved able to generate.

The present institutional provisions, given the lack of convergence on crucial political issues (mainly on CFSP) along with different geopolitical priorities and opt-outs from the EMU, the form of 'enhanced cooperation' or the application of 'flexibility clause' might help overcome some obstacles. Yet, it should be handled with delicacy, on a case-by-case basis.[31] Given the notion that 'enhanced cooperation' might facilitate the absorption of new members, it cannot be applied to the *acquis communautaire* which is the essence of any accession negotiation.[32]

The original aim of the six founding Member States of

the EC was to create a customs union and free trade between them, which would act as an effective antidote to nationalism. As mutual interdependence increased, the process of integration became irreversible—pursuing national interest within a collective framework. European Union with its increased Member States and a long queue of applicant countries waiting in the wings, has come a long way. However, it still has to create a collective unit with a common identity out of an enormous diversity of national and regional collectivities and identities.[33] As Jean Monnet wrote, "the European Community is part of and responds to the changing world order,.... its final destination is not known."[34] The process of EU integration strongly reveals that with every aspect of political and economic development and forging common policies, it is directly affected by inter-governmentalist sensitivities of the Member States, revolving around the Franco-German core. It is this on-going debate between supranational and inter-governmental interest that will determine the pace of integration and the future architecture of the EU.

NOTES

1. See, S. Hoffman and R. Keohane (ed.), *The New European Community: Decision-Making and Institutional Change* (Boulder: Westview, 1991).
2. See, Andrew Moravcsik, "Preferences and Power in the EC: A Liberal Intergovernmentalist Approach", *Journal of Common Market Studies,* vol. 31, no. 4, December 1993, pp. 473-524.
3. Dominique Moisi and M. Mertes, "Europe's Map, Compass and Horizon", *Foreign Affairs,* vol. 74, no. 1, January-February 1995, p. 132.
4. Cf. Pia Christina Wood, "The Franco-German Relationship in the Post-Maastricht Era", in Carolyn Rhodes and Sonia Mazey (ed.), *The State of the European Union* (Boulder: Lynne Rienner, 1998) pp. 221-243.
5. Wood, no. 4, p. 225.
6. During the Franco-German Summit in Mulhouse in May 1994, Mitterrand and Kohl agreed to support Belgian Prime

Minister Jean-Luc Dehaene but this was objected by the UK and the Netherlands. Britain, in fact vetoed the candidacy at the Corfu Summit. Since this was subject to unanimity rule, the British threat of non-agreement brought France and Germany in the bargaining table and the best 'compromising' candidate, Jaques Santer who was approved by all, was selected.

7. Interview with Dr. Ulrika Guerot, former Member of Christian Democratic Union (CDU) Parliamentary Group, Haus der Deutschen Wirtschaft, Berlin, 1 December 1999 and Dr. Thomas Schiller, Spokesman, Office of Karl Lamers, CDU, Berlin, 30 November 1999.
8. Cf. Y. Devuyst, "The Community Method after Amsterdam", *Journal of Common Market Studies,* vol. 37, no. 1, March 1999, p. 112. Also interview with Dr. Chrisoph Jessen, Head of Second Division in the Directorate of Foreign Affairs, Foreign Office, Berlin, 30 November 1999.
9. Interview with Dr. Carlos Jahnsen, European Affairs Advisor, Social Democratic Party (Germany), Berlin, 2 December 1999. The CDU/CSU has been particularly critical of this and also argue that there has been a change in the momentum in the Franco-German relation under the Schroeder government. Interview with Dr. Ulrika Guerot, Haus der Deutschen Wirtschaft, Berlin, 1 December 1999.
10. Interview with Hubert Knirsch, Foreign Affairs Directorate, Chancellor's Office, Berlin, 1 December 1999.
11. See David Buchan, *Europe: The Strange Superpower* (Dartmouth: Aldershot, 1990) p. 173.
12. See, M. Dauderstaedt, "European and German Interests in Central and Eastern Europe compared to the Mediterranean" in Harmut Elsenhans (ed.), *A Balanced European Architecture* (Paris: Publisud, 1999).
13. EC, "Widening and Deepening of the EU: Economic and Political Challenges", Address by M.B. McGeever, Ambassador, Head of the Delegation of the European Commission in India, *Europe Forum,* JNU, New Delhi, 24 February 1998, p.8.
14. See, Moise and Mertes, n. 3, p. 127.
15. Cf. McGeever, n. 13, p. 13.
16. Elsenhans (ed.), n. 12, 224 pp.
17. *Financial Times,* 12 December 1994.
18. See, Buchan, n. 11, p. 90.

19. L. Friss and Anna Murphy, "The EU and the CEEC : Governance and Boundaries", *Journal of Common Market Studies,* vol. 37, n. 2, June 1999, p. 226.
20. Stefan A. Schirm, "Europe's Common Foreign and Security Policy: The Politics of Necessity, Viability and Adequacy", in Carolyn Rhodes (ed.), *The EU in the World Community* (Boulder: Lynne Rienner, 1998).
21. See, for background, *Financial Times* (London), 14 December 1994.
22. See, Schirm, n. 20, pp. 74-80.
23. See, K. Hughes, "The 1996 IGC and EU Enlargement", *International Affairs,* vol. 72, no. 1, January 1996, p. 3
24. Interviews with Prof. Michael Kreile, Humboldt Universitaet, Berlin, 15 November 1999 and Christian Sterzing, Member of the Bundestag and European Policy Spokesman, The Green Party (Germany), Berlin, 29 November 1999.
25. *Europe-Hebdo Overseas Selection,* no. 832, 7 July 1997, p. 3.
26. See, Friss and Murphy, n. 19, p. 224.
27. See, L. Tindemans, "EU: Report to the European Council", *Bulletin of the EC,* (Luxembourg: Office for the Official Publications of the EC, 1976).
28. EC, "Reflections on European Policy", Paper submitted by the CDU/CSU to the Bundestag, 1 September 1994, Agence Europe, *Europe Documents,* no. 1895/96, Brussels, 7 September 1994.
29. The notion of *a la carte* Europe was first discussed in Ralf Dahrendorf, *A Third Europe?,* Jean Monnet Lecture (Florence: European University Press, 1979). Also see for debates on "variable geometry", Helen Wallace and Adam Ridley (ed.), *Europe: The Challenge of Diversity* (London: RIIA, Chatham House Papers 29, 1985).
30. See, Michael Dauderstaedt and Barbara Lippert, *Europe 2000: The German Presidency and Beyond* (London :FES, 1999) pp. 19-21.
31. See, Antonio Missiroli (ed.), *Flexibility and Enhanced Cooperation in European Security Matters: Assets or Liabilities,* Occasional Papers (Paris: ISS/WEU, 1999), pp. i-xviii.
32. See, Francoise de La Serra and Helen Wallace, "Flexibility and Enhanced Cooperation in the EU: Placebo rather than Panacea?" Research and Policy Papers, no. 2, Paris, September 1997, p. 37.
33. See, R. Muench, "Between Nation-Sate, Regionalism and

World Society", *Journal of Common Market Studies*, vol. 34, no. 3, September 1996, p. 380.

34. Jean Monnet, *Memoirs* (Translated by R. Mayne) (New York: Doubleday and Company, 1978), pp. 523-524.

Select Bibliography

PRIMARY SOURCES

Balladur, Edouard, "Major Guidelines for Institutional Reforms for the Union and the Future Structure of Europe : Workings and Dimensions", *Le Monde,* 30 November 1994, as reproduced in Agence Europe (Brussels), 2 December 1994, pp. 1a-1b.

EC, "Expectation of the EU Commissioner on 1996 IGC", Speech by Franz Fischer, Konrad Adenauer Foundation, Brussels, Speech 96/75, *Press Release,* 29 February 1996,.

EC, "The Enlargement of the European Union : The Conditions for Success", Speech by Hans van der Broeck, Member of the Commission, SB Forum, London, *Embargo,* 17 November 1995, 9 pp.

EC, *Treaty of Amsterdam* (Luxembourg: Office for Official Publications of the EC, 1997).

EC, "EC-Turkey Association Agreement", Official Journal of the EC, no. 217, 29 December 1964.

EC, "Why should we ratify the Maastricht Treaty?" Extract from Speech by Sir Leon Britain, EC Commissioner for External Economic Affairs of Liverpool Chamber of Commerce, 19 February 1993", *Press Release,* 1 P (93) 116, Brussels, 19 February 1993.

EC, "Commission's Opinion on Reinforcing Political Union and Preparing for Enlargement", Brussels, 29 February 1996, COM (96), 90 final, 19 pp.

EC, "The Economic and Political Challenges facing Europe", Speech by Jacques Santer, *Conference on European Economic and Political Perspectives,* Copenhagen, 11 April 1996, Speech 96/83, *Press Release,* p. 7.

EC, "EU-Russia : A Challenging Partnership", Speech by Hans van der Broeck, Carnegie Foundation, Moscow, Embargo, no. 96/66, 18 March 1996.

EC, "Europe's Economic Challenges and the role for the EURO", Speech by Jacques Santer, President of the Europe Symposium, Wassenaar, Embargo, Speech 96/86, *European Commission Spokesman Service,* 15 April 1996.

EC, "Commission Presents Opinion on IGC", IP/96/179, *Press Release,* Brussels, 28 February 1996.

EC, "Green Paper on Introducing the Single Currency", *Press Release,* 18/95/541, Brussels, 31 May 1995.

EC, *Background Report : The IGC,* B/2/97, London, January 1997.

EC, "Relations between European Parliament and National Parliaments", Speech by European Parliament President, Klaus Haensch, Brussels, 23 January 1995, *Europe Documents,* no. 1920, 27 January 1995, 7 pp.

EC, *1996 IGC, Reflection Group Report and other Reference for Documentary Purpose,* General Secretariat of the Council of EU, Brussels, December 1995.

EC, "The Issues as the Amsterdam Summit Approaches", Speech by Padraig Flynn, European Commission for Empowerment and Social Affairs, Institute of European Affairs, Dublin, 18 April 1997.

EC, "The Challenges of the Intergovernmental Conference", Speech by Erkki Likkanen, Member of European Commission at the Nordic Council Conference on European Questions, Copenhagen, Speech/96/60 4 March 1996.

EC, "Final Communique of the Denver Summit of the Eight", no. D/97/4, (Brussels: Official Publications of the EC, 23 June 1997).

EC, *Presidency Conclusions of the Amsterdam European Council, 16 and 17 June 1997,* Doc/97/2, Brussels, 18 June 1997.

EC, *The European Union's Common Foreign and Security Policy,* (Luxembourg: Office for the Official Publications of the EC, 1996).

EC, "IGC, Amsterdam European Council Draft Treaty", Brussels, 17 June 1997, *General Secretariat of the Council of the EU,* Information Policy, Transparency and Public Relations, Official Publications of the EC, 145 pp.

EC, "Resolution adopted by European Parliament on Single European Act, 11 December 1986", *European Political Cooperation* (Bonn : Press and Information Service, 1988), pp. 395-398.

EC, "Declaration of the Heads of State and Government at the

North Atlantic Council Meeting, Brussels, 10-11 January 1994", *Atlantic Document*, no. 83, 12 January 1994.

EC, "The Political Agenda for Europe in the Presidency Conclusions, 15/16 December 1995", *Agence Europe*, 17 December 1995.

EC, "Petersburg Declaration of the WEU Ministerial Council, 19 June 1992", Part II, Par. 4, *Europe Documents*, no. 1787, 23 June 1992.

EC, *Commission Opinion in the Application by the Republic of Cyprus for Membership*, COM (93), 3/3 final, Brussels, 30 June 1993.

EC "European Council Presidency Conclusions", Turin, 29 March 1996, *Agence Europe* 30 March 1996.

EC, "Commission Report to the Council on the implementation of Economic Reform in Malta", *Press release*, IP/95/198, Brussels, 1 March 1995.

EC, Commission, "From the Single Act to Maastricht and beyond : The means to match our ambition", *Agence Europe*, Document, no. 1962/63, 19 February 1992.

EC, "Commission adopts report on the functioning of the Maastricht Treaty", *Press Release*, (Brussels), no. IP/95/65, 10 May 1995.

EC, "Research after Maastricht; an assessment, a strategy", *Bulletin of the European Communities*, (Commission of the European Communities), Supplement 2, 1992.

EC, *Presidency Conclusions of the European Council in the Amsterdam Summit, 16-17 June 1997*, Brussels, Document no. 97/2, 18 June 1997.

EC, L. Tindemans, "EU : Report to the European Council", *Bulletin of the EC* (Luxembourg : Official Publications of the EC, 1976).

EC, Commission, "The Europe Agreements and Beyond: A Strategy to prepare the countries of Central and Eastern Europe for Accession", *Communication from the Commission to the Council*, com (94) 320 final, 13 July 1994, 6pp.

EC, "Resolution adopted by European Parliament on European Political Cooperation and the role of the European Parliament, 9 July 1981", *European Political Cooperation* (Bonn : Press and information Service, 1988), pp. 390-393.

EC, "Opinion on the 1996 IGC: Role of the Commission", *Economic and Social Committee of the EC*, Brussels, 22-23 November 1995, CES 1312/95, 11 pp.

EC, "Outlook for European Agriculture and Agricultural Policy with the CEEC", Speech by Rene Steichen, Centre for

Agricultural Strategy, Agence Europe, *Europe Documents,* no. 1914, 7 December 1994.

EC, Commission, "Reflections on European Policy", Paper submitted by the CDU-CSU to the Bundestag, 1 September 1994, Agence Europe, *Europe Documents,* no. 1895/96, Brussels, 7 September 1994.

EC, Commission, "EU-Russia Relation", *Press Release,* MEMO/96/26, Brussels, 15 March 1996.

EC, "Conclusions of the Presidency of European Council of Edinburg 11-12 December 1992", *Agence Europe* (special ed.), 13 December 1992, pp. 9-11.

EC, "The Political Agenda for Europe : Presidency Conclusions, 15/16 December 1995", Agence Europe, *Europe Documents,* 17, December 1995.

EC, "Widening and Deepening of the EU: Economic and Political Challenges", Address by M.B. McGeever, Ambassador, Head of the Delegation of the European Commission in India, *Europe Forum,* JNU, New Delhi, 24 February 1998.

EC, "Kohl-Mitterrand Letter", Agence Europe, *Europe Documents,* no. 5238, 20 April 1990.

Embassy of France, Speech of Roland Dumas, French Foreign Minister to French Senate, 27 June 1990, *Bulletin Information* (Paris: Foreign Ministry, 28 June 1990).

Germany "Address by Willy Brandt, Federal Chancellor to the European Parliament, Strasbourg, 13 November 1973", *European Political Cooperation* (Bonn : Press and Information Service, 1988), pp. 312-314.

Germany "Statement by Alois Mertes, Minister of State on behalf of the German Presidency in the debate of European Parliament on the Report: 'EPC and European Security', Strasbourg, 13 January 1983", *European Political Cooperation* (Bonn : Press and Information Service, 1988) pp. 324-325.

Germany "Statement by Walter Scheel, Federal Minister for Foreign Affairs in the Bundestag on policy toward Europe, Bonn, September 1973", (excerpts), *European Political Cooperation* (Bonn : Press and Information Service, 1988), pp. 310-311.

Germany "Decision of 28 February 1986 adopted by Ministers' Meeting in the Framework of EPC on the occasion of the signing of the Single European Act", *European Political Cooperation* (Bonn : Press and Information Service, 1988), pp. 87-97.

Germany "First Report of the Foreign Ministers to the Heads of

State and Government of Member States of the European Community, Luxembourg Report, 27 October 1970", *European Political Cooperation* (Bonn : Press and Information Service, 1988), pp. 24-30.

Germany "Report on European Political Co-operation issued by the Foreign Ministers of the Ten on 13 October 1981, London", *European Political Cooperation* (Bonn : Press and Information Service, 1988), pp. 61-69.

Germany "Communique of the Conference of the Heads of State and Government of the Member States of the European Community, Copenhagen, 15 December 1973", *European Political Cooperation* (Bonn : Press and Information Service, 1988), pp. 5-55.

Germany "Communique of the Conference of the Heads of State and Government of the Member States of the European Commission, The Hague, 2 December 1969", *European Political Cooperation* (Bonn : Press and Information Service, 1988), pp. 24-23.

Germany "Statement by Hans-Dietrich Genscher, Federal Minister for Foreign Affairs to the European Parliament, Strasbourg, 29 June 1983", *European Political Cooperation* (Bonn : Press and Information Service, 1988) pp. 326-337.

Germany, CDU/CSU Fraktion des Deutschen Bundestages, "Uberlegungen zur europaeischen Politik vorschlaege fuer ein Reform der Europaeischen Union", *CDU/CSU Documentation,* January 1995.

Germany, "Declaration of the Ministers of Affairs on the Strengthening of Franco-German Cooperation on Foreign Policy, Bonn, 3 July 1997", www.info-france-usa.org/news/statements/Germany/fral0797.htm

Laeufer, Thomas, (ed.) *Vertrag von Amsterdam Texte des EU Vertages und des EG-Vertrages,* Press and Information and der Bundesregierung (Bonn : Europa Union Verlag, 1998).

SECONDARY SOURCES
BOOKS

Avery, Graham & Cameron, Fraser, *The Enlargement of the European Union* (Sheffield : Sheffield Press, 1998).

Barbour, P. (ed.), *The EU Handbook* (Illinois: Fitzroy Dearbon, 1996).

Baring, Arnulf (ed.), *Germany's New Position in Europe: Strategies for Differentiated Integration* (Gutersloh: Bertelsman Foundation,

1997).

Blacksell, M & Williams, A.M. (ed.), The *European Community* (Oxford: Oxford University Press, 1994).

Bocquet, Dominique (ed.), *The Future of the Franco-German relation: Three Views* (London: RIIA, 1997).

Brechtfeld, J., *Mitteleuropa and German Politics* (London: Macmillan, 1990).

Buchan, David, *Europe: The Strange Superpower* (Aldershot: Dartmouth, 1993).

Buzan, Barry & Kelstrup, M., *The European Security Recast* (London: Pinter, 1991).

Cafruny, Alan and Rosenthal, Glenda, The *State of the European Community : The Maastricht Debates and Beyond,* (Boulder: Lynne Rienner, 1993).

Chirac, Jacques, *Une nouvelle France : reflexions* l' (Paris: Nil Editions, 1994).

Cobb, R., *French and Germans, Germans and French* (London: Branders, 1983).

Cole, A., *Francoise Mitterrand* (Keele : Keele University Press, 1994).

Colomer, Joseph (ed.), *Political Institutions in Europe* (Barcelona: Spanish Higher Council of Scientific Research, 1995).

Crouch, Colin & Marquand, David (ed.), *Towards a Greater Europe?: A Continent without an Iron Curtain* (Oxford: Blackwell, 1992).

Dauderstaedt, Michael and Lippert, Barbara, *Europe 2000 : The German Presidency and Beyond* (London: FES, 1999).

Deubner, Christian, *Deutsche Europapolitik: Von Maastricht nach Kerneuropa?* (Baden-Baden: NOMOS, 1995).

Dinan, Desmond (ed.), *Encyclopedia of the European Union* (Boulder: Lynne Rienner, 1998).

Dreyfus, Francois-Georges, and Morizet, J., *France and EC Membership Evaluated* (London: Pinter, 1993).

Duff, A., & Pinder, J. (ed.), *Maastricht and Beyond* (London: Federal Trust, 1994).

Eekelen, W. van, *Debating European Security: 1948-1998* (The Hague : SDU Publishers, 1998).

Ehrmann, Henry, *Politics in France* (Boston: Little Brown, 1983).

Eliassen, Kjell., A. (ed.), *Foreign and Security Policy in the European Union* (London : Sage, 1998).

Elsenhans, Hartmut (ed.), *A Balanced European Architecture: Enlargement of the European Union to the Central East European Countries and the Mediterranean* (Paris: Publisud, 1999).

Engles, C., & Wessels, W., *From Luxembourg to Maastricht Institutional*

Change in the European Community after the Single European Act (Bonn: European Union Verlag, 1992).

Friend, Julius, *The Linchpin: Franco-German Relations 1950-1990* (New York: Praeger Publishers, 1991).

Ganz, N. & Roper, J. (ed.), *Towards a New Partnership: US-European Relations in the Post Cold-War Era* (Paris: WEU/ISS, 1993).

Godt, Paul (ed.), *Policy-making in France: From de Gaulle to Mitterrand* (London: Pinter, 1989).

Grandbard, R. Stephen (ed.), *Eastern Europe, Central Europe.... Europe* (Boulder: Westview Press, 1991).

Haig, Simonian, *The Privileged Partnership: Franco-German Relations in the European Community* (New York : Clarendon Press, 1985).

Haas, Ernst, *The Uniting of Europe: Political, Economic and Social Forces 1950-1957* (Standford: Standford Press, 1958).

Haywood, Jack & Page, Edward C. (ed.), *Governing the New Europe* (Cambridge: Polity Press, 1995).

Herol, Gunilla (ed.), *EU Enlargement and Flexibility* (Stockholm: The Swedish Institute of International Affairs, 1998).

Holland, Martin, *The EC and South Africa: European Political Cooperation under Strain* (London: Pinter, 1988).

—, *Common Foreign and Security Policy: The Record and Reforms* (London: Pinter, 1997).

—, *European Integration: From Community to Union* (London : Pinter, 199).

—,(ed.), *The Future of European Political Cooperation* (London: Pinter, 1991).

Keohane, R. & Hoffman, S. (ed.), *The New European Community : Decision-making and Institutional Change* (Boulder: Westview, 1991).

Kolodziej, E.A., *French International Policy under de Gaulle and Pompidou* (New York: Cornell, 1974).

Kulski, W.W., *De Gaulle and the World* (New York: Syracuse, 1966).

Laird, Robbin (ed.), *Strangers and Friends: The Franco-German Security Relationship* (London: Pinter, 1989).

Larres, Klaus, *Germany Since Unification* (New York: St. Martin's Press, 1998).

Laurent, Pierre-Henri & Maresceau, Marc (ed.), *The State of the European Union* (Boulder: Lynne Rienner, 1998).

Laurent, Rene, *France and Germany: Franco-Geman relations and the problems of Modern Europe* (London: Blandford Press, 1965).

Lewis, Derek & Mckensie, John, R.P. (ed.), *The New Germany* (Exeter:

University of Exeter Press, 1995).

Mazey, S., & Newman, M. (ed.), *Mitterrand's France* (London: Croom Helm, 1987).

Mc Carthy, Patrick (ed.), *France-Germany: 1983-1993* (New York: St. Martin's Press, 1993).

Michalski, Anna, & Wallace, Helen, *The European Community : The Challenge of Enlargement* (London : Royal Institute of International Affairs, 1992).

Missiroli, Antonio (ed.), *Flexibility and Enhanced Cooperation in European Security Matters: Assets or Liabilities* (Paris: Institute for Security Studies/WEU, January 1999).

Morgan, Roger (ed.), *The Third Pillar of the European Union* (Brussels : European Interuniversity Press, 1995).

——, *Partners and Rivals in West Europe* (Aldershot: Gower, 1986).

Neil, 'O', M., *The Politics of European Integration* (Nottingham : Trent University Press, 1995).

Nicoll, W., & Salmon, T.C., *Understanding the European Community* (Maryland: Barnes & Noble, 1990).

Nugent, Neil (ed.), *The European Community 1991* (Oxford: Blackwell, 1993).

Nutal, S., *European Political Cooperation* (Oxford: Clarendon, 1992).

Owen, David, *Balkan Odyssey* (New York: Harvest, 1995).

Palmer, John, *The Future of the European Community: Trading Places* (London: Radius Publishers, 1988).

Paxton, John, *The Future of the European Community and Eastern Europe* (London: Pinter Publishers for Royal Institute of International Affairs, 1991).

Peterson, John & Sjursen, Helen (ed.), *A Common Foreign Policy for Europe? Competing Missions of the CFSP* (London: Routledge, 1998).

Pryce, Robert, *The Dynamics of European Integration* (London: Routledge, 1993).

Redmond, J., *The Next Mediterranean Enlargement of the European Community: Turkey, Cyprus and Malta?* (Aldershot: Dartmouth, 1993).

Redmond, J. & Rosenthal, Glenda (ed.), *The Expanding European Union: Past, Present, Future* (Boulder: Lynne Rienner, 1998).

Regelsberger, E. (ed.) *European Political Cooperation in the 1980's: A Common Foreign Policy of Western Europe* (Dordrecht: Nijhoff, 1988).

Rhodes, C. & Mazey, S. (ed.), *The State of the European Union* (Boulder: Lynne Rienner, 1998).

Rhodes, Carolyn (ed.), *The European Union in the World Community* (Boulder : Lynne Rienner, 1998).

Robertson, Patrick (ed.), *Reshaping Europe in the 21st Century* (London: Macmillan,1992).

Ross, G., & Hoffman S. (ed.) *The Mitterrand Experiment (Cambridge*: Polity Press, 1987).

Rotfield D & Stuetzle, W., Germany *and Europe in Transition* (New York: Oxford, 1991).

Rummel, Reinhardt (ed.), *Toward Political Union* (Baden-Baden: Nomos, 1992).

_____ ,*Towards Political Union: Planning a Common Foreign and Security Policy in the European Community* (Baden Baden: Nomos, 1992).

_____ , *The Evolution of an International Actor: West Europe's new assertiveness* (Boulder: Westview, 1990).

Sampedo, L.J.(ed.), *The Enlargement of the European Community* (London : Macmillan, 1983).

Sandholtz, M., Alberta (ed.), *The Euro-Politics, Institutions and Policy-making in the New European Community* (Washington D.C.: Brookings Institution, 1992).

Seers Dudley & Vaitos, Constantine (ed.), *The Second Enlargement of the EEC: The Integration of Unequal Partners*, (London : Macmillan, 1982).

Tiersky, Ronald, *France in the New Europe: changing yet steadfast* (New York: Wadoworth, 1994).

Twitchet, Carol (ed.), *Building Europe: Britain's Partners in the EEC* (London: Europe, 1981).

van Ham, Peter, *The European Community, Eastern Europe and European Unity: Discord, Collaboration and Integration since 1947* (New York: Pinter Publishers, 1993).

Wallace, William, & Herreman, I. (ed.), *Policy-making in the EC* (London: John Wiley, 1983a).

_____ , *The Wider Western Europe*, (London: RIIA Pinter Publishers, 1991). *A Community of Twelve? The Impact of Further Enlargement on the European Community*, (Bruges: Belgium De Tempel, 1978).

_____ , *The Government and Politics of the EC* (Durham: Duke University Press, 1991).

Wallace, Helen, Ridley, A., *Europe: The Challenge of Diversity*, Paper 29, (London: Routledge, 1985).

Wallace, William, (ed.), *The Dynamics of European Integration* (London: Pinter Publishers, 1990).

Webber, Dougles (ed.), *The Franco-German Relationship in the EU* (London: Routlede, 1999).

Weidenfeld, Werner, *Europe 96: Reforming the EU* (Guetersloh: Bertelsmann Foundation, 1994).

Weidenfeld, Werner & Wessels, Wolgang, *Jahrbuch des Europaeischen Integration 1997/98* (Bonn: Europa Union Verlag, 1998).

Welsh, Michael, *Europe United* (London: Macmillan, 1996).

Wessels, W. (ed.), *The EU in the 1990s-Ever Closer and Larger* (Bonn: Europa, 1993).

Young, Thomas-Durell, *The Franco-German Relationship in the Transatlantic Security Framework* (Strategic Studies Institute: Army War College, 1991).

JOURNALS AND ARTICLES

Adenauer, Julanta, "East and Central Europe and the European Community: A Polish Perspective", *London: RIIA Discussion Paper,* no. 4, 1993, pp. 1-33.

Agnella, G., "Europe of 1992", *Foreign Affairs,* vol. 68(4), Fall 1989, pp. 61-70.

Alexander, B., "EC and the Yugoslav Crisis", *Review of International Affairs,* vol. 43, no. 1009-11, 1992, pp. 18-21.

Allen, David, "EC in the New Europe: Bearing the Burden of Change", *International Journal,* vol. 47 (1), Winter 1991-92, pp. 1-28.

Alter, R., "New Challenges in Eastern Europe: Investment and Restructuring", *Intereconomics,* vol. 27, no. 1, January-February 1992, pp. 16-19.

Aluko, O., "France and South Africa", *Jerusalem Journal of International Relations,* vol. 12, no. 4, December 1990, pp. 59-76.

Arnold, E., "German Foreign Policy and Unification", *International Affairs,* vol. 67, no. 3, 1991, pp. 453-472.

Asmus, Ronald, & Larrabee, Stephen, "NATO and the have nots: Reassurance after Enlargement", *Foreign Affairs,* vol. 75, no.6, November-December 1996, pp. 13-20.

Baldwin, Robert, "Inland: Economics and Politics of EU Accession: A Comment", *The World Economy,* vol. 17, no. 5, September 1994, pp. 711-714.

Barkan, J., "End of the Swedish Model?", *Dissent,* vol. 2, Spring 1992, pp. 192-1998.

Barlow, Omer, "Nations in Arms: Germany and France, 1789-1939",

History Today, vol. 4, no. 9 September 1994, pp. 27-33.

Beloff, Max, "Tocqueville and the odd couple", *The National Interest,* no. 55, 1999, pp. 60.

Bertram, Christoph, "German Question", *Foreign Affairs,* Spring 1990, pp. 45-62.

Beyme, von Klaus, "United Germany preparing for the 1994 Elections", *Government and Opposition,* vol. 29, no. 4, Autumn 1999, pp. 445-60.

Birand, M., "Turkey and the European Community", *The World Today,* vol. 34, no. 2 February 1978, pp. 52-61.

Birnabaum, Pierre, "Nationalism : A Comparison Between France and Germany", *International Social Science Journal,* vol. 1332, August 1992, pp. 375-84.

Blaisse, M., "Mitterrand's dilemma", *European Affairs,* vol. 4, 1990, pp. 64-65.

Bluth, C., "Germany: Defining the National Interest", *The World Today,* vol. 51, no. 3, March 1995, pp. 51-55.

Bok, S., "German Question: Pressing and Complex" *Review of International Affairs,* vol. 41, no. 958, March 1990, pp. 11-12.

Bolz, Klaus, "Implications of the EC Internal Market for Relations with Eastern Europe", *Intereconomics,* January-February. 1990, pp. 36-43.

Bowler, S. & Farrel, D. "Organising of the European Parliament Committees, Specialization and Co-ordination", *British Journal of Political Science,* vol. 25, no. 2, April 1995, pp. 219-43.

Brendt, von, Staden, "Nothing Less than the whole of Europe will do", *Aussen Politik,* vol. 41, no. 1, Quarterly 1990, pp. 24-37.

Brewin, C., "The European Community: A Union of States without Unity of Government", *Journal of Common Market Studies,* vol. 25, no. 1, September 1987, pp. 1-25.

Buiter, Willem, H., "Alice in Euroland", *Journal of Common Market Studies,* vol. 37, no. 2, June 1999, pp. 181-209.

Bulmer S. & Paterson, W., "Germany in the European Union: Gentle Giant or Emergent Leader", *International Affairs,* vol. 72, no. 1, January 1996, pp. 9-32.

Campannella, M.L., "Getting to the Core: A neo-institutionalist approach to the EMU", *Government and Opposition,* vol. 30, no. 3, Summer 1995, pp. 347-69.

Cassen, Bernard, "How large is Europe?", *European Affairs,* vol. 5, no. 4, August-September 1991, pp. 6-11.

Chopra, H.S., "European Union in 1992: A Regional Integrative

Process for Peace and Development", *Strategic Analysis,* vol. 13, no. 10, January 1990, pp. 1047-58.

Church, Clive, "The Politics of Change: EFTA and the Nordic Countries: Responses to the EC in the Early 1990s", *Journal of Common Market Studies,* vol. 28, no. 4, June 1990, pp. 401-429.

Claes, Willy, "Europe as an Unfinished Symphony", *The World Today,* vol. 3, March 1994, p. 5.

Cohen, L.J., "Bosnia and Herzegovina: Fragile peace in a segmented State", *Current History,* vol. 95, no. 599, March 1996, pp. 103-112.

_____ ,"Disintegration of Yugoslavia", *Current History,* vol. 91, no. 568, November 92, pp. 369-375.

Cole, Alistair, "Studying political leadership : the case of Francois Mitterrand", *Political Studies,* vol. 42, no. 3, September 199, pp. 453-68.

Cordell, Karl, "Birth-Pangs of the new Germany", *International Relations,* vol. 11, no. 4; April 1993; pp. 381-92.

Costa, Carlos S., "EMU: Its Benefits Outweight its Costs", *European Affairs,* 4 March 1990, pp. 22-27.

Croft, Stuart, "European Integration, Nuclear Deterrence and Franco-British Nuclear Cooperation", *International Affairs,* vol. 72, no. 4, October 1996, pp. 771-89.

Dauderstaedt, Michael, "Can the democracies of East-Central Europe cope with the double impact of Transformation and Integration?" Paper presented at the Conference on *Political and Social Change in Central Europe,* Prague: FES, 8-10 May 1996, p. 30.

_____ , "Foreign Trade option for Central and Eastern Europe", *Intereconomics,* vol. 29, no. I, January-February 1994, pp. 401-429.

Davidson, I, "Search for a New Order in Europe", *International Affairs,* vol. 66, no. 2, April 1990, pp. 275-284.

De Michels, G., "Reaching out to the East", *Foreign Policy,* vol. 79, Summer 1990, pp. 44-55.

Delors, J., "Europe's Ambitions", *Foreign Policy,* vol. 80, Fall 1990, pp. 14-27.

Devuyst, Y., "The Community-Method after Amsterdam", *Journal of Common Market Studies,* vol. 37, no. 1, March 1999, pp. 109-120.

Dicke, Hugo, "Europe 92 : An Obsolete Integration Concept", *Aussen Politik,* vol. 42, no. 2, Quarterly 1991, pp. 162-171.

Diepgen, Eberhard, "Berlin and the new European era", *NATO Review,* vol. 42, no. 5, October 1994, pp. 18-20.

Doder, D., "Yugoslavia: New war, old hatreds", *Foreign Policy,* vol. 91, Summer 1993, pp. 3-23.

Dyba, Karel, & Svejnar, Jan, "Czechoslovakia: Recent Economic Development and Prospects", *American Economic Review,* vol. 81, no, 2, May 1991, pp. 185-190.

Eberstadt, N., "How not to aid Eastern Europe: Continental Drift?", *European Affairs,* vol. 5, no. 6, December 1991, pp. 4-47.

Eichenberg, R. & Dalton, J.R., "Europeans and European Community: The dynamics of public support for European integration", *International Organization,* vol. 47, no. 4, Autumn 1993, pp. 507-534.

Eichengreen, Bary, "European Monetary Unification", *Journal of Economic Literature,* vol. 31, no. 3, September 1993, pp. 1321-57.

Eiff, Hansjorg, "German Unification and Integration Processes in Europe", *Review of International Affairs,* vol. 42, no. 981, 20 February 1991, pp. 8-11.

Elgie, Robert, "French Presidency: Conceptualising Presidential power in the Fifth Republic", *Public Administration,* vol. 74, no. 2, Summer 1996, pp. 275-291.

Fagerberg, J., "Processes of Economic Integration in Europe: Consequences for EFTA Countries and Firms", *Cooperation and Conflict,* vol. 26, no. 4, 1991, pp. 197-215.

Fenske, John, "France's uncertain progress toward European Union", *Current History,* vol. 90, no. 559, November 1991, pp. 358-362.

Frenkel, Jacob, A. & Goldstein, Morris, "Monetary Policy in an emerging European Economic and Monetary Union: Key Issues", *International Monetary Fund Staff Papers,* vol. 38, no. 2, June 1991, pp. 356-73.

Friss, L. & Murphy, Anna, *"The EU and Central and Eastern Europe Journal of Common Market Studies,* vol. 37, no. 2, June 1999, pp. 210-232.

Frowein, Jochen Arb, "Reunification of Germay", *American Journal of International Law,* vol. 86, no. 1, January 1992, pp. 12-62.

Garland, James, "New Germany", *Social Studies.* vol. 82, no. 1, January-February 1991, pp. 5-6.

Gazdag, F., "Does the West understand Central and East Europe?", *NATO Review,* vol. 40, no. 6, December 1992, pp. 14-19.

Geipel, Gary L. "Germany: Urgent Pressures, Quiet Change",

Current History, vol. 93, no. 96, November 1994, pp. 358-3.

Geotz, Klaus H., "National Governance and European Integration: Intergovernmental Relations in Germany", *Journal of Common Market Studies*, vol. 33, no. 1, March 1995, pp. 91-116.

Gloannec, Anna-Marine Le, "Europe by other means?", *International Affairs*, vol. 73, no. 1, January 1997, pp. 83-98.

Gnesotto, N., "European Union after Minsk and Maastricht", *International Affairs*, vol. 68, no. 2, February 1992, pp. 223-231.

Gordon, Philip H. "Normalization of German Foreign Policy", *Orbis: A Journal of World Affairs*, vol. 38, no. 2, Spring 1994, pp. 225-44.

Gow, J., "The Use of Coercion in the Yugoslav Crisis", *The World Today*, vol. 48, no. 11, 1992.

Gros, D. & Thygesen, N., "Institutional Approach to Monetary Union in Europe", *Economic Journal*, vol. 100, no. 402, September 1990, pp. 925-35.

Gstohl, S., "EFTA and the European Economic Area or the Politics of Frustration", *Cooperation and Conflict*, vol. 29, no. 4, 1994, pp. 333-361.

Guehenno, J.M., "France and the WEU" *Nato Review*, vol. 42, no. 51, October 1994, pp. 10-12.

Guerin-Sendelbach, Valerie & Rulkowski, J., "Euro-Trio France: Germany and Poland, " *Aussen Politik*, vol. 45, no. 3, 1994, pp. 246-53.

Gunlicks, Arthur, E., "German Federalism after Unification: The legal/constitutional response", *Publis*, vol. 24, no. 2, Spring 1994, pp. 81-96.

Guth, E., "Assessing the effects of EFTA-EC Integration on EFTA Countries", *Journal of Common Market Studies*, vol. 28, no. 4, June 1990, pp. 379-400.

Hamilton, D., "A more European Germany or a more German Europe?", *Journal of International Affairs*, Summer 1993, pp. 1-18.

Hanrieder, Wolfarm, F., "Germany, the new Europe, and the Transatlantic connection", *International Journal*, vol. 46, no. 3, Summer 1991, pp. 394-419.

Hansen, L. & Williams, M.C., "The Myths of Europe" Legitimacy, Community and the 'Crisis' of the EU", *Journal of Common Market Studies*, vol. 37, no. 2, June 1999, pp. 233-249.

Harrison, Martin, "French Constitutional Council: A Study in Institutional Change", *International Journal*, vol. 46. no. 3,

Summer 1991, pp. 394-419.

Hanse, L. & Williams, M.C., "The Myths of Europe : Legitimacy, Community and the 'Crisis' of the EU", *Journal of Common Market Studies*, vol. 3, no. 2, June 1999, pp. 23-249.

Harrison, Martin, "French Constitutional Council: A Study in Institutional Change", *Political Studies*, vol. 38, no. 4, December 1990, pp. 603-609.

Hartley, Anthony, "Reinventing the Politics of Europe", *The World Today*, vol. 57, December 1993, pp. 21-27.

Hassner, Pierre, "Europe Beyond Partition and Unity: Disintegration or Reconstruction", *International Affairs*, vol. 66, no. 3, July 1990, pp. 4612-47.

Havel, Vaclav, "A Call for Sacrifice: The Co-responsibility in the West", *Foreign Affairs*, vol. 73, no. 2, March-April 1994, pp. 2-7.

Haywood, E., "The European Policy of Francoise Mitterrand", *Journal of Common Market Studies*, vol. 31, no. 2, June 1993, pp. 270-276.

Heath, E., "European unity over the next ten years: From Community to Union", *International Affairs*, vol. 6, no. 2, Spring 1988, pp. 199-207.

Heilbruner, R., "Rethinking the Past, Reshaping the Future", *Social Research*, vol. 57, no. 3, Autumn 1990, pp. 579-586.

Heilbrunn, Jacob, "Germany's New Right", *Foreign Affairs*, vol. 75, no. 6, November-December 1996, pp. 80-98.

Heisbourg, Francois, "The European-U.S. Alliance: Valedictory Reflections on Continental Drift in the Post Cold War Era", *International Affairs*, vol. 4, 1992, pp. 665-678.

Henrich, Francine, "European Union and Global Interdependence", *World Affairs*, vol. 3, no. 2, December 1994, pp. 17-18.

Heseltine, M., "EC: First deeper than wider", *European Affairs*, vol., no. 2, Summer 1990, 8-12.

Hill, Christopher, "The European Community towards a CFSP", *The World Today*, no. 71,1991, pp. 189-1993.

_____ , "The Capability-Expectation Gap or Conceptualizing Europe's International Role", *Journal of Common Market Studies*, vol. 31, no. 3, September 1993, pp. 305-328.

Hine, R.C., "Customs Union, Enlargement and Adjustment: Spain's Accession to the European Community", *Journal of Common Market Studies*, vol. 28, no. 1, September 1989, pp. 1-28.

Hoffman, S., "European Community and 1992", *Foreign Affairs*, vol. 68, no. 4, Fall 1989, pp.27-97.

_____ , "Reflection on the German Question", *Survival,* vol. 32, no. 4, July-August 1990, pp. 291-98.

Holliday, Jan,, "Dealing in green votes: France 1993", *Government and Opposition,* vol. 29, no. 1, Winter 1994, pp. 64-79.

Holst, J.J., "Uncertainty and Opportunity in an era of East-West Change", *Adelphi Paper,* vol. 247, Winter 1989-1990, pp. 66-80.

Hoogendijk, O.F., "There is no European House", *European Affairs,* vol. 4, no. 1, Spring 1990, pp. 36-40.

Howe, Paul, "A Community of Europeans: The Requisite Underpinnings", *Journal of Common Market Studies,* vol. 33, no. 1, March 1995, pp. 27-46.

Howorth, Jolyon, "France since the Berlin Wall: Defence and Diplomacy", *The World Today,* vol. 46, no. 7, July 1990, pp. 126-30.

Ireland, Patrick, R., "Tracing the true Fortress Europe: Immigrant Politics in the EC", *Journal of Common Market Studies,* Summer 1991, pp. 457-480.

Jain, R.K., "Migration in Germany: Issues and Responses", *India International Centre Quarterly,* Winter 1993, pp. 19-38.

_____ , "Enlargement of NATO: Partnership for Peace and After", *Strategic Analysis,* vol. 18, no. 3, June 1995, pp. 407-32.

_____ , "Germany and the European Union", Paper Presented in the International Seminar on *Germany in the Nineties,* School of International Studies, JNU, 4-5 November 1996, 31 pp.

_____ , "European Security after the Cold War", *International Studies,* vol. 31, no. 4, September 1994, pp. 399-42.

Janning, Josef, "German Europe or a European Germany? On the debate over Germany's Foreign Policy", *International Affairs,* vol. 72, no. 1, January 1996, vol. 3-42.

_____ , "Am Ende der Regierbarkeit? Gefachrliche Folgender Erweiterung der Europaeischen Union", *Europa-Archive,* 22, 1993, pp. 645-653.

Jeffery, Charles, "Towards a third level in Europe: The German Lander in the EU", *Political Studies,* vol. 4, no. 2, June 1996, pp. 253-66.

Joffe, Josef, "After Bipolarity: East-West Europe Between Two Ages", *Adelphi Paper,* vol. 247, Winter 1989-1990, pp. 81-91.

_____ , "Once more the German question", *Survival,* vol. 32, no. 2, March-April, 1990; pp. 219-40.

_____ , "The New Europe: Yesterday's Ghost", *Foreign Affairs,* 993, pp. 29-43.

Jones, P.N., "Recent ethnic German Migration from East-Europe to the FRG", *Geography*, vol. 75, no. 3, July 1990, pp. 249-252.

Jopp, M., "Langer Weg-Kuehnes Ziel: Gemeinsame Verteidigungs Politik", *Europa-Archive*, 13/14, 1994, pp. 397-404.

Jorg, H. & Eckermann, Henry, "Eastern Europe's long and winding road to market economy", *Aussen Politik*, vol. 2, no. 2, Quarterly 1991, pp. 183-193.

Kedourie, Elie, "De Gaulle", *Commentary*, vol. 95, no. 1, January 1993, pp. 43-49.

Kenen, Peter, B., "European Central Bank and Monetary Policy in Stage Three of EMU", *International Affairs* (London), vol. 68, no. 3, July 1992, pp. 457-7.

Kennedy, D., "Integration: East Europe and the European Economic Community", *Colombia Journal of Transnational Law*, vol. 28, no. 3, 1990, pp. 633-676.

Kesper, Christine, "European Development Policy after Maastricht", *Aussen Politik*, vol. 4, April 1993, pp. 403-411.

Kinkel, Klaus, "Peacekeeping Missions: Germany can now play its part" *NATO Review*, vol. 42, no. 5, October 1994, pp. 3-6.

Koester, Ulrich & Cramon-von Taubadel, S. "EC, Agricultural Reform ad Infinitum?", *Intereconomics*, vol. 27, no. 4, July-August 1992, pp. 151-156.

Kovally, P., "Central and East European: The Opening Curtain", *Studies in Soviet Thought*, vol. 44, no. 1, July 1992, pp. 51-66.

Kramer, Steven Philip, "France faces the new Europe", *Current History*, vol. 89, no. 550, November 1990, pp. 365-68 and 384-86.

_____ , "Western Europe's Eastern Question", *The World Today*, vol. 47, no. 12, December 1991, pp. 212-215.

Kramer, H., "EC's response to the New Eastern Europe", *Journal of Common Market Studies*, vol. 31, no. 2, June 1993, pp. 213-244.

_____ , "EC and Stabilization of Eastern Europe", *Aussen Politik*, vol. 43, no. 1, January 1992, pp. 12-21.

_____ , "Turkey and EC's Southward Enlargement", *Aussen Politik*, vol. 35, no. 1, January 1984, pp. 99-116.

Kreile, Micheal, "Globalization and European Integration", Paper presented at the 3rd German-Japanese Symposium on *Japanese and German Foreign Policies in Comparative Perspective*, Tuebingen, 21-23 September 1998, 18 pp.

_____ ,"The Influence of Domestic, Political and Economic Actors and Germany's European Policy", Working Paper 7-15,

Centre for German and European Studies, University of California, Berkley, April 1996, 28 pp.

Kuhnhardt, Ludger, "Germany's Role in European Security", *Strategic Analysis,* vol. 8, no. 4, July 1995, pp. 553-72.

Kurth, James, "Germany and the Re-emergence of Mitteleuropa", *Current History,* vol. 94, no. 545, November 1995, pp. 384-385.

Ladrech, R., "Europeanization of Domestic Politics and Institutions: The Case of France", *Journal of Common Market Studies,* vol. 32, no. 1, March 1994, pp. 69-88.

Laffan, Brigid, "The Politics of Identity and Political Order in Europe", *Journal of Common Market Studies,* vol. 34, no. 1 March 1996, pp. 81-102.

Lane, Sarah, "The Pattern of Foreign Direct Investment and Joint Ventures in Hungary", *Communist Economies and Economic Transformation,* vol. 6, no. 3, 1994, pp. 341-366.

Langguth, Gerd, "Germany, the EC and the Architecture of Europe", *Aussen Politik,* vol. 42, no. 2, Quarterly 1991, pp. 137-146.

_____ ,"Single European Market-Also an Opportunity for Eastern Europe?", *Aussen Politik,* vol. 43, no. 2, 1992, pp. 107-114.

Laurent, P., "European Community: Twelve becoming One", *Current History,* vol. 87, no. 532, November 1988, pp. 1357-60.

Laursen, Finn, "EC and its European Neighbours: Special Partnership or Widened Membership", *International Journal,* vol. 47, no. 1, Winter 1991-1992, pp. 29-63.

_____ , "The Community Policy Towards EFTA: Regime Formation in the EES", *Journal of Common Market Studies,* vol. 28, no. 4, June 1990, pp. 303-326.

_____ , "The Maastricht Treaty: Implications for the Nordic Countries", *Cooperation and Conflict,* vol. 28, no. 2, February 1993, pp. 115-137.

Lewis, F., "Bringing in the East", *Foreign Affairs,* vol. 69, no. 4, Fall 1990, pp. 15-26.

Lovett, A.W., "United States and the Schuman Plan: A Study in French Diplomacy 1950-52; *Historical Journal,* vol. 39, no. 2, June 1996, pp. 425-455.

Ludlow, P., "The Maastricht Treaty and Future of Europe", *The World Quarterly,* no. 4, 1992, pp. 119-137.

Mackay, R. Ross, "Europe of the Regions: A Role for Non-Market Forces?" *Regional Studies,* vol. 27, no.5, 1993, pp. 19-31.

Macleod, Alex, "French Policy toward the war in the former

Yugoslavia", *International Journal,* vol. LII, no. 2, Spring 1997, pp. 243-264.

Malcom, Noel, "The Case Against Europe", *Foreign Affairs,* vol. 74, no. 2, March/April 1995, pp. 52-68.

Margo, A., "Greek-Turkey unfriendly allies", *The World Today,* vol. 43, no. 8-9, 1997, pp. 144-147.

Marks, Gary, Hoogie, Liesbet, & Blank, Kermit, "European Integration from the 1980s: State-Centric versus Multi-level Governance", *Journal of Common Market Studies,* vol. 34, no. 3, September 1996, pp. 341-374.

Mates, Leo, "German Reunification", *Review of International Affairs,* vol. 41, no. 958, March 90, pp. 9-11.

Mc Carthy, Patrick, "France in the mid-1990's : Gloom but not doomed", *Current History,* vol. 93, no. 586, November 1994, pp. 364-68.

Mechel, M., "Europe's destiny will be decided in Eastern Europe", *Polish Review,* vol. 37, no. 4, 1992, pp. 489-500.

Meier-Walswer, Reinhardt, "Germany, France and Britain on the threshold to a New Europe", *Aussen Politik,* vol. 43, no. 4, 1992, pp. 334-342.

Menon, Anand, "NATO : the French way from Independence to Cooperation: France, NATO and Europe Security", *International Affairs,* vol. 71, no. 1, January 1995, pp. 19-34.

Meridan, Trevor, "How will the EFTA Four affect the EU Twelve?", *European Tends,* (European Intelligence Unit), 2nd quarter 1994, pp. 53-62.

Mey, Holger & Ruehle, M., "German Security Interests and Nuclear Strategy", *Aussen Politik,* vol. 42, no. 1, 1991, pp. 20-30.

Mierlo, Hans-van, "WEU and NATO : Prospects for a more balanced relationship", *NATO Review,* vol, 43, no. 2, March 1995, pp. 7-10.

Millioń, Charles, "France and the renewal of the Atlantic Alliance", *Nato Review,* vol. 44, no. 3, May 1996, pp. 13-16.

Moisi, Dominique, "French Answer to the German Question", *European Affairs,* vol. 4, no. 1, Spring 1990, pp. 1-35.

Moravcsik, Andrew, "Negotiating the Single European Act: National Interests and Conventional Statecraft in the European Community", *International Organisation,* vol. 45, no. 1, Winter 1991, pp. 19-56.

_____ , "Preferences and Power in the European Community", *Journal of Common Market Studies,* vol. 31, no. 4, December 1993, pp. 473-524.

Moravcsik, Andrew, & Nicolaidis, K., "Amsterdam: Interests, Influence, Institutions", *Journal of Common Market Studies,* vol. 37, no. 1, March 1999, pp. 59-85.

Morgan, Roger, "Rise and Decline of the Fifth French Republic", *Government and Opposition,* vol. 27, no. 4, Autumn 1992, pp. 511-517.

Mortizen, Hans, "The two Musterknaben and the Naughty Boy: Sweden, Finland and Denmark in a Process of European Integration", *Cooperation and Conflict,* vol. 28, no. 4, December 1993, pp. 373-408.

Muench, Richard, "Between Nation-State, Regionalism and World Society: The European Integration Process", *Journal of Common Market Studies,* vol. 34, no. 3, September 1996, pp. 379-399.

Nair, Sami, "France : A Crisis of Integration", *Dissent,* Summer 1996, pp. 75-78.

Nell, Phillipe: "EFTA on the 1990's : The Search for a New Identity", *Journal of Common Market Studies,* vol. 28, no. 4, June 1990, pp. 327-358.

Nelson, D., "Europe's Unstable East", *Foreign Policy,* vol. 82, Spring 1992, pp. 69-73.

Nesteenko, A., "Europe's Unstable East", *Foreign Policy,* vol. 82, Spring 1992, pp. 69-73.

Nesterenko, A., "Western Aid: Hopes and Doubts", *Socialism: Theory and Practice,* vol. 12, no. 209, December 1990, pp. 69-73.

Neumann, B.I., "The European Free Trade Association: The Problems of an all European Role", *Journal of Common Market Studies,* vol. 28, no. 4, June 1990, pp. 359-377.

Neunreither, Karltheinz, "Democratic Deficit of the European Union: Towards Closer Cooperation between the European Parliament and the National Parliaments", *Government and Opposition,* vol. 29, no. 3, Summer 1994, pp. 299-314.

Nicolaides, P., & Close, A., "The Process and Politics of Enlargement", *European Trends,* (European Intelligence Unit), 1st Quarterly 1994, pp. 70-80.

Noetzold Juergen, "The Eastern Part of Europe: Peripheral or Essential Component of European Integration? "*Aussen Poliik,* vol. 44, April 1993, pp. 326-334..

Nowak, J. Z., "Eastern Europe Return to Europe: Back to the Future?", *Polish Review,* vol. 37, no. 4, 1992, pp. 549-555.

Oliver, Peter, "French Constitution and the Treaty of Maastricht", *International and Comparative Law Quarterly,* vol. 33, no. 1,

January 1994, pp. 1-25.

Osmundsen, T., "A United Europe: Where does EFTA Fit in?", *European Affairs*, vol. 4, no. 2, Summer 1990, pp. 73-77.

Pauly, Louis W., "Politics of European Monetary Union: National Strategies, International Implications", *International Journal*, vol. 47, no. 1, Winter 1991-92, pp. 93-111.

Pederson, Thomas, "Problems of Enlargement : Political Integration in a Pan-European EC", *Cooperation and Conflict*, no. 2, 1990, pp. 83-99.

Petkovic, R., "Role of the European Community and the United Nations in Solving the Yugoslav Crisis", *Review of International Affairs*, vol. 43, no. 1002, 1992, p. 3.

_____, "Neutral and Non-Aligned Countries: Can they join the EEC?" *Korean Journal of International Studies*, vol. 20 (3), Fall 1989, pp. 501-512.

Philippart, E. & Edwards, G., "The Provisions on closer Cooperation in the Treaty of Amsterdam", *Journal of Common Market Studies*, vol. 37, no. 1, March 1999, pp. 87-108.

Pijpers, A., "The Treaty of Maastricht and European Foreign Policy", *Jerusalem Journal of International Relations*, vol. 14, no. 2, 1992.

Pinder, John, "The future of the European Community: A Strategy for Enlargement", *Government and Opposition*, vol. 24, no. 4, Autumn 1992, pp. 415-432.

Pinter, Joseph, "Neutrality, European Community and World Peace", *Journal of Peace Research*, vol. 26, November 1989, pp. 413-418.

Popovic, T., Yugoslavia and the EU", *Review of International Affairs*, vol. 47, no. 1044, 15 May 1996, pp. 14-18.

Pradetto, A., "Transformation in Western Europe and International Cooperation: German Position", *Studies in Comparative Communism*, vol. 25, no. 1, March 1992, pp. 23-30.

Preston, C., "Obstacles to EU Enlargement", *Journal of Common Market Studies*, vol. 33, no. 3, September 1995, pp. 451-464.

Regelsberger, E. & Wessels, W., "The CFSP Institutions and Procedures: A Third Way for the Second Pillar", *European Foreign Affairs Review*, vol. 1, Jan 1996, pp. 29-54.

Remington, R. A., "Eastern Europe after the Revolution", *Current History*, vol. 90, no. 559, November 1991, pp. 379-813.

Riegler, J., Sereda, S. & Osasdghiy, S., "Austria in Europe of Today and Tomorrow with the Mediterranean on one mind", *International Affairs* (Moscow), vol. 9, September 1990, pp. 35-39.

Rose, R. & Haerper, C., "Democracy and Enlarging the EU Eastwards", *Journal of Common Market Studies,* vol. 33, no. 3, September 1995, pp. 427-450.

Ross, George, "Hard Choices for Europe", *World Policy Journal,* vol. 9, no. 3, Summer 1992, pp. 487-514.

_____ ,"Chirac and France: Prisoners of the past", *Current History,* vol. 96, no. 608, March 1997, pp. 104-110.

Ruhle, Michael & Williams, N., "NATO Enlargement and the European Union", *The World Today,* vol. 57, no. 5, May 1995, pp. 84-88.

Rummel, R., & Noetzold, J.,"On the Way to a New European Order", *Aussen Politik,* vol. 41, no. 3, 1990, pp. 212-224.

Sadurska, R., "Reshaping Europe or how to keep poor Cousins in (Their) Home :A Comment on Transformation of Europe", *Yale Law Journal,* vol. 199, no. 8, June 1991, pp. 2501-2509.

Salmon, T.C., "Testing Times for European Political Cooperation : The Gulf and Yugoslavia", *International Affairs,* vol. 68, no. 2, 1992.

Sandholtz, Wayne, "Membership Matters: Limits of the Functional Approach to European Institutions", *Journal of Common Market Studies,* vol. 34, no. 3, September 1996, pp. 403-428.

_____ ,"Choosing Union: Monetary Politics and Maastricht", *International Organisation,* vol. 47, no. 1, Winter 1993, pp. 1-39.

Sapir, Andre & Jacquemin, Alexis, "Europe Post 1992: Internal and External Liberalisation", *American Economic Review,* vol. 81, no. 2, May 1991, pp. 166-170.

Sapir, Andre, "European Integration or World Integration", *Review of World Economics,* vol. 124, no. 1, 1988, pp. 127-139.

_____ ,"Regional Integration in Europe", *Economic Journal,* vol. 102, no. 415, November 1992, pp. 1491-1404.

Scharping, Rudolph, "New Challenges, for Franco-German Cooperation", *Aussen Politik,* vol. 45, no. 1, 1994, pp. 3-9.

Schear, J.A., "Bosnia's Post-Dayton Traumas", *Foreign Policy,* vol. 104, Fall 1996, pp. 87-101.

Schleiber, T., "New Europe Faced With Crisis", *Review of International Affairs,* vol. 4, no. 979, 20 January 1991, pp. 17-18.

Schmidt, Max, "German Unification: Problems and Prospects", *Korean Journal of International Studies,* vol. 21, no. 4, Winter 90, 471-96.

Schmidt, Peter, "French Security Policy Ambition", *Aussen Politik,* vol. 44, no. 4, 1993, pp. 335-43.

_____ ,"Franco-German Defence & Security Council", *Aussen Politik,* vol. 40, no. 4, 1989, pp. 360-71.

Schopflin, G., "The End of Communism", *International Affairs,* vol. 66, no. 1, Fall 1990, pp. 3-16.

Scharrer, Hans-Eckart, "A hard-core for the European Union", *Intereconomics,* vol. 29, no. 5, September-October 1994, pp. 109-210.

_____ ,"The Mixed Blessings of Enlargement", *Intereconomics,* vol. 29, no. 2, March-April 1994, pp. 53-54.

Schroeder, K., "Western Financial Assistance for Reforms in Eastern Europe: Conditions and Risks", *Aussen Politik,* vol. 42, no. 4, Quater 1991, pp. 336-343.

Simic, P., "Challenges of Possible Eastern Enlargement of the EC", *Review of International Affairs,* vol. 42, no. 998, 1991.

_____ , "Europe and the Yugoslav Issue", *Review of International Affairs,* vol. 43, no. 1001, 1992, pp. 1-5.

_____ , "Third Europe?", *Review of International Affairs,* vol. 42, no. 981, 20 February 1991, pp. 11-14.

Sloane, Stanley, R., "Nato's future in a New Europe", *International Affairs,* vol. 3, 1990.

Smith, D. Anthony, "National Identity and the idea of European Unity", *International Affairs,* vol. 68, 1992, pp. 55-66.

Smith, Michael, "The EU and a Changing Europe", *Journal of Common Market Studies,* vol. 34, no. 1, March 1996, pp. 5-28.

Sodersten, B., "The Historical Relations between the Nordic Countries and the European Community", *The World Economy,* vol. 17, no. 5, September 1994, pp. 643-650.

Spath, L., "Europe is both East and West", *International Affairs,* vol. 5, May 1990, pp. 43-50.

Spaulding, R.M., "German Trade Policy in East Europe, 1989-1990", *International Organisation,* vol. 45, no. 3, Summer 1991, pp. 343-368.

Stone, M., & Schmartz, G., "Beyond Stabilisation: The Economic Transformation of Czechoslovakia, Hungary and Poland", Communist Economies and Economic Transformation of Czechoslovakia, Hungary and Poland", *Communist Economies and Economic Transformation,* vol. 6, no. 3, 1994, pp. 291-314.

Stevens, Strommanna, R., "German Unification and Europe's Integration", *The World Today,* vol. 47, no. 10, October 1991.

Subedi, S.P., "Neutrality in a Changing World", *International and*

Comparative Law Quarterly, vol. 42, no. 2, April 1993, pp. 238-268.

Susan Nell, "Some Recent Developments in EC and East European Economic Relations", *Journal of World Trade*, vol. 24, no. 1, February 1990, pp. 5-24.

Sutton, Michael, "France: Who beats the nationalist drum?", *The World Today*, vol. 47, no. 6, June 1991, pp. 98-101.

_____ ,"France and the European Union's Enlargement Eastwards", *The World Today*, vol. 50, no. 8-9, August-September 1994, pp. 153-57.

Taylor, Trevor, "West European Security and Defence Cooperation: Maastricht and beyond", *International Affairs*, vol. 70, no.1, January 1994, pp. 1-16.

Taylor, Christopher, "EMU : The state of play", *The World Today*, vol. 51, no. 4, April 1995, pp. 75-77.

Tewes, Henning, "Between Deepening and Widening: Role Conflict in Germany's Enlargement Policy", *IGC Discussion Papers Services*, Number 97/14, University of Birmingham, 1998 pp. 1-27.

Thies, Jochen, "German Unification: Opportunity or Setback for Europe?", *The World Today*, vol. 47, no. 1, January 1991, pp. 8-10.

_____ , "Germany: An era draws to a close", *The World Today*, vol. 50, no. 12, December 1994, pp. 222-23.

Thygesen, Niels, "Delors Report and European Economic and Monetary Union", *International Affairs*, vol. 65, no. 41, Autumn 1989, pp. 637-52.

Tietmeyer, Hans, "Reunification and Beyond: Europe's Economic Union must be built on solid foundations", *European Affairs*, vol. 5, no. 4, August-September 1991, pp. 6-11.

Tovias, A., "EC and Eastern Europe: A Case Study of Hungary", *Journal of Common Market Studies*, vol. 29, no. 3, March 1991, pp. 291-316.

Ungerer, W., "Development of EC and its Relationship to Central and East Europe", *Aussen Politik*, vol. 41, no. 3, March 1990, pp. 225-235.

Vernet, D., "Dilemma of French Foreign Policy Restructuring in the cases of Great Britain, France and West Germany", *Journal of Politics*, vol. 53, no. 3, August 1991, pp. 615-43.

Vredin, Anders, "EMU: Economic Substance or Political Symbolism: A Comment", *World Economy*, vol. 17, no. 5, September 1994, pp. 663-66.

Walker, David, B., "Germany: Confronting the aftermath of Reunification", *Current History,* vol. 91, no. 568, November 1992, pp. 359-63.

Wallace, Helen & Serre, Francoise de la, "Flexibility and Enhanced Cooperation in the European Union : Placebo rather than Panacea?", Research and Policy Papers, no. 2, *Groupment d'etudes et de Recherches "Notre Europe"*, Paris, September 1997, 38 pp.

Wallace, W., & Menon, A., "A Common European Defence", *Survival,* vol. 3, Autumn 1992, pp. 98-118.

Webber, Douglas, "Franco-German Bilateralism and Agricultural Politics in the European Union: The Neglected Levcl", *West European Politics,* vol. 22, no. 1, January 1999, pp. 45-67.

Weiler, J.H.H., "European Integration in the Nineties and the more to Flexibility", Paper Presented on the Jean Monnet Lecture, 24 November 1999, http:///www.law.harvard.edu/programs/Jean Monnet/papers/98/98-13-2.html.

Wettig, Gerhard, "Security in Europe: A Challenging Task", *Aussen Politik,* vol. 1, January 1992, pp. 3-31.

_____ ,"Europe faced by a two-fold Challenge", *Aussen Politik,* vol. 42, no. 2, Quarterly 1991, pp. 107-115.

_____ , "Political Implications of Changes in East Europe", *Aussen Politik,* vol. 41, no. 2, 2nd Quater 1990, pp. 107-117.

Willeman, P.R., "German Contribution Toward Overcoming the Division of Europe", *Aussen Politik,* vol. 41, no. 1, 1990, pp. 15-23.

Wincott, Daniel, "Is the Treaty of Maastricht an Adequate Constitution for the European Union?", *Public Administration,* vol. 72, no. 4, Winter 1994, pp. 573-90.

Yilmaaz, B., "Turkey's New Role in International Politics", *Aussen Politik,* vol. 45, no. 1, 1994, pp. 90-98.

Yost, D., "France and West European Defence Identity", *Survival,* vol. 33, no. 4, July-August 1991, pp. 327-51.

Young, Richard, "The Politics of the Single Currency : Learning the Lessons of Maastricht", *Journal of Common Market Studies,* vol. 37, no. 4, June 1999, pp. 295-316.

NEWSPAPERS & MAGAZINES

European Voice (London).

Frankfurter Rundschau (Frankfurt)

Frankfurter Allgemeine Zeitung (Frankfurt).

Politique Etrangere (Paris).
Le Figaro (Paris).
Le Monde (Paris).
Suddeutsche Zeitung (Munich).
The Economist (London)
The Times (London).
The Wall Street Journal (New York).
The Guardian Weekly (London).
The Irish Times (Dublin).
Financial Times (London).
International Herald Tribune (Paris).
The Daily Telegraph (London).

Index